HUMAN RIGHTS
Perspectives and Challenges

HUMAN RIGHTS
Perspectives and Challenges

Rajindar Sachar
Former Chief Justice, High Court of Delhi

GYAN

Human Rights : Perspectives and Challenges

ISBN: 81-212-0830-0

Reprinted in 2012 in India by
Gyan Publishing House
23, Main Ansari Road, Daryaganj,
New Delhi - 110002
Phone : 23282060, 23261060
Fax : (011) 23285914
E-mail : books@gyanbooks.com
Website: gyanbooks.com

Printed at: Chawla Offset Printers, Delhi

To my wife Raj for her understanding and my father Shri Bhim Sen Sachar, whose commitment to moral values have been my beacon light and to my mother who taught me how to face confidently the vicissitudes of public life.

Contents

Introduction

A book on Human Rights has necessarily to wade through and clear a lot of misconceptions Average person seems to feel that a Human Right activists is no patriot – that his loyalty to the State is not to be taken for granted. One may understand this reaction though it is thoroughly wrong and baseless.

Writing on Human Rights is to wrestle within you to strive to remain firm to commitment to unvarnished truth, even when people may misinterpret your motives including some time hurl calumnious accusations. But that is a price one must be willing to pay in the firm belief of victory of our National motto *Satya Mave Jaite*. A nation which does not keep the flag of Human Right aloft in the direst of circumstances will never reach the height of its spiritual legacy – I believe India is entitled to so reach the pinnacle. It is in that humility that this book attempts to raise and answer some of these perpetual questions troubling our generation.

This book was not planned. I am no professional writer. Basically having been brought up in a family involved in freedom struggle and public life, public issues were a normal part of my daily feast. Though to a normal youngster these issues may sound uncanny and strange, fortunately for me these were normal events. So in the earliest age, though they may not have been totally understood they left an indelible impression motivating me automatically to taking interest in public matters. So right from earlier age I did read the newspapers and a certain kind of humble vanity and self-projection made me dabble in letters to the Editor Column. If my memory does not fail me I remember having joined the debate in 1938 then raging when British Govt. wanted to introduce law to give inheritance rights to Hindu daughters in their fathers' properties. I remember (though a boy of 15 years) a lot of discussion used to take place

– as far as I remember Hindu society was quite conservative and was opposed to the bill as such. I remember the usual refrain of my mother's generation was that by this law love between brothers and sisters would be divisive. I was so upset at this denial to women rights that I shot off a letter to the Tribune (our foremost paper in Punjab) saying that if love between brothers and sisters is dependent on denying a sister a right to equal share in fathers property then this brotherly and sisterly love is a mere façade while in fact it should be automatic and genuine.

Since some time in the recent past a hollow question has been deliberately raised. It is suggested that in developing countries, the stress should be on economic rights; in the process if political rights and civil liberties are curtained this price must be accepted temporarily. Such a sharp cut division is clearly a myth. No such artificial conflict of choice between economic and political freedoms ever existed, as is made clear the Vienna Declaration on Human Rights 1993 which has accepted the universality and indivisibility of all Human Rights, political and economic.

Bread and liberty are two sides of the same coin, and deprivation of either must inevitably damage the fabric of the other. The freedom to agitate for bread and sustenance to fight for one's liberties are concomitant. As a matter of fact the Universal Declaration of Human Rights 1948 encompasses within itself the political rights of life, liberty and security of person (Article 3), and the economic right that everyone has the right to work and protection against unemployment (Article 23). The compulsions of economic rights are recognized by the discerning even in so-called affluent countries. Chapter 1 brings out this core theory of Human Rights.

Freedom of an individual, which is the postulate of human rights, obviously can have no meaning so long as the poor in the country do not have their economic conditions improved and the discrimination based on privilege do not become mere memories instead of becoming more and more aggressive as time passes on. The present situation must cause concern to all human right activists.

Government conveniently invokes the sensitive ground of national security to silence the media from reporting human rights violations in affected areas. Unfortunately, the media, by and large has a tendency to accept this gratuitous advice without much demur. But this kind of yielding is totally counter to the spirit and confidence with which our Constitution gave the free press the protection, it needed to fulfill its essential democratic role.

A good percentage of the press has also gone along with the vicious executive propaganda that human rights organizations are concerned with the rights of terrorist rather than that of the victims of terrorism. This is untrue, considering that established human rights bodies like Peoples Union for Civil Liberties (PUCL) have unequivocally condemned the killing and taking of hostages by terrorist, whether in Jammu & Kashmir or the northeast. The painful part is that even when the statements by the NGOs condemning the killing by terrorists of human rights activists in various parts of the country is published in newspapers nevertheless the media because of its prejudice against the human rights organizations continues to present this wrong picture of the human right activists.

Taking into account the ground reality that in a developing country like ours where the impact of public opinion is weak and the maneuvering by the politician-criminal-bureaucracy nexus continues to be strong, both the media and the NGOs have a common stake in the preservation of human rights.

The media, I have no doubt, will play extra attention to the betterment of the conditions of the people and the safeguarding of the human rights of the 40 per cent of people who are below the poverty line.

It is a truism that just as human rights cannot be safeguarded unless there is a free press, there cannot be a free press, if the human rights of the majority of the people continue to be violated, because then there will be no democracy which alone is a condition precedent to preserving both.

Meeting the challenge of Terrorism requires determination, proper utilization of intelligence information and support of public and not these draconian laws violating the human rights of citizens.

Loud Noise that POTA even if it denies civil rights is necessary for protecting freedom can be dismissed in the words of Mr. Muggeridge, former Editor of Punch (UK) when he warned – "the choice for us is between security and freedom. And if we ever ceased to prefer the later, we should soon find that we had nothing of any worth left to secure anyway."

Human rights organizations firmly believe that by indulging in violence the militants clearly violate the human right of the individuals in the society. But this does not mean that unlawful excesses by the State agencies are justified or can be condoned, even though one appreciates the strains and risks under which these agencies operate. Any such condonation will destroy the fabric of democratic institutions.

In any democratic society whenever such things happen it is the duty of an alert citizenry to protest, and of any responsible democratic government to take note of it. In fact in my view refusal of the governments to own up such excesses only creates a credibility gap between the government and the masses.

For decades sociologists have wrestled with the question whether death penalty is consistent with human dignity. The most formidable challenge to the retention or death penalty is the arbitrariness and freakishness in the sentencing mechanism.

The evil of discrimination in death sentencing is enhanced in societies which have a mixed racial population like U.S.A. where be Intent and open racial discrimination dominates the sentencing procedure. This has been admirably brought out in the recent compilation of international commission of Jurists, Geneva, from which reference is made in the book.

The evidence suggests that race – especially that of the victim – has an important bearing on the likelihood of a death sentence being imposed, particularly in the southern states of USA. Although blacks and whites are the victims of homicide in almost equal numbers, most offenders who are sentenced to death are convicted of murdering whites (86 per cent in 1987). Forty-five of the 98 prisoners executed between January 1977 and May 1988 were black or Hispanic, and 84 had been convicted of killing white victims.

It is universally accepted that the ability of the State to protect human rights is an important indicator of the quality of life enjoyed by citizens in any country.

Torture is defined to mean any act by which severe pain or suffering, whether physical or mental, is intentionally inflected on a person for such purposes as obtaining from him or a third person information or a confession, at the instigation or with consent or acquiescence of a public official.

I know the police in their defence maintain that they resort to torture because they are under pressure from their superiors including politicians to show visible results and obtaining forced confessions is the easy way out. But this is indefensible. Article 2 of the Convention Against Torture clearly says that no exceptional circumstances whatsoever, even if these be of a state of war or a threat of war internal political instability or any other public emergency, may be invoked as justification of cases of torture. Article 2(3) of the Convention further warns that an order from a superior officer or a public authority may not be invoked as a justification for torture.

The Court has firmly held that a custodial death is perhaps one of the worst crimes in a civilized society governed by the rule of law.

Calling globalization "the central challenge we face today", world leaders attending the United Nations Millennium Summit in the evening of 8 September 2000 had to recognize that "For while globalization offers great opportunities, at present its benefits are very unevenly shared, while its costs are unevenly distributed".

To speak of globalization with regard to increase integration of the world economy is misleading, there is a process of concentration of capital which only benefits three principal regions (North America, Europe and East Asia), whilst the rest o the globe (particularly Africa) becomes more and more marginalized. (We can include Indian along with Africa).

The Human Development report 2000 has commented acidly that global inequalities in income increased in the 20th century by orders of magnitude out of proportion to anything experienced before. The discrepancy if incomes of the richest and poorest countries was about 3 to 1 in 1820 to 35 to 1 in 1950, 44 to 1 in 1973 and 72 to 1 in 1992.

The "global marketplace" is not necessarily a place of equality, with benefits and rewards equaliably shared by all those who participate in it. In the case of the Asian "tigers" the consequences of financial liberalization have been mixed at best and absolutely catastrophic at worst. The North American Free

Trade agreement (NAFTA) has led to serious social and political problems in certain regions of America. Unemployment, homelessness and reduction in social services are not confined to any one geographical area.

To speak of globalisation with regard to increased integration of the world economy is misleading, there is a process of concentration of capital which only benefits three principal regions (North America, Europe and East Asia) whilst the rest of the globe – particularly Africa – becomes more and more marginalised and we can include India along with Africa. The situation deteriorates for the disadvantaged when deregulation is followed by a reduction of social services. In other words, globalisation entails not only a growing inequality between regional groups and countries but also within the nation itself.

Seventy per cent of the Indian population is primarily engaged in agriculture in the rural areas. To improve their lot, subsidies and concessions to the agriculture sector are essential, but under the cover of the World Trade Organization and globalization serious constrains have been placed on third World Governments, forcing them to open their markets for unrestricted imports from the developed world. The assault on the indigenous market through the removal of quantitative restrictions, causing a surge of imports, has threatened the very fabric of the Indian economy. The net effect will be the pauperization of the peasantry and the working class both in the unorganized and organized sectors. Mr. Stiglitz Nobel laureate and former World Bank chief economist has condemned it strongly, pointing out that "while preaching free market doctrines abroad, the U.S bails out its airlines and increases agricultural subsidies at home. Even before these increases, subsidies to agriculture by the advanced industrial countries were enormous – exceeding the total income of Sub-Saharan Africa. The rich effectively close their markets to many goods that represent the comparative advantage of the poor."

All Governments since 1991 have spread the canard that the break-up of the USSR showed that socialism as a political philosophy is unworkable notwithstanding the mandate in the preamble of our Constitution that India is a socialist Republic. This is a distortion. The USSR failed not because socialism is a lost philosophy, but it failed because without democracy, socialism cannot grow. Stalinism and not socialism was the cause of the break-up of the USSR.

The public sector is being deliberately maligned by some votaries of liberalization, though the reality is otherwise. During the preceding Economic Policy period (1985-86 and 1989-90), the Government gave about Rs. 25,537 crores as budgetary support to the PSUs while the PSU's contribution to the Central exchequer was Rs. 70,893 crores. In 1991-92, the budgetary support was Rs. 3,617 crores and the PSUs' contribution to the public exchequer Rs. 20,366 crores.

The arguments that the public sector is a drag on the economy is calumny. During the year ended March 1997, the LIC paid Rs.199 crores to the government as its share of valuation surplus. It distributed to policyholders a bonus of over Rs. 3700 crores in 1996-97. The figure rose steadily from Rs. 2250 crores in 1992-93.

The insidious attempt to deliberately link environment with international trade is one of single most important weapon in the hands of developed countries against the developing countries. It is this aspect which requires deep consideration, namely, how alibi of environmental jurisprudence should not be used as a trade barrier against the developing countries.

The cynical disregard for environmental clearances (though loudly shouting its commitment by rich countries) is hollow if one notes that since 1989 more than 500 attempts have been made to export toxic waste from OECD countries to non-OECD courtiers OECD members generate 98% of all hazardous waste.

In fact environment related manufacturing industry is the fastest growing in the developed world.

According to the World Resources (1994-95),-C2 emission per capita of six major countries, that of United States is more than 5 MT of carbon followed by Japan of about 2.3 M.T while that of India is the lowest at about 0.02. M.T.

USA alone is responsible for about 25% of the world's Green House Gas emissions. It has ironically increased the emissions by 6% during the period 1990-95 that is even after Montreal Protocol had been signed. The developed countries make two-thirds to three-fourths of current emissions.

Similarly, in regard to water U.N. Guidelines mandate that the Government should ensure supply distribution and quality of drinking water and strengthen the National Policy in this regard. Unfortunately here also the present situation in India is woeful. According to one Government estimate about 57 per cent of the total population is not covered by supply of safe drinking water. The per capita norm for water consumption should be 300 liters per day whereas on an average, the urban population is supplied only 145 liters per capita per day in Class-1 cities. As many as 31 per cent of the households have to walk up to 100 feet to collect water and many among the poor – women and children – had to cover the distance not once but several times a day to collect the daily requirements. That for the overwhelming majority of the slum dwellers, the availability of water may be lesser than 20 liters per capital per day.

"Instead of Building Bunkers, the Government should First Provide Basic Amenities".

I was appalled at a news item that an insane exercise is being carried out by the Health and Transport Ministries to build bunkers and provide safe covers to ministers and senior government officials and their colleagues in case of a nuclear attack by Pakistan at Delhi.

It is a matter of shame that an administration that cannot ensure even proper water and power supply arrogates to itself the right to conduct such a highly sensitive defence study. With hindsight, however, we know that there must be the temptation to be able to spend millions, with a large chunk of it obviously remaining unaccounted. Do these worthies have the least idea that it is universally recognized that there is no defence against the madness of nuclear attack.

Some Corporate friendly tend to maintain that in these heady day of globalization and neo economic liberalization, legislations like Consumer Protection Act is an unnecessary intervention in the functioning of the market, and that consumers need no special protection; all can he safely left to the market. But the perfect market is an economist's dream and consumer's sovereignty a myth. In real life, products are complex and of great variety and consumers and retailers have imperfect knowledge. Suppliers may often have a dominant buying position. As a consequence, bargaining power in the market is generally weighed against the consumer.

In this context, we in India, have a serious problem where notwithstanding the official minimum of 25 per cent to 30 per cent of population being below the poverty line to whom food purchase is grave problem, but food is not being made available to them notwithstanding the bursting storage of food grain running over to millions of tonnes involving the cost of storage alone running into hundreds of crores. Suggestions have been given by PUCL and large number of NGOs to start a project for food for work in which public works are started by the Government so as to give food as part of the daily wages. Surprisingly, the matter still remains at the discussion stage of Inter-Governmental Agencies. This is a grave violation of Consumer Protection guidelines framed by the U.N. and runs counter to the established principle that giving protection to a consumer is part of Human Right Jurisprudence.

The hope that politics may become cleaner if younger people come forward has also been belied. The 1996 elected Lok Sabha had half the members who were in the age group 25-45. Notwithstanding this, the stink of corruption, irresponsibility and the lack of consideration for the public interest exhibited by the members of the dissolved House have beaten the records of any previous Lok Sabha.

The slogan of stability given by the BJP and the Congress (I) as an automatic solution to the people's problems is a myth. A mere stable government is no guarantee of good governance. Notwithstanding stable Congress (I) Governments in the past. India still continues to be shamed by the lack of drinking water to half the villages and the prevalence of illiteracy among half the population.

It is unfortunate that the question of empowerment of women has been a victim of hypocrisy of all the political parties. All of them make very high sounding promises to act to give powers to the women but all this remains a hollow wordy promise but does not result any action.

Women are not asking for grace and charity. Their contribution in building the nation exceeds that of men. International Labour Organisation study shows that "while women represent 50 per cent of the world adult population and a third of the official labour force, they perform nearly two-thirds of all working hours, receive a tenth of world income and own less than one per cent of world property." Therefore, reservation for women is not a bounty but only an honest recognition of their contribution to social development.

Their contribution to the cause of nation building exceeds that of men. They also played a vital role in the constitution making which gives special consideration for the development and empowerment of women. And yet not only amongst lay men but also amongst judicial circles we continue to repeat slavishly that constitution was given to us by our founding fathers-this phrase is copied from U.S. Court decisions, which rightly refer to founding fathers because there were no women members in the American constitutional convention. But that analogy does not apply to India because we had very distinguished women members in the constituent assembly. Our constitution therefore is a product of the philosophy and sacrifice of both our founding fathers and mothers- I wish in future this in justice of non-reference to the mothers of our constitution is not repeated. Let the present generation make amends for this in-justice to our founding mothers by this small step of passing the women reservation bill.

I firmly believe that reservation for women would check the muddy politics that the men folk have brought about. It would bring social consciousness to political life. It will also help in breaking criminal-politican-nexus- the real danger to our democracy.

It is my conviction that empowerment of women in both the urban and rural fields is probably the only instrument which can release the social forces which can act as a bulwark against the manipulation and criminalisation of politics. Just as in the past when we needed the surgical operation of Mandelisation/ Dalitisation to release the social forces to highlight some aspects of social justice, the country now needs an infusion of fresh blood in the body politic by way of women's empowerment to break the shackles of stratification and the danger of caste and money politics, and may also spur the country on to value-based politics.

The menace of Communalism unless checked will eat into the vitals of our nation. Every spiritual soul in each religion having reached the height of communion with Universal Soul has the same message of universal love, common humanity and the acceptance that same divine power runs through all human beings though outwardly professing different religion and practices.

Thus Hinduism's "Vasudhaiva – Kutumbakam" (world is one

family) is equally reciprocated in the Quran which says, "All the created ones belong to the family of God ... so, an Arab has no precedence over a non-Arab, a White over a Black". And Christ said succinctly, "All are children of God."

Evidently, all great souls and prophets have the same vision of God. There is that indissoluble unity of thinking that no religion whether Hinduism or Islam can claim to be the sole interpreter of God's Vision. Their paths to reach God may differ, but the goal is the same – mainly how to obtain God's mercy and blessings.

The callous indifference of people in general to the plight of these slum dwellers is borne out of colossal ignorance of the phenomenon of Slum creation. Somehow a false impression is created as if the pavement dwellers are unsocial elements, a majority of whom are criminals and unemployed and not interested in work. This is sheer slander. The pavement dwellers are an important part of the daily economy of city life. They are in reality the victims of unjust social order.

The compulsions of why these squatter colonies exist was highlighted by Economic Commission of Europe, which said: "High levels of squatter housing indicate that the formal land market does not provide affordable residential land for housing, forcing households to occupy land illegally. High levels of this indicator also suggest that eviction may not be a realistic option, but rather calls for policies and programmes which lead to strengthening tenure security in squatter settlements, thus facilitating higher levels of housing investment".

Admittedly 40 per cent of the population is below the poverty line. The disparities in wealth/ income in our society are horrendous. Five per cent of our top in society enjoy 33 per cent of the national wealth as against the bottom who own only .001 per cent wealth, similarly 20 per cent of the bottom population share seven per cent of the national income against 10 per cent of the top population which shares 34 per cent. One-fourth of the villages have no driking water supply and three-fourths no all-weather roads, even in Punjab, the pride of Green Revolution, 40 per cent of those working in agriculture own less than seven per cent of the land. Each of them owns less that one hectare of land which has no marketable surplus. The disparities of consumption are a standing fester on our body politik. The share of consumption of top 10 per cent rose from 20 per cent in 1950 to 60 per cent in 1980. Our democracy cannot live with this humiliating poverty, the deprivation of human rights and the prevention of social relations. But to bring a change requires hard political choices to be made high—level of taxation, a strong curb on conspicuous consumption by the affluent sections of society.

We have consciously to decide whether we are to build a society – a State where 100-150 million people will enjoy European standard of living or we will so utilize our resources as to uplift 800 millions of our countrymen to a respectable human existence. In my view, the latter can only be done if both social justice and equity become an integral part of the growth strategy. It is a specious argument that urges that poverty is a long–term problem and that current deficits are short-term emergency—that poverty can wait but deficits cannot. This is muddle-headed thinking. To reduce and eliminate massive absolute poverty line at the very core of development itself. It is critical to the survival of any decent society.

I believe that a human right activist has to have anger and compassion-anger at injustice in one eye and compassion for the downtrodden in the other. It is the sincerity of this approach that will determine the commitment to human right.

This book is modest attempt to answer some of the questions, which constantly arise in the society. I am not vain to think that they are necessarily the only ones. But I place them in the market place of ideas- for the benefit the readers the ultimate sovereign who will judge for himself/herself.

Though in the end, but never the less equally strongly I must thank my daughter Madhavi and my grand daughter Shreya daughter of my son Sanjiv who have done the tedious and tough task of going through my random jottings and the manuscript so as to put it in a proper shape. My thanks are also due to my son Sanjiv and My daugher-in-law Sita for choosing the title of the book.

1
Human Rights : Present Day Challenges

1.1 Human Rights in India—Different Facets

Talk of Human Rights these days is not a forbidden topic even amongst the fashionable crowd. But there is a real danger that this may reduce the concept of Human Right to a mere goody goody sentiment and not recognize it as an instrument of social justice. It is this aspects which constantly needs to be assessed.

Another misconception is to assume that recognition of Human Right is an emanation from west and only came to be known to the rest of the world when U.N. General Assembly adopted on 10th December, 1948 as a Universal Declaration of Human Rights.

This according to me is merely self flaggestion of the west. Human existence and flights of spirit are too ancient to accept that the concept of universalism is only a 20th Century concept. On the contrary this concept has to origin in antiquity.

Ancients always maintained "Vasudhaiva Kutumbakam" meaning all world is one family.

Thus thousand of years back, "Atharva Veda" said as the cow protects her new born even at the risk of her own life so one should enlarge one's heart infinitely with compassion for all sentient beings". The words of Christ are equally apposite when he said "Do not do unto others what is hateful to you. The God will know. Do unto others as you would have them do unto to you". Similarly in the Holy Qoran there is an injunction that all men are brothers and that non-Muslims should be treated with no less dignity and respect for their personality than Muslims. The Qoran prohibits discrimination against all persons whether white or black. In the west, Rousseau, Locke, Thomas Jefferson in 17th and 18th centuries kept up the flame.

In the 20th century emphasis on human rights owes its origin to the Charter of the United Nations, which in the Preamble has reaffirmed to people "fundamental human rights, in the dignity and of human person, in the equal rights of men and women and of nations large and small". Upon this declaration, a Commission on Human Rights was created to draft an "International Bill of Human Rights". The first segment, the Universal Declaration of Human Rights was adopted by the General Assembly on 10th December, 1948. The Declaration when accepted constitutes an obligation on the members of the international community. A step towards concretizing of these human rights was effected when the United Nations Assembly on 16 December, 1966 unanimously adopted the International Covenant on Economic, Social and Cultural Rights, the International Covenant on Civil and Political Rights and the Optional Protocol to the later.

It is obligatory on the States which ratify these covenants to ensure that their citizens are able to exercise the enshrined human rights to the full. With all the talk about commitment to the protection of human rights, these covenants ought to have been ratified by the various nations straightway. But alas! hiatus between precept and practice is a weakness not just of individuals but also of nations. It took almost a decade (1976) before these instruments were ratified by 35 members of the United Nations, a minimum to bring them into force. India whose Constitution has provided for almost all the human rights specified in the covenants defaulted inexcusably and only ratified the two covenants in 1979. It has not yet ratified the Optional Protocol.

Only a small number, i.e., 39 countries have ratified or acceded to the Optional Protocol. This is to be regretted because the Optional Protocol to the Covenant on Civil and Political Rights permits individuals under certain circumstances to file complaints of human rights violation by ratifying States. Any nation which prides itself on its record of protection of human rights can scarcely refuse to ratify the Optional Protocoal. Curiously in this regard India shares the doubtful honour of non-ratification with USA, UK, Pakistan and USSR.

The position in USA is incomprehensible. It refused to ratify either Covenant on Economic, Social and Cultural Rights or the Covenant on Civil and Political Rights, when they were passed though it has made human rights one of its main planks of foreign policy. Even when President Carter in his message to the American Senate on 6 December, 1979 requested its advice and consent to the two covenants, the Senate refused, notwithstanding that President stated:

"In making these anniversaries, we renew our dedication both to our own liberties and to the promotion of human rights everywhere on earth".

President Carter aptly commented:

"The Universal Declaration of Human Rights sets global standards that reflect the same vision that inspire our own Bill of Rights. Almost every country has endorsed the Declaration. Yet in too much of the world its promise is mocked".

Unfortunately America, which prides itself on its concern for human rights, refused to bind itself to the covenants, thus laying itself open to charges of double standards. It is only in 1992 that USA ratified civil covenant—it is refusing and has not ratified Economic Covenant which is the life blood for developing countries as it casts obligation on developed countries like USA to aid in development process.

Since some time in the recent past a hollow question has been deliberately raised. It is suggested that in developing countries, the stress should be on economic rights; in the process if political rights and civil liberties are curtailed this price must be accepted temporarily. Usually, it is presented as a competition between the European model of supremacy of political rights and the communist model of priority of economic rights. Such a sharp cut division is clearly a myth. No such artificial conflict of choice between economic and political freedoms exist. This argument has no basis left after the Vienna Declaration on Human Rights which has accepted the universally and indivisibility of all human Rights, political and economic.

Bread and liberty are two sides of the same coin, and deprivation of either must inevitably damage the fabric of the other. The freedom to agitate for bread and sustenance to fight for one's liberties are concomitant. As a matter of fact the Universal Declaration of Human Rights encompasses within itself the political rights of life, liberty and security of person (Article 3), and the economic right that everyone has the right to work and protection against unemployment (Article 23). The compulsions of economic rights are recognized by the discerning even in so-called affluent countries.

Rule of law is the foundation of Human Rights. How strong is the foundation is to be judged both by substantive law and procedural remedies.

In any democratic state the state of human right is judged by the conduct of one of the coercive manifestation of state-namely the police. It is more so in a country like India, with illiteracy of 50 per cent and extreme poverty. In that context police in our country has a poor record. In this I can do no better than quote from the latest assessment made by National Human Rights Commission (India) itself. The largest chunk of the complaints received by the NHRC concern police with most of these complaints relating to custodial violence. The following data on death in police custody and complaints of illegal detention given in the Annual Reports of the NHRC clearly indicate that despite a growing human rights movement in the country, the police brutality is continuing unabated.

	1996-97	*97-98*	*98-99*	*99-2000*
Death in police custody	136	193	183	185
Illegal detention	282	330	436	1157

A serious source of violation of Human Rights is thus misuse of police power to avert, harass under the influence of political influence or money power. National Police Commission had found that 60 per cent of the arrests made by the police which accounted for 43.2 percent of expenditure on jails are either unnecessary or unjustified.

The entitlement to compensation against police brutality has been recognized by the Courts through the instrumentality of Public Interest Litigation - NHRC has been following this practice - it is stated to have awarded compensation of about 4 crores in 360 cases.

Another human violation of Human Rights in the continuation of Torture methods by police in spite of the Convention against Torture and Other Cruel, Inhuman or Degrading Treatment of Punishment' which entered into force on 26th June 1987.

In spite of massive public demand Government of India is stubborney refusing to ratify convention against torture - a ventable blot on its Human Rights record. (1996) *Pasthim Berpal Mazdoor* Vs. *State*.

The Supreme Court of India has shown sensitivity in the matter of torture and illegalities by the police. In a path breaking judgement (Joginder Kumar) the Court speaking through Mr. Justice A.S. Anand (as his lordship then was) said "No arrest can be made because it is lawful for the police officer to do so. The existence of the power to arrest in one thing. The justification for the exercise of it is quite another .... No arrest should be made without a reasonable satisfaction reached after some investigation as to the genuineness and bona fides of a complaint and a reasonable belief both as the person's complicity and even so as tc the need to effect arrest. Denying a person of his liberty is a serious matter".

In spite of the dismal record Government go on trying to give more powers to the police by passing laws like TADA. Its working was so obnoxious to the Human Rights that NHRC publically lent its support to the voice of NGOs like Peoples Union for Civil Liberties and others that there has been great misuse of TADA is clear from the figures which show that of the total of over 52,000 persons proceeded under TADA in 1993, 14,451 are from Punjab, that 14,049 were proceeded in Gujarat is the climax of abuse of power, because not even the best friends of government will claim that Gujarat is 'terrorist infested'. The practical utility of this draconian measures is nil because during 1985-93, conviction rate of those arrested has never exceeded 0.89 per cent.

It has however to be recorded that Members of Parliament

did not cover themselves with glory on the passing of TADA. Thus, unfortunately, members of Parliament seemed to have lapped up the false pleas of the Government. That alone can explain that discussion in Parliament on TADA from 1985 to 1993 has veried between 1 hour and ten minutes (1993) to a maximum of 8 hours in 1985. The participation of MP's further shows the scant concern of our lawmakers for the liberties of citizens, it has varied for 8 MP's to a maximum of 34 in 1985. It would seem that gradually the sensitivity of MP's at the deprivation of basic rights of citizens been dulled into indifference.

Notwithstanding this experience Government of India is thinking of revising it though camouflaging it under the enactment called Criminal Law Amendment Bill. Country wide agitation by Human Rights Activists have uptill now been able to stall it. PUCL intends to activate this movement and hopes that with the apposition from NHRC, this ugly legislation may be avoided.

Judicial delay is also one of the deprivation of Human Rights. According to an official release reported in the press, a total of 21,567 cases are pending disposal in the Supreme Court as on 1 November 2000. Of these 8,472 cases have been pending for more than two years and 645 for more than 10 years. The backlog of cases before the various High Courts are reported to be around 18.86 lakhs pending for more than two years, and about five lakhs pending for more than ten years. Whereas, of a total of 2.01 crore cases pending before the district and subordinate courts, 1.93 crore cases have been pending for less than ten years, and 8.19 lakh cases for more than ten years. A report by Mrinal Pandey the eminent journalist shows that the malnutrition among young mothers and children remains rampant, as high as 48 per cent in Orissa and 44 per cent in West Bengal. Citing a recent study — Second National Health Survey (1998-1999) fifty per cent of women are still married off illegally before the age of 18. A disturbing trend on gender equality.

There is no reliable data on the exact number of children being exploited at work. The estimate range from 20 million (official) to 100 million (NGO). They are engaged in a variety of industries or vocations - matches and fireworks, carpet making, glass bangle making, brassware's, plastics and rope weaving, salt extraction, incense stick production.

The Alternative Report on India submitted by the Butterflies, an Indian NGO, submitted to the UN Rights of the Child Committee in 1998 (in parallel to the official report submitted by the Government of India). Largely indicted the Government for the failure of the political leadership and bureaucracy (both of whom continued, according to the report, to be titled in favour of the privileged classes) and for its eagerness to withdraw from the social sector under the structural adjustment programmes.

Disabled

Although the disabled are expected to be beneficiaries of Parts III and IV of the Constitution, social prejudices more than anything else stand in the way of the strife of the disabled to achieve equality of status and of opportunity. On the occasion of the International Day for Persons with Disabilities on 3 December 2000, the Union Ministry of Social Justice and Empowerment has rededicated itself to its commitment "to provide equal opportunities, protection of rights, full participation and all round development of persons with Disabilities Act, 1995 in the new millennium." The Act, which was passed with much fanfare, however, remains in the statute book without much implementation on the ground.

About 6 per cent of India's population is estimated to be disabled. They have attracted the government's attention only in the 1990's. Less than two per cent of them have had access to education. Most public places and transport systems are inaccessible to them, although the Disabilities Act assures them of a right to "barrier-free-environment".

According to a 1991 survey, there are about seven million employable disabled person (and this figure could increase with the introduction of appropriate technologies) but the placement rate has been no more than 4000 a year. The Chinese have tapped the potential of its disabled by finding productive employment for 70 per cent of them.

The menace of communalism is on the rise. It is a matter of profound shame that we still witness riots and terrorist violence in the name of religion. Communalism still stalks our land. All over the country we see different religions veering towards fundamentalism. The growing trend of communalism is tearing asunder the unity of our country and posing a grave threat of India's integrity. Different kinds of communal organizations and religious "Bodies" are raising their ugly heads all over the country. It is my belief that those who talk of a state founded on religion are working for the disintegration of India and are violating the letter and spirit of our Constitution.

We need to work towards establishing just and equal society inshrined in our Constitution. If we go on fighting each other in the name of religion we shall never be able to begin our march for establishing such a society. Today, all Hindus, Muslims, Sikhs, Christians all Indians—have to wage a concerted struggle for social justice and equalitarianism. They have to make a reality of the society envisioned in our Constitution.

Is it now the foremost duty of those believing in Human Rights to put up a spirited fight against this menace of communalism lest this menace eat into the very vitals of our democracy.

Communal strife acts as a barrier in the way of every kind of struggle for a better life for the vast majority of our people. It disrupts common struggle against poverty and exploitation. At a more fundamental level, communalism has to be fought because it is profoundly anti-human. It has caused, and cannot but cause, untold suffering, repeated riots, millions of refugees, persistent threats of violence, and squeezing of employment and economic opportunities purely because you happened to be a member of a particular community.

Though the Indian Constitution declares equality in the eye of law, entitled to equal treatment, in fact the prevailing social system gives no solace to a believer in human rights. Swami Vivekananda said decades ago that a tyranny of the majority is the worst form of tyranny. The masses who comprise the lowest castes have had their dignity trampled upon through the blows and kicks dealt to them by the higher castes. We have every day to hang our heads in shame at the treatment meted out to the scheduled castes in large parts of rural India. Even now there are places where they do not have village lanes without covering their heads, and they have to take their marriage processions on certain routes. Where they dare disobey, carnage and murder follows.

Recently a campaign has been started against Reservation in jobs for Dalits by camouflaging it under the bald slogan of efficiency. These are the old exploded excuses and against facts. Hardly 2 per cent Dalits are able to take advantage of job reservation both in states and the center. In my opinion past and continuing unjustice to Dalits mandates a positive social justice approach.

Arguments apparently attractive, are raised that the solid test for any preferential treatment at the hands of the State should be the economic, but this ignores the social domination of caste system in our society. We have still not got out of feudal set up and to ignore the shackles of caste is to ignore reality. But courts must be vigilant not to fall in for this apparently attractive, though unsound argument, namely as to why in the matter of allotment of surplus land in the village preference should be given to the landless Harijans but that the test should be only that of economic penury. The strategies even today need to be the same as I expressed in one of my judgments in Delhi High Court way back in 1982 thus "it was urged that there was no reason why persons other than Harijans if they were landless should not be allotted land. We feel that the paucity of land being there and it being impossible to fulfill the desire of every landless, preference must be given to those who are landless labourers belonging to Harijans and Backward Classes residing in the village and who would earn their living by land. The allotment of land is not merely a matter of earning a living or an asset creating issue for landless ones in the village but is in a more important sense an aspect of recognition of their dignity and status in the village community. As the land which is available for allotment is very much less even to meet the requirements of the Harijan and the weaker sections of the community in the village, we cannot subscribe to the suggestion that priority should not be given to Harijan community, but all castes should be eligible for the allotment financial penury being the sole test. Though in theory financial penury will weigh equally heavily on all the castes, it would be unrealistic not to accept that Harijans are the worst sufferers of poverty. The other castes have only financial exploitation to resist. Harijans have to be brought out of not only the financial but social outcastism to which they have been condemned for centuries. In the matter of alleviation of any misery a country with limited resources has necessarily to evolve priorities in each sector. Our social system has, it must be remembered to live down the centuries of caste exploitation and sub-human existence to which this large chunk of our population, i.e., Harijans were condemned. Giving preference for allotment of land to those landless Harijans is only a recognition of our responsibility to create equal, casteless society to which our Constitution is committed. Our Constitution not only permits but demands an affirmative action in favour of the Harijans and other similar weak classes".

It may be asked whether protagonists of human rights should concern themselves with this. The answer is an emphatic yes. The denial of human rights to such large segments, if not resisted, will stultify the fight for human rights.

Believers in human rights must be ever vigilant to resist any onslaught on the civil and political liberties of the individual. There can be no compromise in their essentialities. It is necessary that these rights so far as developing countries are concerned must be correlated with another major aspect of human rights, namely, the development of the economy and the responsibility of society to feed, clothe, house, and maintain a people, free from starvation, free from pollution in the air and water, able to bring up one's children and oneself in a decent healthy environment, and to have the maximum conditions of good health.

The horror of poverty was highlighted in a message given on 17th October in observance of International day for the Eradication of Poverty by the UN Secretary-General, who reminded us as to "how many times have we said that it (poverty) was incompatible with human dignity. But billions of people are still trying to survive on less than three dollars a day, with no drinking water, health care, or access to education, still denied the jobs that would help them escape their impoverished state, and thus, still deprived of some of their most basic rights".

Freedom of an individual which is postulate of Human Rights obviously can have no meaning so long as the poor in the country do not have their economic conditions improved and the discrimination based on privilege do not become memories of the past rather than becoming more and more aggressive as the time passes on.

Unfortunately, the solutions being suggested are illusion. Thus the must touted claim by the propagandists of globalization that it will accelerate progress in developing countries is belied by UNDP's Tenth Human Development Report of 1999, which says that "market dominated globalization has led to growing marginalisation of poor nations and people, growing human insecurity and growing unequal with benefits accruing almost solely to the richest people and countries and that the global gap between the haves and have-nots is widening."

HDR 1999 has commented tersely "the benefits of globalization in the past decade have been so unevenly shared that the very word has come to acquire in certain quarters a pejorative tinge". The present situation must cause concern to all Human Right activists.

The richest fifth have an income 74 times that of the poorest fifth.

One per cent of the wealth of the 200 richest people, or $ 8 billion, could provide universal access to primary education for a year - but no political party is seeking to correct this perverted balance - the result a denial of human right of universal education.

The assets of three richest people are more than the combined GNP of the 48 least developed countries.

Calling globalization "the central challenge we face today", world leaders attending the United Nations Millennium Summit on the evening of 8 September 2000 had to recognize that "For while globalization offers great opportunities, at present its benefits are very unevenly shared, while its costs are unevenly distributed".

H.R.D. 2000 has commented acidly that Global inequalities in income increased in the 20th century by orders of magnitude out of proportion to anything experienced before. The distance between the incomes of the richest and poorest countries was about 3 to 1 in 1820, 35 to 1 in 1950, 44 to 1 in 1973 and 72 to 1 in 1992.

The "global marketplace" is not necessarily a place of equlity, with benefits and rewards equitably shared by all those who participate in it.

To speak of globalisation with regard to increased integration of the world economy is misleading; there is a process of concentration of capital which only benefits three principal regions (North America, Europe and East Asia) becomes more and more marginalized. (we can include India along with Africa).

All talk of Human Rights must sound hallow unless the State policy assures a citizen find Housing which is the primary need of an individual or a family.

Now it admits of no doubt that the "Right to adequate housing" which as a distinct and unique component of international human rights law, finds recognition within a broad and diverse range of treaties, declarations, agreements, recommendations, resolutions and other legal texts.

Global strategy for shelter to the year 2000 as adopted by the General Assembly formulates that the right to adequate housing is universally recognized by the community of nations .... All citizens of all States, poor as they may be have a right to expect their Governments to be concerned about their shelter needs and to accept a fundamental obligation to protect and improve houses and neighbourhoods rather than damage or destroy them".

The Housing Policy, 1988 issued by the Ministry of Urban Affairs & Employment, Government of India, itself recognizes the grim housing situation. In its introduction the Government had lamented how Member after member in the Lok Sabhas (Parliament) vividly described the sad and miserable life which millions of our fellow citizens, men, women, and children, are compelled to lead without proper shelter and habitat. The situation is doubtless grim and calls for nothing less than a revolution — "A Housings Revolution". Mere lip service will not do. And yet the dichotomy between words and deeds becomes startling painful by even a routinely observing the actual woeful situation on the ground — the actual reality.

The projection of housing shortage is estimated about 30 million units of which 16.7 millions units are in urban areas. Out of this 15.02 million houses are needed for Low Income Group (L.I.G) and Economically Weaker Section (E.W.S.) - Out of the total of housing stocks in urban area, 76 per cent or so are "pacca" (built of mortar construction). In rural areas the situation is far worse with mortar houses being only about 34 per cent.

This deficit, along with the needs of housing during the Ninth Plan (1997-2002) would need an investment of about Rs. 1,51,000 crores or (37 billion USD). It has been estimated that urban infrastructure alone would need a sum of Rs. 2,50,000 crores about (60 billion USD) in the next ten years. Only ten per cent of this would be available from government sources.

As per the Government programme, it is proposed to facilitate construction of 2 million additional units every year, with emphasis on EWS (Economically Weaker Section) and LIG (Low Income Group) sections of the population as also the needs of Scheduled Castes and Scheduled Tribes SC/ST and other vulnerable groups. Out of 2 million additional houses, 0.7 million houses will be constructed in the urban areas and remaining 1.3 million in the rural areas. This would requires an additional investment of around Rs. 4,000 crores (1 Billion USD).

Now Global strategy defines "Adequate Housing" to mean: "adequate privacy, adequate space, adequate security, adequate basic facilities, all at a reasonable cost".

The distressing reality however is that in India over 45 per cent of households have only one room per capita. Area available to the bottom 40 per cent is 58 sq. metre. Even the Delhi Municipal Corporation prescribes the requirement regarding the minimum size of a habitable room as 60 sq. metre.

A study conducted by the Delhi Development Authority shows that a hut of 2.5 X 3 metres accommodates about four persons. In Delhi nearly one third of the total population live in jhuggi jhopri bustees. (Tin/plastic shacks).

The inequity in the provisions of infrastructure and basic services across the states and size categories of settlements has been accentuated as a consequence of the programme of structural adjustment and consequent withdrawal of the state.

Thus about 40.7 per cent household in the country are living in one room and average household is 5 to 6 persons. About 50 per cent of the dwellers were using open areas for toilet purposes. Sharing of latrines is quite common among poor households as over 60 per cent among them have shared latrines.

In Urban areas of the country private toilets are limited to 15 per cent of the households and community toilets to another 21 per cent whereas more than 60 per cent of the households resort to open spaces for defeaction.

Water, sewage and housing are other critical elements for life, without which there can be neither health nor comfort.

According to one Government estimate about 57 per cent of the total population is not covered by supply of safe drinking water. The per capita norm for water consumption should be 300 litres per day whereas on an average, the urban population is supplied only 145 litres per capita per day in Class-I cities. As many as 31 per cent of the households have to walk up to 100 feet to collect water and many among the poor — women and children — had to cover the distance not once but several times a day to collect the daily requirements.

That for the overwhelming majority of the slum dwellers, the availability of water may be lesser than 20 litres per capita per day.

The present contribution of social housing in meeting the needs of weaker sections is a mere token and was able to contribute only 6.54 per cent of the stock.

The fact that the urban poor constitute about one third of the big city population in countries like India, Pakistan and Bangladesh, and that structural adjustment is unlikely to do them much good, is a matter of concern for economic and urban planners alike.

The entry of foreign capital and real estate developers had meant that land prices in cities are rising further especially at prime locations and in metropolitan centres. Pressure on slum-dwellers and other unauthorized encroachers to vacate their sites is therefore increasing.

For millions of people all over the world, especially in rural areas, land is the principal resource for survival.This dependency on land is not limited to tribal or indigenous populations but uncompasses small and marginal farmers and the rural agricultural labour that depends on land for livelihood. The failure by Governments to either adopt land reforms or implement the existing statues, and the failure to arrest speculation and the commercialization of land, has resulted in a situation today where evictions, landlessness and homelessness are on the increase.

The same is the position in India, Rural poverty is most fundamental reason for the great migration to cities. The vast majority of these men and women are marginal farmers and farm labourers who in their native villages lack resources and opportunities.

Recent trend in slum evictions are on increase. This follows from the usual bureaucratic unsympathetic approach, encouraged by the over enthusiastic but misplaced. Environmental groups, who using the cloak of fear of pollution and over indulgent consideration for the welfare of wild animals seek the aid of courts for direction to evict the poor slum dwellers from the sites they have lived for generations. Somehow, I do not mind confessing that I do feel bitter that these worthies invoke the language of first world and seek to apply the same tests in developing countries that are most inapposite in different situations. After all the greatest violation of Human Right is the poverty, homelessness and not having even ordinary shelter. I may sound a reactionary to these so called animal lovers, but if ever a choice was to be made between preserving the Human Right to shelter of a slum dweller or the so called environmental standards laid down by first world, I would unhesitatingly opt for the former because to me no one takes precedence over human brotherhood.

Fortunately there is authorative support for such a view that it is inequitable and impractical to ask the developing countries to enforce the same rigid environment standards as the developed nations and which was recognized in a study by a GATT on the subject of trade and environment which had concluded that interference with trade is seldom if ever the best way of achieving a particular domestic environmental objective.

Similar approach is recognized in Principal II of the 1992 Rio Declaration on Environment and Development which says "Standards applied by some countries may be inappropriate and of unwarranted economic and social cost to other countries, in particular developing countries".

One of the most unfortunate of such example is taking place in the State of Maharashtra (India), Starting April 20, 2000, the state Government of Maharashtra started bulldozing the homes and evicting over 60,000 slum and shanty dweller families in Mumbai. The drive, executed under the orders of the Bombay High Court, continued with brutal precision with around a 1,000 homes being smashed under the treads of bulldozers everyday in what has become the largest eviction operation independent India has ever seen.

The drive has already seen around four schools catering to over 20,000 children being removed from the face of the earth, and at least two persons dead.

These evictions that are going on even today concern slums that have come up over the years of immigrant populations and have settled of the borders of what is called the Sanjay Gandhi National Park - a forest reserve on the outskirts of the city. Most of the slum dwellers were not aware and are still disputing the ill-defined borders of the national reserve. It is also clear that most of them whose settlements are as old as 10 to 25 years. The number of these evicted families is around 33,000 and about 1,50,000 persons are affected. Govternment with tongue in check proclaimed that they will be relocated/ rehabilitated at Kalyan district. No such area has been legally located or developed. The uprooted lot continue to live exposed to the sky and without a shred of shelter. Besides slum dwellers, the evictions involve the removal of nearly 2,500 'adivasi' or tribal families — whose hamlets occupied parts of the forest even before the area was declared a national part in 1982 are also threatened with eviction.

Equally disturbing is the demolition and police action at Bhimnagar slum (Maharashtra) colony on July 22-23, 2000 in which two persons lost their lives.

The site on which Bhim Nagar once existed is today a hillside of smoking rubble. People crouch under make shift plastic tents and can be seen trying to scavenge whatever they can of their belongings from amidst the ruins of what was once their homes.

The attitude of the urban elite in the matter of slum and pavement dwellers in totally negative. It may sometimes mouth sympathy with them, but they are consistent in their demand that slum dwellers, who are mostly squatters on government and must be forcibly evicted, notwithstanding the lack of my alternative rehabilitation scheme and which would be in defiance of recognized international Human Right Covenants and law. This was exemplified in the instance of slum improvement project Narela which was meant for rehabilitation of about 10,000 units from various parts of the capital (Delhi). The provision on paper showed that for re-locating and re-settling evictees, basic facilities and also provision of school and other facilities would be provided. A visit to the project site however revealed that the slum dwellers allegedly rehabilitated lacked basic amenities. An officers in charge of this project were forced to concede that the basic amenities should have been provided before relocation but offered an untenable excuse of delay on the part of the Government decision. One of the serious criticism against the relocation has always been that the slum dwellers are denied their employment by way of livelihood by being thrown at a very distant place. Even this was conceded by the officer that the slum dwellers faced a genuine problems like lack of employment opportunities. But made a statement with typical cynicism that in the next two years area would have ample employment opportunities and that nothing much can be done soon with regard to the poor in the society.

Mercifully this total indifference has been sought to be retrieved by local Delhi Government on the World Habitat Day on 4th October that any slum dwellers hutments built prior to 1998 would not be demolished but will be provided with electricity, water and sanitation facilities. These announcements, however is to be taken cautiously because the Central Government (belonging to different political party) and which has control over these facilities has not given his approval and affirmation to this policy. Unfortunately electoral publics does play its role in various announcements of local and Central

Government which further hinders the evolving of a long term slum up gradation policy.

Later day planners unfortunately have not sought to fuse the problem of environment with the human problem of poor. The courts somewhat rashly gave direction to shift industries outside the city limits, which will involve dislocation and relocation of about 2,00,000 families. Insistence by Courts even without there being adequate relocation policy, to shift in the shortest of time frame compounds the problem. The poor get the blame for pollution, when the inefficiency and vested interest of government machinery should take the blame.

Also in this apportionment of blame, it is conveniently forgotten as was pointed out in one estimate that 70 per cent of air pollution in Delhi is caused by 30 lakh vehicles (the highest number in the country). And yet planners and politicians seldom talk of having no vehicles zone, planning the vehicles movement and improving the availability of efficient public transport. In their misplaced enthusiasm courts goaded by environmental-cum-business lobby insist on applying Euro-II standard in cars in India with per capita annual income of 350 US Dollars (when the same were introduced in Europe hardly a decade back when per capita annual income was at least 15,000 US Dollars). These rigid standard have resulted in mass unemployment of individual taxi driver and of three wheelers thus seriously jeopardizing the livelihood of hundreds of thousands and consequently violating their Human Right of living and work.

I find this lack of understanding dangerous. I wish the policy makers were to ask themselves the right question so that they can get their sums right.

With the above authoritative formulation it is incumbent on the governments to choose instruments through which to make this right realistic. Most of the Government tend to take the easier, but ineffective course of leaving this right to be exercised through the unsatisfactory mechanism of the market. How wrong! Now free markets, if left to their own devices, can wind up terribly unfree, and government intervention is sometimes necessary to ensure even unfettered competition.

It is now well-established that market alone cannot be the

answer, because as Habitat Review stated: "in order to have progress in urban shelter requires strong Government intervention; it cannot be rectified by markets alone, since markets care little for considerations of equity and sustainability".

It will thus be self-evident that in a poor country like India, without large scale intervention by the State through legislative means, or the construction of public housing units, the provision of housing subsidies or rental protection, much larger numbers of people than at present would become homeless or be forced to stay in inadequate shelters.

A believer in human right has to have anger and compassion — anger at injustice, compassion for the downtrodden. Realism must spill over into the study of human rights. Let not universities and colleges concern themselves only with slavery in Rome, Greece and Fascist Germany, but also with the gross violations of human rights at home. A study of the human rights perspective in India can no longer be the concern of researchers alone — along with research, there must be firm action against the violator of human rights. It is the sincerity of this effort that will determine the commitment to human rights.

1.2 A Visit to Sri Lanka

For two decades, Sri Lanka has suffered under a fratricidal war between the Tamils in the North and the Government in Colombo. A recent visit to the island-nation and interactions with a cross-section of the people including top functionaries of all political parties, the Buddhist clergy, civil society representatives, church leaders and NGOs give hope that events may be taking a turn for the better. This is the result of the peace process, the term used to describe the events taking place in Sri Lanka dating from the ceasefire declaration of December 2001 to the Memorandum of Understanding (MoU) signed in February 2002, and the current Norway-facilitated negotiations between the Government in Colombo and the LTTE.

Though there are lingering doubts, everyone accepts that peace in some form is urgently needed in Sri Lanka to alleviate the human, social and economic costs of the war incurred by all sides. There is near unanimity among all sections of the people, both in the North and the South, that the present peace should not be disturbed. This is the greatest factor after the MoU leading to the optimism that not only will peace continue, it will also bring about a permanent solution satisfactory to the Tamil people and, what is of significance, without in any manner violating the integrity and status of Sri Lanka.

A formal meeting with the top Buddhist leadership in Colombo was rewarding. Buddhist monks are known to have played a very crucial part in influencing the majority Sinhala community and the Government. In a refreshing exchange, the monks frankly admitted that denying Tamil the status of official language was a mistake and undoubtedly contributed to the unfortunate developments. Buddhist monks now accept that there can be no permanent solution without a large devolution of power and functions to the North and the East but insist that it should not in any way affect the integrity of Sri Lanka, which proposition is overwhelmingly accepted by both sides.

Some sceptics seem to suggest that the Government is not genuinely interested in meeting the demands of the Tamils for sharing of power but is going through the motions to prolong the talks in the expectation that time will weaken the hold of the LTTE — there are reports that there is now free movement and some of the cadres of the LTTE are leaving and, hence, it is argued, it will become weaker if later on the Government decides to hang up on it. I do not agree. It has to be remembered that the LTTE's strength was in the perception of injustice to the Tamil people and denial of their rightful participation in the governance of Sri Lanka. If the Government were ever to try to go back on its promises of being serious in conceding genuine Tamil demands, the consequences would be severe. But from our interaction with unbiased observers and close confidants of both sides, it was seen that this assessment about the Government's motives is not shared by any responsible section of the people. As a matter of fact, there is now a close camaraderie between Government officers and the LTTE cadre. Anton Balasingam agreeing to use a Government helicopter to meet V. Prabakaran before the second round of negotiations is cited as an example.

This assessment now finds corroboration from the reports of deliberations at the second round of talks in Thailand at which an agreement was reached between the Government and the LTTE on the broad parameters for the utilisation of international aid and restoration and rehabilitation in disturbed areas. This arrangement has the welcome development of having a Muslim representative from the eastern region being part of a task force along with Tamil and Sinhala representatives.

There is no denying that one of the delicate issues is the question of merger of the North and the East as one region, which to the LTTE is non-negotiable. The Muslims who constitute a big section in the East are somewhat apprehensive about their rights if there is a merger. The result of this latest adjustment among these three sections would act as a boost to peace talks, and also give the necessary reassurance to the Muslims. The Muslims are basically traders and the LTTE has rightly or wrongly a grievance that they did not participate fully in its fight against the Government. This misunderstanding will further get cleared now that the economic package is to be shared equitably.

Some of the human rights activists, though no doubt welcoming the peace talks, emphasised that the MoU does not have a human rights content and that it is necessary that there must be a mechanism by which reports of violations are investigated by an independent body. That is why many feel it will be wrong to give exclusive control to the LTTE in the interim administration that may be formed in the near future. Even Sri Lankan Tamils and other parties sympathetic to the LTTE share the view that there must be some mechanism by which other Tamil organisations and NGOs working among children and women could be associated with the interim administration and the normal civil and political rights of the citizens guaranteed not only by the LTTE but also by the monitoring committee, more especially when the MoU acknowledges international law in accordance with which the parties have agreed to refrain from hostile acts against the civilian population.

The practical wisdom which determines the desire of the Government and the LTTE to continue talks is shown by the fact that the recent judgment of a Colombo court sentencing Mr. Prabakaran to a 200-year jail term has not derailed the talks. Rather, Mr. Balasingam has gone public by asserting that the sentence will not affect the peace talks. Similarly, Lakshman Kadirgamar, former Foreign Minister, said that notwithstanding the verdict the talks would continue.

Paradoxically, one of the road blocks could be the petty politics being played by the UNP and the PA — political parties respectively of the Prime Minister and the President. They indulge in mutual accusations; one threatening to dissolve Parliament and the other moving constitutional amendments seeking to curtail the President's power, when both the parties know well that objective conditions do not permit either of the courses. This attitude, if continued, could damage the peace talks and only encourage anti-peace Sinhala chauvinists.

India is accepted by all shades of opinion as having an abiding interest in the peace prevailing in Sri Lanka. From all signals one got from various sources. India continues to be supportive of peace efforts. India needs to continue to recognise the sensitivity of the situation because sometimes unnecessary motives are attributed to innocent acts. Thus, a normal commercial contract bagged by Indian Oil to supply oil at Trincomalee port, and for which it had been permitted to set up its oil storage tank, was portrayed as if India was being allowed to establish a naval presence.

1.3 Settling the Naga Issue

A deep suspicion, complaints of breach of promises by the Government of India and a confusing situation continue to bedevil the prospect of a solution to the Naga question. A breakthrough was, however, made when the then Prime Minister, Mr. I.K. Gujral, made the following announcement in Parliament on July 25, 1997: "In recent talks with the Isac Muivah group of the National Socialist Council of Nagaland (NSCN), it has been mutually agreed to ceasefire with effect from 1 August, 1997 and initiate discussions at political levels."

The term of talks were agreed as follows: (i) it shall be without conditions from both sides; (ii) it shall be at the highest level, that is, at the Prime Ministerial level; and (iii) the venue shall be anywhere outside India.

In all fairness, it must be recognised that this became possible because of the initiative taken earlier by former Prime Ministers beginning with a meeting between Mr. P.V. Narasimha Rao and the NSCN collective leadership in 1995. Again in February 1997, Mr. H. D. Deve Gowda had a meeting with Mr. Isac Swu, chairman and Mr. Muivah, general secretary, NSCN.

In 1998, the emissary of the Prime Minister, Mr. A.B. Vajpayee, met the NSCN collective leadership thrice at different places outside India .This was followed in September 1998 when Mr. Vajpayee held talks with the NSCN collective leadership in Paris. The Prime Minister's new emissary, Mr. K. Padmanabhaiah, also met the collective leadership in Amsterdam twice in 1999.

Despite some serious effort by both sides, the situation was becoming more critical, especially because the ceasefire was to expire by July 31, 2000, and no extension was being announced. This aspect was overwhelmingly impressed upon me when some of us participated in a consultation organised by the Asia Forum, Bangkok, on July 24, 2000. The meeting appealed to both the NSCN and the Government of India to extend the ceasefire so that the peaceful, constructive dialogue may continue.

One hurdle to the continuation of talks was the arrest and detention of Mr. Muivah by the Thailand Government on the charge of travelling on a fake passport. We were informed by Thai lawyers that if the Government of India had indicated to the Thai Government that it did not wish to have Mr. Muivah prosecuted, Bangkok would have released him on humanitarian grounds as it has done with other political prisoners caught with false travel documents.

The Union Home Minister, Mr. L.K. Advani, was informed of this when we met him recently. I feel that such a gesture by the Government of India, even if the Thai Government does not agree to release Mr. Muivah, will certainly help in restoring the confidence of the Naga leadership in the Union Government's intentions and facilitate talks.

A suggestion was given to Mr. Isac Swu and other members of the NSCN when some of us met them in Bangkok that in the meanwhile talks need not be stalled and Mr. Muivah could nominate a team to continue the dialogue in his absence. A team has since been nominated by Mr. Muivah and talks between them and Mr. Padmanabhaiah have taken place.

However, the biggest impediment in the peace process, as the NSCN sees it, is the refusal of the Government of India to officially extend the ceasefire to all Naga-inhabited districts (Ukhrul, Chandel, Senapati and Tamenglong) in Manipur.

A top political functionary of the Union Government says the Manipur Government fears this may be used as a device to take away these areas. This attitude appears illogical and unhelpful. At present the most pressing need is to maintain peace — in as large an area as possible. The question of reorganisation of States is totally irrelevant in the context of a ceasefire.

The whole rationale of a ceasefire is to create an atmosphere of godwill to facilinate talks. When a ceasefire was agreed to in 1997, the NSCN was operating in all Naga areas, even those outside Nagaland. It makes little sense to say that while both parties will hold their fire within Nagaland, they will continue to fight in areas outside the State. Of course, the Centre can legitimately expect the NSCN to ensure a ceasefire in all these areas by other groups also.

Another cause for disturbance of the peace process was the attempt on the life of the Nagaland Chief Minister, Mr. S.C. Jamir, in an ambush in November 1999. Immediately after this, Mr. Jamir issued a memo to all police stations that all NSCN cadres be arrested, which the NSCN considers a breach of the ceasefire. Nagaland Government representatives also refused to attend some meetings of the ceasefire Monitoring Group.

Subsequently, Mr. Jamir was persuaded to relent and his representatives attended the last meeting of monitoring group in May, 2000. For some administrative reasons, meetings have not been held in June and July, adding to the further distrust of the NSCN. The next meeting is scheduled for the middle of this month. There should, however, be an independent enquiry into the attack on Mr. Jamir since the NSCN has denied a hand in it.

Another unfortunate incident is the killing of 12 NSCN activists by the 17 Para regiment on July 11 in the North Cachar Hills. This has naturally caused a wave of anger amongst Nagas, and is held up as a breach of the ceasefire. The Centre has a different version of the incident, but a high-powered judicial inquiry should be ordered to defuse the situation.

Notwithstanding this disturbing event, it was a relief when we were told by Mr. Rh. Raising, member, NSCN Steering Committee, that "Nagas are totally committed to solve the problem through peaceful means. They want to solve any problem through mutual discussion, understanding, respect and consent". It is not only the NSCN but many other groups and human right activists in Naga areas who believe that continuing violence is ruinous for everyone and that a solution has to be found through talks.

I believe Naga civil society is prepared to play an active, meaningful role towards this end. It is accepted even in the highest Government circles that since the ceasefire, casualties have come down to one-third the pre-1997 period. This alone is justification and compulsion enough for both the Centre and the NSCN to continue their peace talks, not withstanding the provocations from some quarters on political considerations or on wrong analyses. The gun can never solve a problem in the modern world.

1.4 Media and Human Rights

1. All over the world the promotion and protection of human rights is accepted without any debate. Also accepted is the universality of these rights, not just in the present but also since the hoary past of human existence.

2. In the 20th century the emphasis on human rights owes its origin to the Charter of United Nations, which in the Preamble has reaffirmed to people "fundamental human rights in the dignity and of human person, in the equal rights of men and women and of nations large and small."

3. Overwhelmed by the misery and the almost total rout of all civilised and humane existence both within and inter nations, the General Assembly of the United Nations in recognition of the inherent dignity of the individual proclaimed the Universal Declaration of Human Rights (U.D.H.R.) on 10.12.1948. This document is a foundation which emphasised the place of human rights as being essential for the development of individual and society.

4. Article 19 of the declaration mandates that everyone has

a right of freedom of opinion and expression: *and to receive and impart information and idea through any media.*

5. A number of international covenants emphasise the pivotal position of Human Rights, the most notable being International Covenant on Civil and Political Rights. (ICCPR) and International Covenant on Economic, Social and Cultural Rights (ICESCR).

6. India's founding fathers and mothers who framed the Constitution showed similar concern by Incorporating Part III guaranteeing to its citizens the right to equality, to non-discrimination on any ground, freedom of Speech and Association and right to life.

7. Bereft of any embellishment, recognition of Human Rights must proceed on the acceptance of the basic equality amongst all the citizens and to treat each individual as an end in itself. From that flows the inevitable premise that the country must have a democratic set up and as is often said, be a government of laws and not of individuals. Unquestioned acceptance of supremacy of laws over every individual in the society, be of any ideology, wealth, caste or political, social or economic power, is the raw material from which the foundation of Human Rights has been laid. Any slight dent in the acceptance of these postulates would destroy the citadel of Human Rights and a mere husk would gape at us.

8. The role of Indian Press in the earlier period of our Independence in the matter of safeguarding human rights is a mixed one. Though individual cases of police excesses of the poor, or slum dwellers were no doubt reported, but not in the context of Human Rights violation but as an individual police official's aberration.

9. Governments conveniently invoke the sensitive ground of national security to sometime silence the media from reporting Human Rights violations especially from the sensitive areas. Unfortunately, the media by and large have a tendency to accept the gratuitous advice without demur. But this yielding is totally counter to the spirit and confidence which the international covenants repose in free press and the expectation that it will fulfill, its essential role in development of democratic

structure.

10. It is however a matter of satisfaction that media has now become more conscious of its role in the preservation of Human Rights and correspondingly its new language and reporting reflect its realization of what was aptly said long time back by Mr. Muggeridge the Editor, *Punch* weekly "The choice for us is between security and freedom. And if we ever ceased to prefer the latter, we should soon find that we had nothing of any worthwhile left to secure any way."

11. Sometime a hollow question is deliberately posed by those in political power in the developing countries. It is suggested that in developing countries, the stress should be on economic rights, and if in the process of civil liberties are curtailed this price must be accepted temporarily. In my view no such artificial conflict of choice between economic and political rights arises.

12. Bread and liberty are two sides of the same coin, and deprivation of either must inevitably damage the fabric of the other. The freedom to agitate for bread and sustenance to fight for one's liberties are concomitant.

13. Fortunately, this myth of conflict between political or economic rights or artificial prioritization of such rights in developed or developing countries was exploded, when Vienna Declaration and Programme of Action at the World Conference on Human Rights (1973) affirmed that human rights are the birth rights of all human beings and their protection and promotion is the first responsibility of the government and that all the human rights are universal, indivisible and interrelated.

14. Freedom of an individual which is postulate of Human Rights obviously can have no meaning so long as the poor in the country do not have their economic conditions improved and the discrimination based on privilege do not become memories of the past rather than becoming more and more aggressive as the time passes on.

15. If, therefore, I confine myself more with some aspect of human rights peculiar to the developing countries, it is not because of the lack of recognition or the importance of those aspects of the human rights which are more emphasised in

European and American context. It is only because I feel that the benefit of recognition of those aspects of human rights as put forth by the European context will not have large appeal unless the protagonists of human rights in developing countries concern themselves with the actual realities of oppression of the weak and of discrimination in the social set up which stares every one of us in face. Europe and America are concerned with the rights of Gay Group, the rights of unmarried mother, right to abortion or the status of surrogate mother, no doubt important aspects of human rights dimension in their social set up. But should not we of developing countries concern ourselves with more urgent aspect of Human Right.

16. The blessing of Government would degenerate into tyranny of government unless it is accompanied by a recognition that there are certain basic rights which are possessed by all the citizens. Though believers in Human Rights must be ever vigilant to resist any onslaught on the civil and political liberties of the individual and there can be no compromise on their essentiality, it is necessary that these rights, so far developing countries are concerned, must co-relate it with the equally important major issue which is also an aspect of human rights, namely, the development of the economy and the responsibility of the society to feed, clothe, house, maintain its people free from starvation, and able to bring up one's children and oneself in a decent, healthy environment.

17. The horror of poverty was highlighted in a message given on observance of International day for the Eradication of poverty on 17th October 1999 by the UN Secretary-General, who reminded us as to "how many times have we said that it (poverty) was incompatible with human dignity."

But billions of people are still trying to survive on less than three dollars a day, with no drinking water, health care, or access to education, still denied the jobs that would help them escape their impoverished state, and thus, still deprived of some of their most basic rights.

18. Now it is beyond dispute that right to adequate housing is recognised as a Human Right by the International Community, but yet according to indicators complied by the United Nations Centre on Human Settlements, at present over 100 million

people live in a state of absolute homelessness, while an excess of one billion people are forced by circumstances to reside in desperately inadequate housing conditions which threaten their health, security, safety and dignity.

19. It also needs emphasing that a number of such rights that are generally recognised as housing rights are linked to or derived from other human rights, such as equality and non-discrimination, gender equality, property rights, the right to a fair trial, the right to freedom of movement and to choose one's residence, the right to privacy, the right to process and other human rights related to housing.

20. The much touted claim by the protagonists of globalization that it will accelerate progress in developing countries is belied by UNDP's Tenth Human Development Report of 1999, which says that "market dominated globalization has led to growing marginalisation of poor nations and people, growing human insecurity and growing inequality with benefits accruing almost solely to the richest people and countries" and that "the global gap between the haves and have-nots, is widening.

21. The report further says that "the top fifth of the world's people in the richest countries enjoy 82 per cent of the expanding export trade and 68 per cent of foreign direct investment the bottom fifth, barely more than 1 per cent, combined GNP of the 48 least developed countries.".

22. HDR 1999 has commented "the benefits of globalization in the past decade have been so unevenly shared - between countries and regions of the world and between social classes in individual countries - that the very word has come to acquire in certain quarters a pejorative tinge." It has further warned that 'globalization' is not the one-word panacea dogmatists claim it to be. If anything globalization is creating new threats to poor and rich countries alike apart from the danger of financial volatility and the resulting job and income insecurity.

23. Finally, HDR 1999 points out that even supposedly global institutions like the World Trade Organization are dominated by the rich countries and are incapable of articulating or defending the interests of the majority of the world's peoples.

24. Similarly World Development Report 1999-2000 report' identifies "four critical lessons" of the development experience in the past half-century - growth does not trickle down and so development efforts must address human needs directly".

25. The report says, given current projections, the number of people living in absolute poverty will continue to increase. At the start of the new millennium, an estimated 1.5 billion people will subsist on the equivalent of a dollar a day, up from 1.2 billion people in 1987. By 2015 the number of people subsisting below this international poverty line could reach 1.10 billion.

26. About 220 million urban dwellers, 13 per cent of the developing world's urban population, lack access to safe drinking water and about twice that number lack access to even the simplest of latrines. That ugly reality made Mr. Nitin Desai, the UN's Under-Secretary-General for Economic and Social Affairs, to comment acidly that "the world's economic system was alert enough to protect the rich but too tardy to protect the poor. If one looked at financial flows, the net transfer of flows out of developing countries had amounted to nearly $ 60 billion. The goal was not to have a global economy that ended up as a welfare state for the rich. Rethinking was needed on how to make the system more equitable and mindful of long-term concerns".

27. Though developed world pours reams of sympathy for the plight of the poor of the developing world, but ironically the subsidization of agricultural output in the North not only shuts out imports from developing countries but also leads to unfair competition in the latter's own markets.

28. Northern producers continue to benefit from protection. Clothing and textile producers are still protected both by high tariffs and by stringent quantitative restrictions on imports from developing countries, and they will continue to enjoy high tariff protection even when all quota restrictions are removed in 2005.

29. US excludes most textiles and clothing products from its scheme, and its Most Favoured Nations (MFN). As a matter of fact it has been calculated that restrictions on imports of textile from developing countries cost the consumers in USA as high as 27 billion US Dollars. If quotas were removed, textile

prices would be reduced by 50 per cent for the US consumer.

30. Another denial of human rights is to the half of the population, that is the women. The burden of deprivation, poverty and violence is the heaviest on them. In most parts of the world, men refuse to accord equal status to women in matters of public life, employment and decision making.

31. An International Labour Organisation study shows that "while women represent 50 per cent of the world adult population and a third of the official labour force, they perform nearly two-thirds of all working hours, receive a tenth of world income and own less than one per cent of world property".

32. In most countries women have neither a right to the home in which they were born nor to the home they live in after marriage. This essential homelessness of women is a major factor in limiting the valuable contribution women can make towards gaining and retaining a home and, in turn, in building society. This critical factor has the effect of perpetuation of gender inequality and poverty.

33. Admittedly women face discrimination and marginalisation in subtle as well as in flagrant ways. Women constitute 70 per cent of the world's poor. The media needs to take seriously the lament of Platform for Action adopted by Fourth World Conference of Women held at Beijing, China (1995) wherein it pulled up the media by pointing out that "the lack of gender sensitivity in the media is evidenced by the failure to eliminate the gender based stereotyping that can be found in public and private local, national and international media organisations".

34. Though Vienna Declaration and Programme of Action, 1993 adopted at the World Conference of Human Rights resonantly affirms that speedy and comprehensive elimination of all forms of racism and racial discrimination, xenophobia and related intolerance is a primary task for the international community, but the ground reality and conspiratorial silence from rich world's quarter where much is endemic, is greatly disturbing.

35. Taking into account the ground reality that in developing countries where the impact of public opinion is weak and the

indifference of politico-cum-bureacratic nexus is proverbial both the media and the NGOs have a common stake in the preservation and protection of human rights.

36. It is therefore a matter of satisfaction that during the last 25 years, NGOs have contributed to international and national discourse on issues of global scope such as eradication of poverty and the promotion of gender, equality, peace, sustainable development and human rights. The UNDP Report of 1993 cites 50,000 NGOs worldwide.

37. Globalisation reinforces the tenuous relationship between States and the NGOs. Although States are necessary agents for the implementation of human rights policy they are also among their chief violators or accomplices to such violators.

To maintain such control, governments use different means to hamper, disturb or stop NGO activities. They may challenge the credibility or legitimacy of an NGO or its actions by using legal or sometimes illegal means to ban NGOs from operating in the country to intimadate or arrest NGO personnel.

38. The elimination of child labour has been the priority item of the agenda of NGOs in India much earlier than the recent international onslaught on this item, by developed countries, a pressure which unfortunately is motivated more by their desire to corner a greater share of increase in International Trade and Commerce than for their alleged commiseration for the children.

39. This approach of the North was trenchantly criticized by Professor Jagdish Bhagwati, who regretted that "this sentiment was then picked up by NGOs and given the colour of moral objectives like ending child labour (leading to social clause). Bhagwati argued that NGOs movements also had a nationality, the protest over hormone injected beef was launched by European NGOs while the American ones were silent.

40. Professor Bhagwati also came out heavily against an extended protection of Intellectual Property Rights that has to come to be accepted and argued that economic logic did not justify such protection.

41. Now, undoubtedly - right to healthy environment is a human right. But in this garb the developed countries should

not be permitted to pressurise the developing countries in such a manner that their economic development suffers. One of the very seriously debated agenda is the question of global warming. All kinds of pressures are being put on the developing countries to reduce the emission of green gases while completely ignoring that the six major countries specially U.S.A. has an emission rate of 5 metric tonnes of carbon whereas that of India is the lowest at 0.02 metric tonne. 80 per cent of the current emission comes from the industrial nations which have only 25 per cent of the world population. Some calculations have been made to show that the taking of the average cost of emission even at a minimum of 20 U.S. $ per tonne the South is sending about 60 billion U.S. $ to the North and as there is no assistance coming from the North such a burden cannot possibly be taken by the developing countries. It is here that the role of NGOs in the developing countries must visualize and prioritize their own plan of action and not merely echo the programme put by NGO of North. Even the World Bank has recognized that where the objectives of developing countries conflict with global environment such as the mitigation of green gases the development takes priority.

42. The brazenness of this unconcern by the developed nations is again highlighted by the latest guidelines finalised by Japanese government for its policy to be made effective from 1998, namely: Nations seeking Japanese Official Development Assistance (ODA) for environment and anti-pollution projects will now have to make obligatory purchases of goods and services from Tokyo. That environment standard insistence is a neat way of trade advancement, is clear from the fact that Japanese government plans to limit "tied ODA loans" to projects related to anti-pollution and other environmental protection projects and measures.

43. In situations where there is more political space and less oppression, the most common method the governments use to limit the space for NGOs in civil society is to place NGOs in the box of social service providers. This approach is often used by governments in developing countries and is supported by the IMF and other major donors. Governments use this classification politically and often accuse NGOs of over stepping

their mandate when they raise issues of civil or political rights. In extreme cases, NGOs will be identified as a part of the political opposition.

44. Mr. Peter Van Tuige in his Article "N.G.O. and Human Rights sources of Justice and Democracy", published in *Journal of International Affairs* (1999), notices that this goes hand in hand with a drive to centralise and homogenise government-NGO relationship. While this approach has also been supported by NGOs because it allows them to step to tap increasing flows of official donor money. It has created a new problem of accountability to the population they serve".

45. Mr. Tuige gives a thought provoking warning to the effect that "NGOs in developed countries have better access to foreign governments, international organisations, multinational corporations and the media and can bring pressures to bear. They can spot advocacy opportunities at international and global levels. The danger is that they will dominate the agenda especially since they have much greater political and financial resources than the local and national NGOs in the developing world. Thus transnational networks may be dominated by strong NGOs".

46. A review of NGO access to official financial resources already warns of a threating oligopoly of a limited number of Northern based NGOs or NGO networks which have become market leaders each controlling annual budgets of approximately $ 500 million.

47. In India, the involvement of NGOs has received fillip by the innovative method of Public Interest Litigation (P.I.L) fashioned by the Supreme Court by relaxing the vigour of locus standi as is usual under the Anglo Saxon jurisprudence. Thus, NGOs and even public spirited individuals, are permitted to intervene in human right matters seeking directions from the High Courts and the Supreme Court whenever Human Rights are being violated on the principle that the poor and deprived sector of the society by themselves have not the resources and expertise to obtain relief by themselves.

48. Thus, important changes in the law of rape and crime against women were initiated under the pressure of women

NGOs.

49. In India, we don't have a specific law of privacy. But it is now recognized that right to privacy is one of the human rights. People Union for Civil Liberty (PUCL) - which I am associated took up the matter to the Supreme Court against the practice of telephone tapping by the law enforcement agencies. Though we did not succeed fully but still good deal of safeguards against arbitrary and uncalled for wire tapping have been laid down by the Supreme Court thus reducing the rigor of the arbitrary functioning by the law enforcement agencies.

50. Similarly NGO, have either by court action or creating public opinion have succeeded in pressurizing Indian Government to make beneficial changes and observance of Human Rights to undertrials, child labour, displaced victims and of development programmes.

51. Amnesty International fight for preservation of a human right for the abolition of death penalty - is of unique contribution.

52. The role played by Habitat International Coalition and other NGOs to get Istanbul Declaration of Acceptance of Human Right of Housing is another landmark.

53. As a U.N. Special Rappoertuer on Right to Adequate Housing I received tremendous help from the NGOs in preparation of my report, and I acknowledge the same in my final report which was published by the Centre for Human Rights in Geneva in 1996 in para 227 I said: Throughout my reports I have recognised the catalytic role played by civil society and non-governmental and community-based organizations in bringing housing rights to the forefront of concern and action at local, national and international levels. I must place on record my appreciation of the assistance accorded to me, especially by way of information received from these groups. Although the work of these groups continues to be indispensable for progress on developing a wide acceptance of housing rights and on these rights being understood in a larger canvas, a number of additional practical strategies need to be followed".

54. I may quote from Mr. Amartya Sen, Nobel Laureate who said "It is often claimed that non-democratic systems are better in bringing about economic development", but

immediately repudiated this by firmly opining that "There is, in fact, no convincingly general evidence that authoritarian governance and the suppression of political and civil rights are really beneficial in encouraging economic development. Indeed, the general statistical picture does not permit any such induction".

55. I myself also strongly believe that just as human rights cannot be safeguarded unless there is a free press, and a strong public opinion reflected by NGOs similarly there cannot be a free press, or independent functioning of NGO if human rights of the majority continue to be violated, because then there will be no democracy and which alone is a condition precedent to preserving both. It is the depth and the sincerity of media and NGOs in this regard that will determine the course of Preservation and Protection of Human Rights not only in developing countries but even in the rest of the world.

1.5 Human Rights and Minorities

In any country the faith and the confidence of the Minorities in the impartial and even functioning of the State is the acid test of being civilized State. This is accepted wisdom, and was expressed succinctly by Lord Acton as follows:

"A state which is incompetent to satisfy different races condemns itself; a state which labours to neutralize, to absorb or to expel them is destitute of the chief basis of self-government", we need only substitute minorities for races in the above quotation to apply the test in India.

International Covenant on Civil and Political Rights 1966 (ICCPR) Article 27 is too accepted as a foundation for all minority rights.

"All persons are equal before the law and are entitled without any discrimination to the equal protection of the law. In this respect, the law shall prohibit any discrimination and guarantee to all persons equal and effective protection against discrimination on any ground such as race, colour, sex, language, religion, political or other opinion, national or social origin, property, birth or other status."

"We the people of India have given to ourselves the

Constitution which is not for any particular community or section but for all. Its provisions are intended to protect all, minority as well as majority communities.... We conceive, the duty of this Court to uphold the fundamental rights and thereby honour the sacred obligation to the minority communities who are our own".

The same sentiment was emphasised by the Supreme Court when it said.

"It is clear from the constitutional scheme that it guarantees equality in the matter of religion to all individuals and groups irrespective of their faith emphasizing that there is no religion of the State itself. The Preamble of the Constitution read in particular with Articles 25 to 28 emphasizes this aspect. The concept of secularism is one facet of the right to equality woven as the central golden thread in the fabric depicting the pattern of the scheme in our Constitution."

The Court stressed that:

"The purpose of law in plural societies is not the progressive assimilation of the minorities in the majoritarian milieu. This would not solve the problem; but would vainly seek to dissolve it."

Posing the question what is the purpose it referred with approval to the test laid down by Lord Scarman of House of Lords UK, (Minority Rights in a Plural Society, p. 63).

'The purpose of the law must be not to be extinguish the groups which make the society but to devise political, social and legal means of preventing them from falling apart and so destroying the plural society of which they are members'.

Secularism is thus more than a passive attitude of religious tolerance. It is a positive concept of equal treatment of all religions. This was emphasized in no uncertain terms in Bommai case 3 when Ahmadi J after referring to Articles 25 to 30 of the Constitution as being basic structure of the Constitution reminded us that this casts a duty on every citizen to cherish and follow the noble ideals which inspired our national struggle for freedom, to uphold and protect the sovereignty, unity and integrity of India, to promote harmony and the spirit of common brotherhood amongst all the people of India transcending religious, linguistic and regional or sectional diversities, and to value and preserve the rich heritage of our composite culture.

He also quoted Gandhiji writing in 1908 "Indian cannot cease to be one nation, because people belonging to different religions live in it."

The Supreme Court upheld the dismissal of State Government on the reasoning that the acts of a State Government which are calculated to subvert or sabotage secularism as enshrined in our Constitution, can lawfully be deemed to give rise to a situation in which the Government of the State cannot be carried on in accordance with the provisions of the Constitution.

Ordinarily 'minority' means a group of individuals smaller in number as against the numerically dominant group in a population within a defined area. Such a group possesses stable ethnic, religious or linguistic traditions or characteristics markedly different from those of the rest of the population, and it wishes to preserve them.

Judicially it has been held that 'minority, means a "community which is numerically less than fifty per cent" of the total population.

"Minority" as defined by European standards shall mean a group which is smaller in number than the rest of the population of a State, whose members, although nationals of that State, have ethnical, religious or linguistic features different from those of the rest of the population, and are guided by the will to safeguard their culture, traditions, religion or language.

This tested it means that it is only non-Hindu who can constitute a religious minority in India. Of course, in the question of linguistic minority both Hindus and Non-Hindus could constitute linguistic minority in a defined area according to the Supreme Court.

But that definition cannot apply as such to linguistic Minorities in India. There are of course religious minorities like Muslims, Sikhs, Christians. But they do not necessary share the same language or culture. Thus, a Kerala Muslim is a part of linguistic group of Malayalam speaking of which even a Hindu is a part their culture is also different from the culture from that of Muslim of UP.

Similarly Punjabi Hindu and Sikh and even Muslims of West Pakistan have different religions, but their language and culture is very common. Punjabi has incorporated good vocabulary from person, while Malayalam has lot of Sanskrit words. For that matter is not the language (Urdu) of UP Hindus, Muslim and also of good part of Punjabi, Hindu and Sikhs in the North the common legacy, while a Karnataka or Tamilian Muslim cannot even speak Urdu. He may be a conreligionist of North Muslim, but he is a linguist majority in those states. While a North Indian Muslim and Hindu is a linguistic minority in those states.

UN Declaration of the Rights of persons belonging to National or Ethnic, religious and linguistic minorities 1992 mandates in Article 1 that States shall protect the existence and the national or ethnic, cultural, religious and linguistic identity of minorities within their respective territorial, and shall encourage conditions for the promotion of that identity.

Our Constitution is suffused with unadulterated commitment to the equality of status and the responsibility of State to preserve, protect and assure the rights of minorities in the matter of linguistic, religion, culture. That is why our National leaders have emphasized the doctrine of unity in diversity. But it needs to be emphasized that India is not a multi- ethnic nation. Possibly there may be some small ethnic groups in the North East, but in the rest of the country, ethnicity is the distinguishing feature of religion and language. But, I am of the view that there is a confusion in equating ethnic with religious minorities. This is a concept borrowed from West where colonization by Europeans in countries of Africa and Asia in fact brought forth the question of local and indigenous people of a colony being exploited by ruling class which had come from outside. Thus native Indians in USA, aborigines in Australia, New Zealand, Canada are ethnically different. But in India no doubt we are a multi-religions, multi-lingual people, but our ethnicity and race is the same. We are all the proud product of over 5000 years of residence in this country. Muslims are not outsiders. Not even 1 per cent of Muslims are of Turkish, Arabic, origin even they have been for over 500 years and adopted India their permanent home. Thus all the Muslims have the same dignity of residence in this country as any Hindu.

The Muslims have as much claim to the wealth, and fruits of India as any one. Simply because they belong to the minority religion of Islam in no way makes their status less equal to the majority population belonging to Hindu Religion. This country is not and will never be a Hind state. Of course, battle against obscurantism will have to be fought continuously. But that should in no way create apprehension amongst the minorities that their guaranteed rights will be curtailed or that Indian state in any way will discriminate against the minorities. In India it has to be remembered and that is of significance that the biggest minority, i.e., Muslim is over 12 per cent. For hundreds of years even in Minority, Muslims Rulers ruled over the country and thus Muslims belonged to the religion of the ruling class—there could not be any inferiority complex to them during that period. Of course, there is no denying that mass of people whether Hindus or Muslims have to fend for their existence, irrespective of whether there are Muslim or Hindu rulers. The loss of ruling privilege was a psychological setback—Muslim withdrew from modern education and developed inwardness unfortunately led to backwardness in education and inevitably led to being the loser in economic share in the country. Even since Sir Sayyad Ahmed the gap is being filled up. The best in the field of profession, service, arts are to be found amongst Muslims. The problem, however, is in the large mass of Muslims who have not taken to education are seriously compounded by the poverty level being high amongst compared to other communities.

There is no doubt that minority have inherent tendency to react - may be sometimes unreasonably to even discuss some aspects of their practices which they feel would endanger their religion. Thus eminent journalist M.J. Akbar writing in *Asian Age* of 3.3.2002 talks about the irrational conduct of Muslim fundamentalist reaction to Shah Bano judgment and the opening it gave to Mr. Advani and RSS to raise hysterics about Ayodha says "a Section of the country's self-appointed Muslim leaders thought they had found a route map back to relevance. This judgment, instead of being addressed with a sense of responsibility, was turned into a weapon to challenge the

Constitution of India. There is sufficient space in Islamic jurisprudence for interpretation according to changing norms in social law: every Muslim country has made place for reinterpretation in its legal code. Certain Muslim leaders, decided that the proper response to the Supreme Court was hysteria designed to provoke a virtual revolt of Muslims against the Indian state. It was as unprecedented as it was artificial, of separatism and the clerics dusted off that old and paradoxical cry that Islam was in danger. If L.K. Advani, whose party, the BJP, had been reduced to two seats in the 1984-85 Lok Sabha (even Atal Behari Vajpayee had been defeated, in Gwalior) had beamed at that point, he would have been fully justified. He now decided to teach the Government of India, which had bowed to Muslim fundamentalists, just how powerful Hindu hysteria could be."

It is in such circumstances that the test for leadership of minority arises. But the reaction is understandable though efforts should be made to remove any misapprehension. In that context, I recollect that in 1990 I was told by Lawyers from Bangladesh that at an NGO meeting called to make changes in personnel law, the response from Muslims was encouraging. But the Hindus protested that there should not be any change in their personnel law as it would be interference with Hindu Religion - ironically forgetting that in India with overwhelming Hindu population we had made for more radical changes in personnel law applicable to Hindus since 1956 - without fearing that it was attack on Hindu Religion or old shastras. But this would not open an opportunity for Hindu fundamentalist to try to make changes in Muslims Law - that must be initiated by Muslims themselves - as it is increasing number and encouragingly many of them have realized that working for gender equality and which opposing practices which discriminate against women is not against the teaching of Islam - a religion which was the first amongst all the religions of her to give a status as a person and dignity as a human being and legal rights of inheritance as far back as about 1400 years ago.

Many so called liberal Hindus tend to advice Muslims purporting to suggest as if Hindu have a monopoly of nationalism. This is not as is reported by Pt. Nehru who said:

"In a country like India, which has many faiths and religions, no real nationalism can be built up except on the basis of secularism. Any narrower approach must necessarily exclude a section of the population, and then nationalism itself will have a much more restricted meaning than it should posses."

Prof. V.K.R.V. Rao's expressed thus:

"Muslims of India constitute an integral part of the nation. Their history is a part of Indian history and their blood has mingled with the rest of Indian blood in common causes... The majority have a duty, and they must perform it to the minority, not only for the sake of the latter but for their own sake and for the larger interests of the nations as a whole."

In the report of working group on Minorities formed by U.N. Sub Commission on Protection of Minorities, it was the unanimous view that the assimilative approach was not one promoted by the United Nations, and that formal recognition of minorities is the first crucial step towards their effective participation in society. This means not only participation in governance, but also involvement in the economy. Also accepted was the need for multi-lingual education and respect for cultural identity of minorities and the need to ensure fair representation of minorities within the law enforcement system and the workplace.

The basic task is to reconcile the pluralism which then exists in that State, and the need to respect the identity of the various groups, with the overall concerns of non-discrimination, equality, national security, territorial integrity, and political independence.

Such is the intermingling of the people of India that finding solution in the peculiarity of Europe would not take us anywhere.

One set of problems arises from the process of economic development. Conflicts are likely to intensify when there is unequal development and some ethnic groups or minorities lag behind others in the overall national development. It is aggravated in times of economic recession when some groups experience more deprivation than others. When this manifests itself in a higher rate of unemployment, it is likely to generate unrest among unemployed youth, whose frustration and anger unfortunately often are diverted into irrational ethnic conflict. Ideally, development processes should remove or reduce economic and social obstacles to co-operation and mutual respect among all groups in national society; if development processes are misdirected, they may unfortunately have the opposite effect. It is this aspect which is important and needs to be addressed so as to give confidence to the minorities.

The solution lies in the poor and disadvantaged amongst all the groups both of Minority/Majority to make common cause to wage a fight to demand a more equitable and caring society wedded to the directive principles of our Constitution where justice, equality and economic freedom are the equal right guaranteed to all citizens of the Republic.

Let us remember that Aziz Prem (Muslim) Birla (Hindu) have a common link and comradeship notwithstanding their different religion from that of a Nathu (Hindu) labourer and Rahim (Muslim) a weaver. The later have a common brotherhood, interest - to the extent this unity comes about will it be a solution to the artificially created Minority/Majority conflict, and will bring economic prosperity to the disadvantaged to the poorer sections of minorities and majorities alike.

Of course, though we must remain optimistic, current situation of the danger signals at Ayodhya and the tragic happenings in Gujarat showing unfortunately the communal divide and those in authority fanning the communal fire are warning signs and naturally cause great apprehension in the minds of the minority. The apprehension of the minorities are understandable and justifiable. Fortunately, overwhelming section of the majority has expressed is deep indignation and horror at activities of those who are out to create hostility between two communities. Though immediately one feels quite downcast but one has full faith that the land of Gandhi who was able to quell the fire of Kolkata and Noakhali still survives amongst our hearts and we shall be able to overcome this communal fury and stop the poison from spreading.

This is a task which is a common of both majority and minority. It is a joint task because we are all Indians and have common interest in the welfare and progress of our common motherland—India.

1.6 Women Empowerment - The Sathins

It is now universally accepted that Women's Empowerment Programme is a crucial component of any development programme. Women's Development Programme (WDP) was started in 6 districts of Rajasthan in 1984 with the financial assistance given by the UNICEF.

WDP was conceptualised with the broad objective of reaching the socially backward and underprivileged women of Rajasthan and, through the process of empowerment bringing them into the mainstream of the development process. The agent of social change and empowerment at the grassroots level was the *sathin* (friend). She was looked upon as a grass-root volunteer who would catalyse the shift from acquiescence to self-assertion among women from the deprived and underprivileged sections of society. She was to create consciousness and organise women in appropriating their rightful shares of fruits of development as well as to fight injustice being done to them.

UNICEF discontinued its financial assistance in 1991. And no sooner when in 1992, Rajasthan government took over the entire financial burden of programme, the programme was put in reverse gear. The first casuality was non-recruitment of any more Sathin and refusal to increase the pittance of honorarium of Rs. 250, which all NGO were unanimously demanding because of the increase of workload of Sathings. According to Dr. Arti Sawhney, State General Secretary, Sathin, Karamchari Sangh, the State Government demands performance of tangible tasks and a Sathin is asked to report monthly compliance with a list of 62-63 tasks.

The National Commission for Women which fully recognised the need for improvement of conditions of Sathin, conducted a study on the role of Sathins in four districts of Rajasthan. An abstract of the study and recommendations forward to the Chief Minister, Rajasthan in March 1996 are confirmatory of the stand of Sathins. It found:

(a) Thus notwithstanding their handicap of little or lack of education, in fact, we have found Sathins to be experienced and articulate in the rural context. In fact World Bank

(1992) Report has demonstrated that illiterate women can be effective organisers.

(b) Sathins are working as catalysts and change agents in the villages.

(c) In fact Sathins can be a great aid and ally to the Panchayat Raj movement in different districts of Rajasthan.

(d) To sum up, the National Commission for Women (NCW) feels that the institution of Sathins should not be abolished, but the State government should further augment their duties and financial compensations.

Evidently Rajasthan Government did not take recommendations seriously. That probably was the compulsion for NCW - to hold a seminar on Women Empowerment - special focus on Sathins in October, 1996 at Jaipur.

The participants included over 100 major women organisations from all over India, including high government officials. All of them were appreciative of the work done by Sathins and the need for continuing the project. Even Chief Guest Ms. Sarala Gopalan, Secretary, Women & Chief Development Department, government of India, accepted that the Sathins have been successful in the community work and consciousness raising, and that the sort of awareness present in the Sathin themselves is not to be found in the employees of any government programme.

The greatest injustice highlighted at the seminar was the grossly insulting allowance of Rs. 250 p.m. being paid to the Sathins, considering that the Rajasthan Government itself has fixed the monthly minimum wages at Rs. 960.

In my opinion denial to pay minimum wages is ethically, morally and legally indefensible.

One would have expected that after indictment by such a high powered group Rajasthan government would show sensitive recognition of the role of Sathins. But NCW was in for a shock when Chief Secretary, Government of Rajasthan by its letter of January 1997 made the uncalled for comments that the programme was now getting more and more stutified and ruling out increase in honourarium for Sathins.

Angered and left with no alternative by the wooden response of Government, Sathin Sangharsh Samiti held a massive protest meeting on 3rd April at Jaipur, which was attended by Leader like Pramila Dandvate and also member of NCW The confidence, the determination and the vigour of protest by Sathins was an exhilarating experience reviving faith in the power of the people.

A delegation also met Chief Minister of Rajasthan in the evening 3rd April 1997. The response was discouraging - the only concession was a vague assurance to possibly consider giving a little more of honorarium after May, 1997.

It is unfortunate that the strategic role of Sathins implementation of WDP has not yet registered on the insensitive bureaucracy. Possibly its opposition is because it is apprehensive of formation of an alternate centre of power which the politicians and bureaucracy will not be able to manipulate.

This makes it all the more imperative for the social activists and informed public opinion to put strong pressure on Government of Rajasthan to fulfil its constitutional obligation for the implementation of Women Empowerment Programme by doing justice to the Sathins, including the enhancement of their honorarium at least to the level of minimum wages.

In my opinion denial to pay minimum wages is ethically, morally and legally indefensible.

One would have expected that after indictment by such a high powered group Rajasthan government would show sensitive recognition of the role of Sathins. But NCW was in for a shock when Chief Secretary, Government of Rajasthan by its letter of January 1997 made the uncalled for comments that the programme was now getting more and more stutified and ruling out increase in honourarium for Sathins.

Angered and left with no alternative by the wooden response of Government, Sathin Sangharsh Samiti held a massive protest meeting on 3rd April at Jaipur, which was attended by Leader like Pramila Dandvate and also member of NCW The confidence, the determination and the vigour of protest by Sathins was an exhilarating experience reviving faith in the power of the people.

A delegation also met Chief Minister of Rajasthan in the evening 3rd April 1997. The response was discouraging - the only concession was a vague assurance to possibly consider giving a little more of honorarium after May, 1997.

It is unfortunate that the strategic role of Sathins implementation of WDP has not yet registered on the insensitive bureaucracy. Possibly its opposition is because it is apprehensive of formation of an alternate centre of power which the politicians and bureaucracy will not be able to manipulate.

This makes it all the more imperative for the social activists and informed public opinion to put strong pressure on Government of Rajasthan to fulfil its constitutional obligation for the implementation of Women Empowerment Programme by doing justice to the Sathins, including the enhancement of their honorarium at least to the level of minimum wages.

2
Housing : A Basic Right

2.1 Need of Legislation and Resources

The International concern for the right to adequate housing was shown by the interest and debate at the just-concluded session of UN Sub-commission on Prevention of Discrimination and Protection of Minorities held earlier this month at Geneva.

According to indicators compiled by the United Nations Centre on Human Settlements, over 100 million people live in a state of absolute homelessness, while the excess of one billion people are forced by circumstances to reside in desperately inadequate housing conditions which threaten their health, security, safety and dignity.

Pious Wishes

That housing rights are recognised and reaffirmed in all international and regional covenants is an old story. However, a teasing question that arises relates to their enforceability in each country. Is the only answer a homeless person can get is that unless these covenants are incorporated into domestic legislation they are only pious wishes? Notwithstanding ratification of these international covenants recognising the right to housing, can state parties continue to ignore these obligations with impunity? Cannot a citizen insist that ratification of these covenants is an obligation the State parties should undertake to adopt, in accordance with their constitutional process, such measures as may be necessary for making this right a reality? The law may not be the perfect instrument for bringing full social justice to the community but it is on the side of the homeless and the inadequately housed.

In India, there may not be a domestic law which compels the state to house the homeless. But the Supreme Court has nevertheless accepted the right to housing by interpreting in an innovative way Article 21 of the Constitution, and holding that the right to life would take within its sweep "the right to food, and reasonable accommodation to live in".

Article 11.1 of the International Covenant on Economic, Social and Cultural Rights mandates that "the State parties to the present covenant recognise the right of everyone to an adequate standard of living for himself and his family including adequate food, clothing and *housing*... and that State parties will take appropriate steps to ensure the realisation of this right..."

It admits of no doubt that covenants fully qualify to be called international law. Courts have evolved a harmonious role of interpretation, namely that an international convention is binding in international law on all countries which have ratified it, and it is the duty of the court to construe legislation so as to be in conformity with international law and not in conflict with it.

Legislation

The comity of nations further requires that rules of international law may be accommodated in municipal law even without express legislative sanction provided they do not run into conflict with Acts of Parliament. The doctrine of incorporation also recognises that rules of international law are incorporated into national law and considered to be part of national law, unless they are in conflict with an Act of Parliament. As there is no law prohibiting the State from making provisions for the housing of its citizens, it is self-evident that no question of any conflict between domestic law and international law can arise.

I am, therefore, of the opinion that ratifying States like India are under a legal obligation to provide adequate housing. Thus, it automatically empowers a citizen to take recourse to law to compel the State to honour its international obligations regarding provision of adequate housing.

Experience the world over has shown that the private sector has been unable to look beyond profit and the inherent monetisation and commoditisation of land and housing. And yet the Government of India recently announced its new housing policy by describing its role as a 'facilitator' and not a 'provider', which is a euphemism to let market forces operate uninterruptedly. This obviously is being done under the conditionalities laid down by the World Bank.

Efficient

The focus of the World Bank as far as housing is concerned is almost exclusively on making the housing market more efficient and removing what it deems as market distortions. While it is widely established that free market approaches to housing have never been adequate for satisfying the housing needs in any given society, particularly of the lower-income groups, the World Bank continues to pursue a largely ideological, purely market-oriented approach which cannot secure adequate housing for all.

When one examines, even in the most rudimentary manner, the housing situation in any country, rich or poor, in the North or South, it is self-evident that without large-scale intervention by the State through legislative means, or the construction of public housing units, the provision of housing subsidies or rental protection, much larger numbers of people than at present would suffer.

The experiences of social housing may vary widely throughout the world, but it has been proved that this housing sector has provided accommodation to many tens of millions of people over the past half a century and earlier who would have had tremendous difficulties gaining access to legal and affordable housing in the open market.

In addition to the unabashedly pro-market housing approach advocated by the World Bank, it can also be argued that the World Bank actually assists in the violation of housing rights when supporting projects involving forced evictions, or what the Bank labels "involuntary resettlement" — the most heart-rending being Narmada Sarovar project. Approximately two million people were being displaced from their houses or lands, or both, under 134 ongoing projects in Asia with resettlement components accounting for only 65 per cent of them.

Although household expenditure on housing often constitutes the most sizeable portion of a person's or families' spending, public expenditure by national governments on housing and related services remains generally much less than is commonly assumed. The global average ranges between two and four per cent of national expenditure.

Resources

The plea of lack of resources sounds hollow in view of the finding of the United Nations Development Programme in 1992 that only a three per cent reduction in arms expenditure per year during the 1990s would make available by the year 2000 an amount of $ 1.2 trillion to the industrialised countries and an amount of $ 279 billion for the developing countries. All efforts, therefore, must be made to convince the national as well international community to accept the urgency of the human rights to adequate housing and to concretize various rights of citizens, as well as duties and obligations of the government.

Platitudes on Housing

The National Housing Policy (NHP) recently approved by Parliament is long on rhetoric and short on substance. Housing is a basic necessity next only to food and clothing. But it is yet to be recognised as a priority sector. That perhaps explains why the government has taken so long even to come up with a comprehensive housing policy. It was the Rajiv Gandhi Government which first tabled the NHP draft in both Houses of parliament in May 1988. But it could not come through as Parliament was dissolved. The second draft NHP which was released in June, 1990 also met with a similar fate. Though the objective and strategies outlined in the NHP are laudable, given the resource crunch and other constraints, the roof over every head by the turn of the century will remain a pipedream. The Government's firm assurance in Parliament that it will not be abandoning the interest of the economically weaker sections of people living in urban centres does not carry much conviction. The national housing policy will make some sense only when the Urban Land Ceiling Act, Agricultural Land Ceiling Act and the Rent Control Act are suitable amended. The Government spending on housing has been steadily declining from 34 per cent in the first five-year Plan to a mere 9 per cent in the Seventh Plan. Currently the Government is spending only 2 per cent of the GDP on housing which is grossly inadequate. The shortage of dwelling units has been increasing with every successive five-year Plan. While in 1951 the shortage was put at 9 million units, the same shot up to 29 million units in 1990. It will be unrealistic to expect the Government to be solely responsible for meeting the shelter needs of the people. But the Government too must go beyond mouthing platitudes on housing.

The price of urban land has increased phenomenally over the years. Since the value of urban land is determined by its location and its potential use, it will go on increasing. Perhaps even with the aid of legal tools and legislative backing the Government may not be able to make land available to the poor at the affordable price. The Rent Control Act is another disincentive for investment in housing. The Government now sees its role as a facilitator of housing activity rather than a builder. It must now take concrete steps to augment the flow of institutional finance, NRI investment and enhanced budgetary support for the housing sector.

2.2 UN Meet to Focus on Urban Management and Housing Development

The gravity of unsatisfactory living conditions in the world had prompted the United Nations (UN) to hold the Conference on Human Settlement Habitat I at Vancouver in 1976. It let to the establishment of the United Nations Centre for Human Settlements (UNCH). A declaration made in the Conference was "Adequate shelter and services are basic human rights which place an obligation in Governments to ensure their attainment by all peoples."

Since the gravity of the situation has deepened over the past few years, the UN plans to hold the Habitat II conference at Istanbul Turkey) in June 1996. Habitat II is a world conference on managing urbanisation and on improving our living environment. Also called the City Summit, this conference aims to promote new policies and strategies for urban management and housing development and to help solve urban environmental problems.

Each country has set up a national preparatory committee for this purpose. Recently, the Swedish preparatory group (Boplats 96) held a seminar at Stockholm in which I was invited. The participants broadly accepted the observation made in the 1995 report of the UN Commission Global Covenance, which states: To keep global resource use within prudent limits, by which people living in poverty can use their living standards, affluent societies need to consume less.

There was a wide agreement that housing right is a human right. This is self-evident. The right to adequate housing, as a distinct and unique component of international human rights law, finds recognition within a broad and diverse range of parties and declarations. Article 11.1 of the International Covenant on Economic, Social and Cultural Rights (ICOE & SCR) 1966 specifically states: The States parties to the present Covenant recognise the right of everyone to an adequate standard of living for himself and his family, including adequate food, clothing and housing.

The right to adequate housing is universally recognised by the community of nations. The global strategy for shelter by the year 2000 as adopted by the General Assembly on December 20, 1988, says: All citizens of all States, poor as they may be, have a right to expect their Governments to be concerned about their shelter needs and to accept a fundamental obligation to protect and improve houses and neighbourhoods rather than destroy them.

Agenda 21 (UNCED, 1972) is even more specific. The right to adequate housing as a basic human right is enshrined in the Universal Declaration of Human Rights and the International Covenant on Economic, Social and Cultural Rights, it states. The UNCH itself passed a resolution on May 5, 1993 entitled "The human right to adequate housing."

There can, in fact, be no doubt that the right to adequate housing can be legally enforced against the states which are not fulfilling their obligations of providing citizens with adequate housing. Also, states must ensure that there are provisions of domestic remedies for each of these fundamental aspects and core contents of such human right.

Unfortunately, at the preparatory meeting of Habitat II held at Nairobi in April 1995, the US persuaded other countries to call in question whether housing is a human right. The document circulated by the US delegation, entitled "Revisions", sought to remove every single reference to the terms "the right to adequate housing" from all Commission documents, and even from ongoing Habitat programmes.

What must be emphasised is that human rights are not a gift from governments. Nor are they supposed to flow solely from any legal document formulated by the states. Human rights are inherent in every person in any civilised society, by virtue of the mere fact that he or she is an individual.

For all these reasons, it is indubitable that when the UN Commission in its resolution of May 1, 1995, cast doubt on whether the right to adequate housing is a human right, it was, with respect, acting beyond its competence.

The plea of lack of resources sounds rather hollow. The UNCHS estimates that about $75 billion dollars are required to meet the needs of housing. The United Nations Development Programme found, in 1992, that only a three per cent reduction in arms expenditure per year during the Nineties would make available US $ 1.2 trillion for the industrialised countries and $ 279 billion to meet the housing requirements of the developing countries.

The Supreme Court of India has included the right to housing in the fundamental rights. In one of the cases, it has said, "the right to life is guaranteed in any civilised society. That would take within its sweep the right to food, the right to reasonable accommodation to live..." The Court has stated clearly that a reasonable residence is an indispensable necessity for fulfilling the Constitutional goal of development of man and should be taken as included in "life" in Article 21.

Thus, inadequately housed or homeless people need not wait for the day the government decides to take a sympathetic attitude to their problem. Their position is, in reality, stronger because housing rights are legally enforceable at the instance of a citizen.

2.3 Housing : A Human Right

The Government of India has with great fanfare announced its long-awaited national housing policy a few months back. The magnitude of the problem can be gauged by the fact that the houseless population is estimated at 23.3 million units (16.3 rural, 7 urban). The cost of providing shelter for this number is estimated at a minimum of Rs. 3000 billion.

The projections show that by the year 2001, about 100 million citizens of India will be without adequate housing. It is obvious that the success of any housing policy will depend on whether the right to adequate housing is accepted as an obligation towards protection of human right or is merely treated as a routine governmental programme. The right to housing is not a new human right.

Article 25 (1) of the Universal Declaration of Rights 1948 recognises that everyone has the right to a certain standard of living...including food, clothing and housing. Internationally, this right to adequate housing finds acceptance in Article 5 (e) of the International Convention on the Elimination of All Forms of Racial Discrimination (CERD), the UN Vancouver Declaration on Human Settlements (1975), and within the Convention on the Elimination of All Forms of Discrimination Against Women (Article 14) and the ILO recommendation No. 115 on worker's housing.

At its 43rd session (1991) the Sub-Commission on the Prevention of Discrimination and Protection of Minorities, by a unanimous resolution affirmed the need for additional human rights activities leading towards full realisation of the right to adequate housing for everyone, and urged all States to pursue effective policies and adopt legislation aimed at ensuring the realisation of the right to adequate housing of the entire population, concentrating on those who are inadequately housed.

This aspect received a great fillip when, at the sixth session of the Committee on Economic, Social and Cultural Rights, held in November-December 1991, it adopted its General Comment No. 4 (1991) on the right to adequate housing (Article 11 (1) of the Covenant). The committee has very significantly observed that the human right to adequate housing, which is derived from the right to an adequate standard of living, is of central importance for the enjoyment of economic, social and cultural rights.

The committee clearly states that the right to housing is integrally linked to other human rights and to the fundamental principles upon which the Government is premised. General Comment No. 4 goes on to stress that the right to adequate housing cannot be viewed in isolation from other human rights contained in the two international covenants and other applicable international instruments.

The importance of this human right was further highlighted in resolution 1992/10, adopted by the Commission on Human Rights at its 48th session, in which it took note with particular interest of General Comment No. 4 on the right to adequate housing. Keeping with this trend, the UN Sub-Commission at its 44th session (1992) decided to appoint one of its members, as special rapporteur to carry out a two-year study on this issue.

'The United Nations' Global Strategy for Shelter unequivocally says : "No nation can claim to have reached the objective of adequate shelter for all citizens, and therefore, no nation can claim to possess the recipe for reaching this objective worldwide".

Recent studies in India indicate the following, largely unrecognised facts:

(i) The share of formal housing agencies (including government, public sector and large, private developers) is less than 15 per cent of the total addition to housing stock since 1951.

(ii) The commercial private sector contributes 18 to 25 per cent. The remaining 65-70 per cent takes place in the community sector (the variation is 85-90 per cent in rural areas and 45-50 per cent in urban areas).

The right to a secure place to live in is a fundamental one. The sense of security, dignity and community, gained from being able to retain a home, is an essential pre-requisite for the pursuit and exercise of a variety of other human rights, including the right to choose one's place of residence, the right to vote, the right to popular participation, the right to health, the right to a safe environment and other rights comprising a dignified life.

While all human rights are clearly indivisible and inter-dependent, the right to housing is a right that everyone is directly involved with, confronts and experiences everyday. Housing is as fundamental a human need as food and clothing. The lack of any of these deprives the human being of the right to live a dignified life.

Since the right to adequate housing is a fundamental requirement related to a primary human need, its lack must be seen as an injustice. And it is a structural injustice, which is part of the unequal distribution of income and consequently of goods and services within and among nations.

In many context States gladly accept international obligations in order to improve their global image, and after ratifying a treaty will conveniently do little to carry out these legal duties. India, which has ratified all these covenants, is no exception to the failure to carry out its obligations to fulfilling the housing rights.

A democratic State must guarantee conditions in which all women and men may gain and retain adequate housing and where they and their children can live with security and dignity. Housing must be seen not simply as the provision of houses, but primarily as an instrument for the promotion of justice, equality and peace.

2.4 Time to Ensure Housing Rights to All Women's Right to Housing

Habitat-II (a follow up of Habitat-I, 1976) which concluded recently at Istanbul (Turkey) addressed two themes of global importance: adequate shelter for all; and sustainable Human Settlements Developments in an urbanising world.

More than one billion people live in desperately inadequate conditions. The World Bank estimates that by the year 2025, two thirds of the developing world's absolute poor will be living in urban areas.

Throughout the developing world, the urban poor live in life threatening conditions. At least 220 million urban dwellers lack access to clean drinking water; more than 420 million do not have access to the simplest latrines. And more than 1.1 billion people live in urban areas where air pollution levels exceed permissible levels.

After sleepless nights, forceful pressure by NGOs resulted in a kind of agreed draft at Habitat-II. No doubt the global plan of action dwells on the urgent needs of the poorer part of population, but I am sceptical about its benefits to the poor. I say so because the agenda does not explicitly recognise that adequate housing is a universal human right, without which all promises to the poor will be an empty formality. On the other hand, it accepts the US Government's position that housing right has no separate existence by itself, but is merely an important component of the right to an adequate standard of living. This is arrogantly unmindful and dismissive of the agony reflected in the people's petition (signed by persons from all over the globe) presented to the Secretary General of Habitat-II, Dr Wally N'Dow, reaffirming that housing is a human right.

Not only that, but the heart rending narrations of forcible eviction and displacement produced at a public hearing organised by Habitat International coalition and NGO Forum before a panel, consisting of three representatives from India, Kenya, and France did not result in any change. The anguished Afro-Americans' plaint of discrimination during forcibel evictions (on the pretext of the Olympic Games being held at Atlanta), while leaving untouched the whites, could not persuade the governments to acknowledge their fundamental obligation to ensure housing rights to all. All that it was prepared to say was that governments have a responsibility in the shelter sector, and appropriate action will be taken in the overall context of the "enabling approach". But this "enablement paradigm is driven by profit motive" as recognised in "Living in Asian cities", a report of the Second Asia Pacific Urban Forum. The prescription of agenda for making housing affordable is to emphasise adopting of policies by governments through appropriate regulatory measures and market incentives. This is very cruel, because—relying on the market to supply houses for the poor is a mirage, with the private sector having a single overriding characteristic, namely profit. Private enterprise will only enter the housing market if it smells a higher return or/and a lower risk, than alternative investments. Thus, crudely, the only supports that can attract a greater private sector investment in low-income housing are financial guarantees. *Living in Asian Cities-1996* clarifies this point. To similar effect is the warning given in the Copenhagen Programme of Action adopted by the World Summit "Social progress will not be realised simply through the free interaction of market forces".

My apprehensions are further reinforced by the opposition to the use of the word 'forcible eviction' notwithstanding that the commission of Human Rights Resolution of 1993, has stated "that the practice of forced eviction constitutes a gross violation of Human Rights, in particular the right to adequate housing". Ultimately, an unsatisfactory compromise was arrived at by qualifying the words 'forced eviction', which are unlawful and to take into account humanitarian law. That this will be a great setback for protection of housing rights is emphasised by the Human Rights Watch, which said, "Avoiding the widely used term" 'forced eviction' obscures the duty of states to provide adequate legal remedies whenever abusive forced evictions occur".

In 1970, compulsions of the cold war made the G-7 countries pledge to devote at least 0.7 per cent of the member nations' GNP to assist developing countries. The reality is that, barring Scandinavian countries, for the others it varies between 0.1 to 0.2 per cent. Strong urgings by the development countries at Habitat-II failed to evince any favourable response from the North, inviting the cynical comment that Habitat-II was concerned more with looking after the needs of Western industry, and for more market expansion, rather than for equitable spread of resources for the developing countries.

Many countries had NGOs in their official delegations. But such is the official caste system that India had neither an NGO representative, nor a representative, NGO women groups (the inclusion of a lady civil officer in the delegation). There is no substitute for giving representation to women who are the biggest sufferers of housing rights violations. Is that why Habitat-II continued the injustice and violation of Human Rights by denying women equal rights, along with men of inheritance, and security of land tenure?

Women's Right to Housing

The continuation of the grave and unsatisfactory living conditions explains why the United Nations will hold Habitat II conference at Istanbul (Turkey) in June 1996. The 1976 declaration had firmly said: "Adequate shelter and services are a basic human right which places an obligation on Governments to ensure their attainment by all people". Against that backdrop, the Government of India held on January 19, 1996 a meeting and concluded with the adoption of a New Delhi Declaration.

Between 1990 and 2030, it is predicted, the world population will rise by 3.7 billion. Ninety per cent of that increase will take place in the developing countries, and 90 per cent of the growth in those countries will occur in the cities. According to the World Bank, 800 million people in developing countries are living in substandard houses. The misery of lack of rights to land and housing weighs the heaviest with women and children.

In most countries women have neither a right to the home in which they were born nor to the home they live in after marriage. This essential homelessness of women is a major factor in limiting the valuable contribution women can make towards gaining and retaining a home and, in turn, in building society. This critical factor has the effect of perpetuation of gender inequality and poverty.

Reference may also be made to the resolution adopted in August 1994 by the UN Sub-Commission on Prevention of Discrimination and Protection of Minorities wherein it said "one of the areas where the indivisibility and interdependence of human rights and of the rights of children becomes most apparent is with respect to the existence of widespread poverty leading to inadequate housing and living conditions."

Though there was the usual mouthful of consideration for the poor and other disadvantaged sections of society, the New Delhi declaration scrupulously avoided even mentioning that right to adequate housing is a human right.

This pusillanimous conduct of the Government of India was

obviously a continuation of the same approach as it took at the Nairobi Prep Com. of Habitat II in April 1995, namely, to curry favour with the USA which had consistently taken a rigid stand that it does not recognise the right to adequate housing as a human right. This is all the more amazing considering that our Supreme Court has categorically held that the right to life guaranteed under Article 21 of the Constitution will take within its sweep "the right to reasonable accommodation to live in."

I understand that the country paper which India is proposing to present at Habitat II has also studiously avoided to refer to the right to housing as a human right.

The deafening silence of this aspect is a matter of anxiety to those who are concerned with the rights of women and children. Of the 12 critical areas of concern highlighted in the Beijing Declaration and the platform of action by the Fourth World Conference on Women, (September 1995) poverty had been identified as the main obstacle to the advancement of women.

It needs to the emphasised that the Copenhagen Declaration (1995), to which USA was an affirming party, had stated that "absolute poverty is a condition characterised by severe deprivation of basic human needs, including food...shelter." Therefore, the stand of the USA in denying the existence of human right to adequate housing is manifestly perverse and untenable.

The final report by the UN Special Rapporteur on the right to adequate housing was submitted to the Sub-Commission which adopted it at its 47th session in August 1995. The resolution by the Sub-Commission categorically stated that it "was disturbed by developments in the preparatory process for the United Nations Conference on Human Settlements (Habitat-II) in which housing has been questioned as a human right."

The Government of India's justification for not accepting a human right to housing rest on a deliberate misinterpretation of the issue as meaning that the Government would have to provide houses at no charge to the entire population, immediately. That this assumption is unwarranted has been clarified by the UN Special Rapporteur on the right to adequate housing in his various reports submitted to the Commission.

Recently, an Expert Group Meeting on Human Rights to adequate housing was organised jointly by the United Nations Centre for the Human Settlement (Habitat II) and United Nations Centre for Human Rights at Geneva on January 18 and 19, 1996. The group has taken a unanimous view that the wording used in the various relevant international covenants would result in the logical conclusion that the right to adequate housing exists, whether as part of broader umbrella right or separately, in either case, it is necessary to treat the right as having a distinct existence.

The group also endorsed the above mentioned view of the UN Special Rapporteur when it clarified that the acceptance of the housing rights should not be interpreted to imply inter alia (a) that the State is required to build housing for the entire population; (b) that housing is to be provided free of charge by the State to all who request it or (c) that the State must necessarily fulfil immediately all aspects of this right.

The right does, however, imply certain obligations for the State. Among the core areas of the State role in realising the human right to adequate housing is the prevention of "illegal and mass evictions, elimination of homelessness". In specific cases, the "State may have to provide direct assistance, including provision of housing units, to the most vulnerable groups of the society".

The Expert Group also recognised the interdependence and indivisibility of certain human rights. A number of such rights that are generally recognised as housing rights are linked to or derived from other human rights, such as equality and non-discrimination, gender equality, property rights, the right to a fair trial, the right to freedom of movement and to choose one's residence, the right to privacy, the right to due process and other human rights related to housing.

The unexplained silence and reluctance of the Government of India to accept human right to adequate housing was the subject of critical comment, and it was recorded as a matter of great disappointment and resentment at a regional seminar on Habitat II held by the All India Women Conference in Delhi on February 20, 1996. It was resolved there that "Housing is one of the most important basic human rights. and the right to housing and equality of rights should be included in the Constitution".

The untenable stand of the government is based on the assumption that the market is the only provider of housing and that the State should have no role to play in the field. This is directly opposed to the conclusion of Habitat Reviews that "in order to have progress in urban shelter requires strong Government intervention; it cannot be rectified by markets alone, since markets care little for considerations of equity and sustainability."

It is to be hoped that strong public pressure, especially from women's groups, will make the government see wisdom and thus avoid sullying the name of India at International meets.

2.5 Role of USA in Housing Problem

The two most important international human rights covenants are the Covenant on Civil and Political Rights (Civil Covenant) and the Covenant on Economic Social and Cultural Rights (Economic Covenant). The United States ratified the Civil Covenant a year back. It is not only not ratifying the Economic Covenant, but continues to maintain that the rights covered in Economic Covenant are not human rights. Thus for the US the gay rights in Army service are human rights, but rights to housing or food are not human rights. As a result, the States are under no obligation to ensure housing rights to the disadvantaged. This approach is both against facts and against all human rights documentation. Thus, the US is persisting in the sterile controversy of the Cold War period which posited Freedom against Bread. This is a false projection. The fact is that freedom has no meaning unless human rights to housing and food are assured to every citizen. Of course, it is equally true that these human rights cannot be obtained or protected unless the political rights of free speech and association are similarly assured. Freedom and bread are the opposite sides of the same coin—there is no dichotomy between the two. They serve the identical purpose—namely the development of harmonious individual personality.

Inter-related

That is why political and economic rights have always been considered to be indivisible and inter-related. This has also been affirmed unanimously by the world conference on Human Rights held at Vienna (1993) to which the US too was a signatory. But the US, which since the end of Cold War has become contemptuous of world public opinion is still determined to make an effort to emasculate the obligations placed on the States under the Economic Covenant.

The latest manifestation of this was demonstrated at the 15th session of the UN Commission of Human Settlement (UNCHS) and the second preparatory committee meeting of Habitat-II at Nirobi (Keyna) in April 1995.

Declaration

The recognition of the human right to adequate housing was further strengthened by UNCHS when it issued the Vancouver Declaration (1976), which was supported by 132 countries. The Declaration was specific: "Adequate shelter and services are a basic human rights." This was followed by the UN Global Strategy for Shelter (GSS) to the year 2000 where it was affirmed: "The right to adequate housing is universally recognised by the community of nations."

In December 1992, the UN General Assembly decided to organise the second United Nations Conference on Human Settlement (Habitat II) which shall take place in Istanbul, (Turkey), in June 1996.

UNCHS informed the world conference on Human Rights (1993) that at its 14th session it had unanimously adopted a resolution on the entitled Human Right to Adequate Housing on May 5, this year. With these precedents, it was only to be expected that the Executive Director of UNCHS when presenting his report on housing strategy to be adopted for Habitat II conference 1996, should entitle it as "Towards a housing rights strategy: practical contributions by UNCHS (Habitat) on promoting, ensuring and protecting the full realisation of the Human Rights to Adequate Housing."

This harmless action set the US delegation in a fury of rage and it acted as a bull when seeing a red rag. It immediately put forward a series of revisions purporting to delete from various documents of preparatory committee of Habitat and Commission, references to the "human right to adequate housing".

Naturally there were some protests over thus seeking to

negate the human right to housing. But the US ignored these protests superciliously. Under threat of disruption of the work of the Commission held out by the US, it was able to steam-roll a resolution adopted by the Commission, which "took note of the report of the Executive Director entitled Human Rights to Adequate Housing, and requested the Executive Director to update the said report... by taking into consideration legal, social, economic, political and practical aspects of the subject and the views and concerns expressed by some member states including those *regarding the existence and/or the legal status of the right to adequate housing (emphasis added).* India, unfortunately, supported the above resolution".

Arrogance

The said resolution represents arrogance and defiance of all human rights jurisprudence. Apart from the self-evident absurdity, the attempt to determine whether right to adequate housing or for that matter any other right is a human right or not, is outside the mandate of the Habitat and its action is an usurpation of jurisdiction vested in other UN bodies.

It is axiomatic that human rights are not a gift from a State, nor are they supposed to flow from any legal document formulated by a State. Human rights inhere in every person in any civilised society by the mere fact that he or she is an individual person. This aspect is affirmed by all international covenants including the Economic Covenant. Indeed the General Assembly in its resolution of Dec. 4, 1986, described the Universal Declaration of Human Rights 1948, which it conceived as a common standard of achievement for all people and nations and providing the basis for the development of international covenants on human rights.

Impermissible

In view of this, the authoritative recognition of the right to adequate housing as a human right by the highest UN body, it is impermissible for any subsidiary United Nations agency like UNCHS to cast doubt about the legality of this human right or to give a different interpretation than that given by the parent body, the General Assembly.

The untenable stand of UNCHS is also opposed to the equally authoritative pronouncement of Commission on Human Rights and UN Committee on Economic Covenant, accepting the right to adequate housing as a human right. India must dissociate itself from the embarrassing position of having supported USA in this interpretation of the Human Right to Adequate Housing which if persisted can only damage the right to social development correctly asserted by the Third World countries.

2.6 Housing Rights Under the International Law

1. The right to adequate housing, as a distinct and unique component of international human rights law, finds recognition within a broad and diverse range of treaties, declarations, agreements, recommendations, resolutions and other legal texts. Nationally, a comparatively large number of states have explicitly codified the right to housing within their national Constitutions and nearly all states maintain legislation relevant in one way or another to the right to adequate housing.

2. Within the system of international human rights law, an analysis of the legal recognition and formulation of housing rights must begin with Article 25 (1) of the Universal Declaration of Human Rights. This article effectively forms the cornerstone of a fundamental aspect of all economic, social and cultural rights; the right to an adequate standard of living, including the right to adequate housing. Article 25 (1) reads: "Everyone has the right to a standard of living adequate for the health and well-being of himself and of his family, including food, clothing and housing".

3. The said Article 25, formed the basis for Article 11.1 of the International Covenant on Economic, Social and Cultural Rights (ICESR) (1966) which states:

"The States Parties to the present Covenant recognize the right of everyone to an adequate standard of living for himself and his family, including adequate food, clothing and housing and to the continuous improvement of living conditions. The States parties will take appropriate steps to ensure the realization of this right, recognizing to this effect the essential importance of international cooperation based on free consent".

4. The process of formulation and the preparatory debates on the Covenant which lasted from 1951 to 1963 reveal the crucial importance placed on the right to housing even in the early

1950s, when the several States argued for a separate article on the right to housing. Even though no agreement could be reached in this respect, there was an insistence on including a separate implementation article, which would minimally ensure that States would adopt legislation securing for everyone a dwelling consistent with human dignity. Such an article was, however, opposed and if the text presented to the General Assembly in 1954 housing was combined with food and clothing, in a format much as it remains today.

5. The drafting debate considered whether the word "decent" was more appropriate than the word "adequate" in highlighting the attributes of housing, food and clothing. 'Adequate' was finally accepted.

6. However, the motion for a separate specific implementation clause for article 11 was struck down, with the Covenant being finally adopted in 1966 and entering into force in 1976.

7. It is clear from looking at the history of the drafting of Article 11.1 that the States were influenced considerably by the wording and the spirit of Article 25 of the Universal Declaration of Human Rights.

8. The range of issues raised and the different visions of the right to housing expressed by the States participating in the debates indicates, however, that a broad interpretation of the right could be derived and has been gradually accepted by international community.

9. Some of the other important texts also refer directly or implicitly to this right of housing:

(a) International Convention on the Elimination of All forms of Racial Discrimination (1965) prohibitation of racial discrimination in the enjoyment of the right to housing.

(b) Convention on the Elimination of All forms of Discrimination against Women (1979, the rights of rural women to adequate housing).

(c) Convention on the Rights of the Child (1989, the duty of states to provide material assistance, including housing to children in need).

(d) Convention relating to the Status of Refugees (1950, equality of treatment as regards housing between refugees and aliens).

(e) International Convention on the protection of the Right of All Migrant Workers and Members of their families (1990, equality of treatment with nationals in relation to access to housing schemes, and protection against exploitation in respect of rents).

(f) International Labour Organisation (ILO) Recommendation No. 115 on workers housing (1961 ensuring that adequate and decent housing accomadation and a suitable living environment are made available to all workers and their families).

(g) Declaration on the Right to Development (1986). equality of opportunity for all in their access to basic resources and housing).

(h) Declaration of Social Progress and Development (1959, the provisions for all, particularly persons in low income groups and large families, of adequate housing, declaration on the Right to Development (1986, equality of opportunity for all in their access to basic resources and housing).

10. The 1976 United Nations Vancouver Declaration on Human Settlements contains a range of clauses relating to housing rights, including Section III (8) and Chapter II (A.3), which state:

"Adequate shelter and services are a basic human right which places on obligation on Governments to ensure their attainment by all people. The human settlement policies must be in conformity with the declaration of principles and the Universal Declaration of Human Rights".

11. The Global strategy for shelter to the year 2000 as adopted by the General Assembly in resolution 34/181 on 20th December 1988 has this to say (the right to adequate housing is universally recognized by the community of nations) .... All citizens of all States, poor as they may be have a right to expect their Governments to be concerned about their shelter needs and to accept a fundamental obligation to protect and improve houses and neighbourhoods rather than damage or destroy them".

12. Agenda 21 (UNCED, 1992) is even more specific, "The right to adequate housing as a basic human right is enshrined in the Universal Declaration of Human Rights and the International covenant on Economic, Social and Cultural Rights".

13. Global strategy defines "Adequate housing" to mean: adequate privacy, adequate space, adequate security, adequate basic facilities, all at a reasonable cost.

14. Additionally, the regional systems of human rights protection have established legal instruments enshrining specific housing rights and related provisions. In the European context, the following texts are relevant: European Social Charter (1961); the European Community Charter of Fundamental Social Rights (1989) and also the final Act of Helsinkin (1975); Conference on Security and Co-operation in Europe (CSCE), Vienna Concluding Document (1989) and Document of the Copenhagen Meeting of the Conference on the Human Dimension of the CSCE (1990, special attention to housing).

15. Although Article 31 (k) of the OAs Charter, of 1948, notes that states agree to dedicate efforts towards adequate housing for all sectors of the population, this formulation falls short of a legal right to adequate housing. A clause similar to Article 25 of the Universal Declaration of Human Rights is found in Article 11 of the OAs American Declaration on the Rights and Duties of Man. However, no subsequent OAs human rights text has explicitly recognized housing rights, including the Additional Protocol to the American Convention on Economic, Social and Cultural Rights. The original drafts of that convention contained such clauses, but they were deleted prior to adoption.

16. Setting however a potentially useful precedent, the United Nations Commission on Human Settlements (UNCHS) adopted its first-ever resolution on housing rights in mid-1993, entitled "The human right to adequate housing.

17. It is correct that earlier European Social Charter (1961), or the European Convention on Human Rights, did not contain an explicit right to adequate housing. But there has been a sea change in thinking on this aspect in recent times. Thus Amsterdam Treaty includes a new clause which states that EU "may adopt measures designed to encourage cooperation between

Member States through initiatives aimed at improving knowledge.... promoting innovative approaches and evaluating experience in order to combat social exclusion". (Article 118)

18. Some housing rights activists insist that all people who are either homeless or poorly housed should be recognised as victims of social exclusion, because having access to decent and affordable housing is an essential condition for full participation in any civilised modern society.

19. The Amsterdam Treaty states that the EU is attached to "fundamental social rights as defined in the European Social Charter", which was agreed at Turin in 1961. In 1977 the Council of Europe produced a revised version of the European Social Charter, including an article on the "right to housing" which refers to the need for measures to "prevent and reduce homelessness". However, until August 1997 the revised Charter had been signed by only 8 of the 15 EU Member States, and had not yet been fully ratified by any one of them. I hope the situation is now somewhat better.

20. However, there is a further welcome development in as much as that the European Parliament has by resolution on May 29, 1997 recognised that: "The lack of decent housing represents an affront to human dignity and on obstacle to participation in political, economic, social and cultural life for the individuals and families concerned". The Resolution sets out proposals for the development of a European housing policy, to be "based on efforts to provide adequate housing for all".

21. Furthermore, the Parliament believes that "housing must be seen as an area of general interest, underpinning all other fundamental social rights, to be taken into consideration at all levels of decision-making in the [European] Union".

22. Again, the Commission on Human Settlement at its 16th session, held in June 1997, resolved to promote the realisation of the human right to adequate housing, thus affirming that housing is a human right and not merely a empty exhortation by the State.

23. It would thus be clear that in view of these various Conventions and Resolutions and also Vienna Declaration having accepted that all human rights are indivisible and inter-

dependant, denial of housing right would be a denial of these admittedly human rights accepted in all societies.

24. It also needs emphasing that a number of such rights that are generally recognized as housing rights are linked to or derived from other human rights, such as equality and non-discrimination, gender equality, property rights, the right to a fair trial, the right to freedom of movement and to choose one's residence, the right to privacy.

25. Now admittedly the various treaties, conventions, covenants have been accepted and ratified by most of the countries of the world, e.g., ICESR has been ratified by 108 countries since last year.

In my view jurisprudentially speaking all these conventions and treaties fulfill the test of being called international law.

26. I say this because "historically, treaties are the second source of international law; they developed as the means whereby states could give to rules for their mutual conduct a greater particularity than was provided by custom".[1]

27. The moral element as foundation for international owes a great deal to the writings of Prof. Brierly. As pointed out by Sir Hersch Lanterpacht, Judge, International Court of Justice, that Brierly emphasised the beneficient potentialities of a revived law of nature as one of the main elements of moral foundation of international law.[2]

28. Of particular importance is the Charter of the United Nations which, in addition to being a treaty embodying the constitution of that organisation, has become the basic legal instrument for the international community.

29. The adoption of the UN Charter and the subsequent enactment of such fundamental international instruments as the Universal Declaration of 1948 and the two Covenants on Human Rights of 1966 had such an impact on the international community that no state currently challenges the concept that human rights must be cherished and respected everywhere in the world. As a result of, on the one hand, those general texts and a host of specific conventions and international resolutions, and, on the other hand, the consistent practice of international bodies - especially the multifarious activities carried out by

various UN organs - a general principle has gradually emerged prohibiting gross and large-scale violation of basic human rights and fundamental freedom.[3]

30. This heightening of the consciousness of human right necessity calls for an instrument of protection.

31. If as pointed out above a claim by citizen for adequate housing is not only a right but a human right certain inevitable conclusions must flow, the topmost being as to what is the implementation machinery to effectuate this human right. Now as Salmond on Jurisprudence says "All rights whatever correspond to duties". The right of a citizen, therefore, corresponds to a duty on the State. Thus as Salmond again puts it "when the law recognises an act as a duty it commonly enforces the performance of it, or punishes the disregard of it."

32. In the search for principle to make international law enforceable big boost was given by what Sir Lauterpacht called Brierly's beneficial doctrine of incorporation according to which "courts apply international law, per se, as being part of the law of the land. It is, in his view, beneficial not only as showing that municipal courts apply international law as authoritative in its own right, but also 'because by asserting that it is part of the law of the land we deny that it has any specific quality which distinguishes it from that law. The doctrine of incorporation has constituted one of the main contributions of the common law to international legal tradition." It is in this light that "Brierly arrived at the affirmation of the essential unity and identity of international and municipal law and the rejection of the then still predominant dualistic view. He deprecated the customary exaggerations of the absence of sanctions of international law and the laxity of its observance."

33. A survey of the varied practice of states show that, except possibly in terms of dialectics, it is impossible to accept the view that rules of international law cannot, without express municipal adoption, operate as part of municipal law, or the opposite view that they always so operate. On the contrary, states show considerable flexibility in the procedures whereby they give effect within their territories to the rules of international law, although a great many states adopt the doctrine that international law is part of the law of the land. But while the procedures vary, the

result that effect is given within states to the requirements of international law is by and large achieved by all states. This result may be called for in relation to almost any held of activity which is regulated by international law, although in certain fields, such as the observance of human rights, it has assumed special importance.[4]

34. And for the protection of human rights generally, have testified to the intimate connection between the interests of the individual and international law. The Charter of the United Nations, with its repeated recognition of human rights and fundamental freedoms', inaugurated a new and decisive departure with regard to this abiding problem of law and government. In some instances - as, for example, in the European convention on Human Rights, and the two United Nations Covenants on Economic, Social and Cultural Rights and on Civil and Political Rights - that development has assumed the complexion of explicit rules legally binding upon States.

35. As Professors Van Dijk and Van Hoof noted: "Nevertheless, it would appear to us that in view of its character the European Convention contains the germs for a gradual development into a common legal system for the contracting States, to which their national law must be subordinate."[5]

36. The two International Covenants namely civil and economic marked a notable step forward in the protection of human rights within the framework of the United Nations, and largely constitute the basic provisions of an International Bill of Rights.

37. The two covenants also demonstrated the way in which the United Nations is overcoming its earlier hesitations about the enforcement of human rights obligations.

38. Ratification is defined in the Vienna Convention on the Law of Treaties 1969 as 'the international act so named whereby a state establishes on the international plane its consent to be bound by a treaty'.

39. Georg Schwarzenberger maintains that a State which has contracted international obligations is bound to make in its municipal law such alterations as may be necessary to ensure the fulfilment of its international obligations.

40. Despite, the inclination of a few observers who continue to suggest the non-justiciability of social-economic human rights, including housing rights, a deeper examination of the normative content of housing rights, decisions and approaches taken by national judiciaries and the jurisprudence of the regional and international human rights bodies especially committee on ESCR reveals that the vast majority of the constituent elements of housing rights as recognized under international and national law are in fact, justiciable.[6]

41. I am inclined to agree with the following: "Denying an individual or group the ability to make constitutional claims against the state with respect to nutrition, housing, health and education excludes those interest from a process of reasoned interchange and discussion, and forecloses a useful forum for the recognition and redressing of injustices."

42. The application of international law as part of the law of the land means that, subject to the overriding effect of statute law, rights and duties flowing from rules of customary international law will be recognised and given effect by courts without the need for any specific act adopting those rules into domestic law.

43. It is self evident that unless the Right to Adequate Housing is legally enforceable by an individual, it will only remain a moral imperative, but of no practical benefit. What then is the position in law.

44. Now as Salmond on Jurisprudence says "All rights whatever correspond to duties". The right of a citizen, therefore, corresponds to a duty on the part of a State. Thus as Salmond again puts it "when the law recognises an act as a duty it commonly enforces the performance of it, or punishes the disregard of it."

45. Now, it admits of no doubt that covenants fully qualify to be called international law. Courts have evolved a harmonious role of interpretation, namely that an international convention is binding in international law on all countries which have ratified it, and it, is the duty of the court to construe legislation so as to be in conformity with international law and not in conflict with it.

46. The comity of nations further requires that rules of international law may be accommodated in municipal law even without express legislative sanction provided they do not run into conflict with Acts of Parliament. The doctrine of incorporation popularised by Brierley also recognises that rules of international law are incorporated into national law and considered to be part of national law, unless they are in direct conflict with domestic law.

47. As a matter of fact jurisprudence under the compulsion of universality of Human Rights is developing into own Human Rights Jurisprudence.

48. As a result of this development, and the compulsion and obligation to comply with international treaties, even when the former seem to be conflict with domestic legislation, it is being accepted even in the United Kingdom, which has had its fundamental basis in the complete sovereignty of its Parliament that conconventions should prevail. This welcome trend has been noted (Wade and Forsyth in *The Administrative Law.* (7th Edition) as follows[7]

"Unlike other States who are parties to the European Convention on Human Rights and Fundamental Freedoms of 1950, Britain has failed to incorporate the Convention into domestic law, so that its status is that of a treaty only and complainants must undertake long and expensive litigation in Strasbourg. But the courts, though unable to enforce the Convention directly, have made some progress towards giving effect to it indirectly. They will take it into account in construing statutes or regulations in cases of ambiguity. In one case Lord Reid said that it was hardly credible that Parliament or any government department would act contrary to it. Several times it has been held that regard ought to be had to the Convention as an aid to interpretation, and in one case under the common law, where arguments were evenly balanced, they treated the convention as decisive. Distinguished judges, speaking extrajudicially, have suggested how this House of Lords, Lord Griffiths acknowledges the responsibility of the judiciary to refuse to countenance behaviour that threatens either basic human rights or the rule of the law."

49. The principle of English Courts has been also aptly put

(Maxwell on Interpretation of Statutes) thus [8]: "Under the general presumption that the legislature does not intend to exceed its jurisdiction, every statute is interpreted, so far as its language permits so as not to be inconsistent with the comity of nations or the established rules of international law and the court will avoid a construction which would give rise to such inconsistency unless compelled to adopt it by plain and unambiguous language."

50. A similar view was expressed in an English case[9]. It was observed "the Warsaw Convention is an International Convention which is binding in International Law and all the countries who have ratified it and it is the duty of our courts to so construe our Legislation so as to be in conformity with the International Law and not conflict with it". *Concocraft Ltd.* vs. *American Airways*: (1969) I AER 80).

51. The European Social Charter of 1961, by Article 16, provides that the contracting parties undertake such means ..... like provision of family housing and also ensures by Articles 19 for migrant workers, treatment not less favourable than that of their own nationals in respect of, amongst others, accommodation.

52. A fair amount of case law on these housing clauses has been generated by the European Committee of Independent Experts responsible for monitoring the Charter. An analysis of the existing case law on Article 19 reveals the following jurisprudential considerations:

(a) It is not enough for a Government to prove that no discrimination exists in law alone; it is obliged to prove in addition that immigrant workers did not in practice suffer any disadvantage in the allocation of low-cost housing despite of de jure equality they enjoyed.

(b) The committee has noted the existence of "concession laws" which frequently appear to distinguish between local residence, other citizens of this state and aliens. Such distinctions, in so far as they affect aliens, would certainly be contrary to the Charter.

(c) In one case, it was decided that a State Party in which alien workers could only be granted public housing if they had lived there for seven years failed to meet the obligations under Article 19 (4).

(d) If a State's legislation discriminates even indirectly between citizens and foreigners in respect to the purchase of real estate, it would be contrary to Article19, to the extent that this discrimination affected access by foreigners to housing.

53. The Committee of Independent Experts has also expressed the opinion that, as regards subsidized housing, where conditions required to obtain such housing (birth or length of residence) are only applicable to nationals of States bound by the Charter, such a situation would not be in conformity with Article 19 (4). Finally, in yet another instance, a state party was deemed not to be complying with the Charter's provisions since "public promotion housing" was allocated only to the nationals of the country concerned.

54. It is pity that most states in Europe though have ratified these documents appear to treat the right to adequate housing as aspirational and have given little, if any, attention to their operation. A few States like Belgium, Portugal, Spain and the Netherlands have enshrined the right to housing in the constitution as the highest law of the land. The right to housing in these countries is integrated in the programme part of the constitution and is established as a statement of intent of commitment to principles, rather than as an entitlement. Individual legal claims to a home cannot be made exclusively upon constitutional provisions.[10]

In 1995 the Constitution of Finland was amended to include the right to a home. This amendment imposes an obligation on the State to further the right of all people to a home and to support people in finding a home. However, this right has not been tested in the courts, and so it is not clear exactly what the State must provide, and where the limits are.[11]

55. France and Belgium have passed laws to transform the right to housing into concrete legal norms. The laws in the two countries assert, clearly and in a detailed manner, the right to housing for all citizens and the obligation of solidarity towards those unable to access the right from their own resources. In the United Kingdom and Ireland, laws have been passed which do not assert the general right to housing but specifically address the condition of homelessness. The legislation in the United

Kingdom puts an obligation on the local authorities to provide housing for those homeless people assessed to be in priority need and found to be unintentionally homelessness. Irish legislation puts a duty on the local authorities to monitor homelessness and assess the housing needs of people excluded from adequate housing.

56. In India, there is no domestic law casting obligation on the State to house the homeless. The Supreme Court has however in an innovative way sought to incorporate this right to housing by so interpreting Article 21 of the Constitution which provides that no person shall be deprived of his life or personal liberty except according to procedure established by law, and interpreting in the context of various International Covenants.

The Supreme Court in (*Jolly George Varghese* v. *Bank of Cochin*: (1980) 2 SCC 360), posed the question from the international law as to whether it is right to enforce a contractual liability by imprisoning a debtor in the teeth of Article 11 of the International Covenant on Civil and Political Rights. The Article reads:

"No one shall be imprisoned merely on the ground of liability to fulfil a contractual obligation."

At that earlier stage though the Court accepted the principle of law that from the national point of view the national rules alone count, but it emphasised that "India is now a signatory to this Covenant and Article 51 (c) of the Constitution obligates the State to "foster respect for international law and treaty obligations in the dealings of organised peoples with another" and invoking the well recognised rule of interpretation, namely, "it is a principle generally recognised in national legal systems that, in the event of doubt, the national rule is to be interpreted in accordance with the State's international obligations" it set aside the detention of the debtor.

57. In the most published case Indian Supreme Court said[13]:

"Eviction of the petitioners from their dwellings would result in the deprivation of their livelihood. There is thus a close nexus between life and means of livelihood. And as such that which alone makes it possible to live, leave aside what makes life livable, must be deemed to be an integral component of the right to life".

58. In another case it was held the right to the life "would take within its sweep the right to .... a reasonable accommodation to live in ....".[14]

59. Indian Supreme Court has been consistently upholding the view that the right to life guaranteed under Article 21 of the Indian Constitution includes the right to a shelter. In this view it invoked to its aid Article 25 (1) of the U.D.R. and Article 11 (1) of ICESR.[15]

60. In another case[16] the Supreme Court read the right of privacy in Indian law though there is no specific rights in domestic law by invoking International Covenants, by observing:

"India is a signatory to the International Covenant on Civil and Political Rights, 1966. Article 17 of the said covenant is as under:"

"Article 17

1. No one shall be subject to arbitrary or unlawful interference with his privacy, family, human or correspondence, nor to unlawful attacks on his honour and reputation.
2. Everyone has the right to the protection of the law against such interference or attacks."

   Article 12 of the Universal Declaration of Human Rights, 1948 is almost in similar terms.

21. International law today is not confined to regulating the relations between the States. Scope continues to extend. Today matters of social concern, such as health, education and economics apart from human rights fall within the ambit of International Regulations. International law is more than ever aimed at individuals.
22. It is almost an accepted proposition of law that the rules of customary international law which are not contrary to the municipal law shall be deemed to be incorporated in the domestic law."

61. Many jurisdictions in Anglo Saxon Law, including India accept that if there is any ambiguity in a statute, and particularly (but not necessarily only) where it is expressly enacted to give effect to a treaty, it will be interpreted in the light of and, if

possible, in such a way as to be consistent with the country's international obligations.

62. One of the helpful and progressive development recently in giving support to the binding effect of right to adequate housing has been the role of United Nations Committee on Economic, Social and Cultural Rights. In its five sessions (eight to twelfth sessions, 1993-1995), the Committee has specifically addressed rights issues, e.g., thus it has held that :

(a) "The Government should ensure that forced evictions are not carried out". (Philippines, twelfth session).

(b) "The Committee regrets that a large number of household have experienced harassment or illegal eviction and notes that the national housing policy is not adequate to address address this problem". (United Kingdom, eleventh session).

(c) "The Committee reiterates the importance it attaches to the right to housing and reaffirms its longstanding view that force evictions are prima facie incompatible with the requirements of the Covenant and can only be justified in truly exceptional circumstances." (Dominican Republic, eleventh session).

(d) "The Committee urges the State party to recall General Comment No. 4 (1991) in which it noted that "the Committee considers that instances of forced eviction are prima facie incompatible with the requirements of the Covenant and can only be justified in the most exceptional circumstances, and in accordance with the relevant principles of international law". (Mexico, ninth session).

(e) "With regard to the right to adequate housing, the Committee notes with great concern that practices of forced evictions without consultation, compensation or adequate resettlement appear to be widespread in Kenya, particularly in Nairobi". (Kenya, eighth session)[17].

63. A more encouraging and forthright push to the Housing rights was given by U.N. Committee came in its General Comment No. 7 on Forced Evictions at its meeting held on 16th May 1997. Wherein in it noted that it should be remembered that that in its General Comment No. 4 (1991), the committee

observed that all persons should possess a degree of security of tenure which guarantees legal protection against forced eviction, harassment and other threats. It concluded that forced evictions are prima facie incompatible with the requirements of the Covenant. The Committee has reiterated that the issue of forced eviction had been the subject matter of serious concern in the year - 1976 Vancouver Declaration on Human Settlements and in other international declarations and agreements.

64. The Committee endorsed the statement of Commission on Human Rights that 'forced evictions' are gross violation of human rights to adequate housing. General Comment No. 7 has given this clarification as a result of various reports of forced evictions received by it in the context of right to adequate housing, found in Article 11 (1) in the Economic Covenant. It has recorded that the right to adequate housing and not to be subject to forced evictions should not be violated by the State and the State must refrain from forced evictions.

65. It has also said that evictions should not result in rendering individuals homeless or vulnerable to the violation of other human rights. Where those affected are unable to provide for themselves, the State must take all appropriate measures, to the maximum of its available resources, to ensure that adequate alternative housing, resettlement or access to productive land is available.

66. The plea of enforceability of housing rights should not now be a matter of debate after Habitate II at Istanbul (1996).

Istanbul Declaration commits the Heads of State Government to the objective principle and recommendations contained in Habitat Agenda and they have pledged their mutual support for its implementation.

Now Habitat Agenda accepts that "everyone has the right to an adequate standard of living for themselves and their families including adequate food, clothing .... *housing*"(emphasise supplied).

Further, there is a promise to implement and promote this objective in a manner fully consistent with human rights standard.

There is a further promise of protecting all people from and providing legal protection and redress for forced evictions that are contrary to law, taking human rights into consideration.

These declarations and promises by the Heads of States create legitimate expectations in the minds of citizens that the State will implement its promise to provide adequate housing. Now, law is well settled that in such situation jurisprudentially a citizen can invoke the jurisdiction of the courts and pray for mandommus to carry out their obligations. In this eventuality the state will be further stopped from pleading any defence against the claim put forth by the citizens.

This further strengthened my conclusions that right to adequate housing can be legally enforced in a court of law.

67. Notwithstanding some irritant hesitations by some courts, I am, therefore, more than convinced that the right to adequate housing can be legally enforced against the States which are not fulfilling their obligations as mentioned above. I also believe that States must ensure the provision of domestic remedies for each of these fundamental aspects and core contents of the human right to adequate housing.

68. This course flows from the indisputable proposition about the indivisibility and interdependence of all human right and the inherent, indispensable and permeable relationship between the full enjoyment of the right to adequate housing and certain civil and political rights. I am convinced that a wide range of civil and political rights like the right to privacy, the right to family law, the right to equal protection and benefit of the law, the right to gender equality, the right to be free from discrimination, the right to property will be seriously compromised in the absence of measures geared towards respecting, protecting and ensuring the right to adequate housing.

69. Although governmental accountability for the respect, protection, promotion and fulfilments of housing rights is now well established under international law, measures of implementation and, in particular, judicial enforcement have remained somewhat hesitant. Despite major progress regarding the definition of housing rights and the concomitant State

obligations, the much enhanced stature of this norm at both the international level will only be possible through an Optional protocol to the International Covenant on Economic, Social and Cultural Rights like the one in covenant on civil and political rights.

70. Judged by the position in law of housing rights in international law, the situation in Israel is indeed unfortunately quite alarming and an example of gross violation of housing rights.

71. On 19th December 1968, the General Assembly, in adopting resolution 2443 (XIII), established the Special Committee to Investigate Israeli Practices Affecting the Human Rights of the Population of the occupied Territories. The Special Committee was asked to report to the Secretary-General as soon as possible and whenever the need arose thereafter.

72. In its various reports, e.g., in 1984 the committee, found that the Israeli Government was continuing "with increasing vigour" its policy of annexation and settlement in the occupied territories. There existed a number of highly organised groups of Israeli settlers whose aim was to consolidate the Israeli presence by terrorizing the civilian population.

73. The situation continued to become worse when in 1991 the Committee reported that between 9 March and 9 April in the West Bank alone, an estimated 68,000 dunums of land were expropriated or surveyed for expropriation seemed to indicate, in the Committee's view, a deliberate will to modify the territories' demographic composition.[18]

74. The situation in territories occupied by Israel as a result of armed conflicts in the Middle East continued to be of concern to the United Nations in 1995.

75. The Committee appealed to Israel to take concrete measures like reviewing its settlements policy, halting the expansion of settlements and ending land confiscation; and ending pressure on Arabs in East Jerusalem to sell their houses.

76. In its annual report, The Special Committee was of the view that Israel's policy of establishing Jewish Settlements in the occupied territories had been since its inception in 1968, at the heart of the Arab-Israeli conflict.

77. On 6 December, 1994, the Assembly adopted resolution 50/29 by which it reaffirmed in particular that the Israeli settlements in the occupied Palestinian territory, including Jerusalem, and the other Arab territories occupied by Israel since 1967 are illegal and an obstacle to achieving comprehensive peace.[19]

78. A report was prepared by the Economic and Social Commission for Western Asia (ESCWA) and submitted in July by the Secretary-General, in accordance with 1994 requests of the Economics and Social Council and the General Assembly.

79. On 28 July, the Economic and Social Council adopted Resolution 1995/49, by which it reaffirmed that Israeli settlements in the Palestinian territory, including Jerusalem and other Arab territories occupied since 1967 are illegal and an obstacle to economic and social development.

80. My own reactions were no less alarming when I as an U.N. Special Rapporteur submitted my final report[20] on the Right to adequate housing, wherein I said: "One of the most poignant examples of the devastating impact of a state of occupation is that of the Palestinians uprooted from their ancestral homes since the occupation in 1967 of East Jerusalem by Israel. Not until he visited that area did the Special Rapporteur realise the deliberate, systematic violation of housing rights undertaken by the Israeli government. The wanton destruction of Arab homes and the takeover of the lands where they have lived for generations to make room for Jewish settlements defies description. Recent studies based largely on official Israeli Government sources demonstrate the systematic policy of discrimination being followed in Jerusalem.." (Para 28)

"In the absence of any censure from the Western nations (the United States even vetoed the resolution of the Security Council asking Israel to halt further confiscation) the Israeli Government publicly announced with fanfare further confiscation of 53 hectares of Arab land in East Jerusalem. The condemnation of the Arab and Asian countries was brushed aside with disdain. The Israeli Government stated that it would go ahead with the confiscation of this area, brushing aside the advice and warnings from Arab States that that might jeopardise the peace accord with the Palestine Liberation Organization." (Para 30)

"The Special Rapporteur believes that all such actions stem from not accepting that violations of housing rights are not merely a breach of any gratuitous promise but are, in fact, violations of human rights violations which no State can be allowed to commit if it wants to remain a member of the community of civilised nations". (Para 31)

81. That the Government of Israel continues to violate housing rights is amply borne out by the concluding observations of the committee on Economic, Social and Cultural Rights held under Articles 16 and 17 of the IESCR on 4th December 1998, wherein it said:

(a) "The Committee takes the view that large-scale and systematic confiscation of Palestinian land and property by the State and the transfer of that property to these agencies, constitute an institutionalized form of discrimination because these agencies by definition would deny the use of these properties by non-Jews. Thus, these practices constitute a breach of Israel's obligations under the covenant".

(b) "The Committee deplores the continuing practice by the Government of Israel of home demolitions, land confiscations, restrictions on family reunification and residency rights".

(c) "The Committee notes that despite State Party's obligation under Article 11 of the covenant, the Government of Israel continues to expropriate Palestinian lands and resources to expand Israeli settlements. Thousands of dunams (hectares) of land in the West Bank have been recently confiscated to build 20 new bypass roads which cut-off West Bank towns from outlying villages and farmlands... The Committee also notes the annual per capita consumption allocation (of water) for Palestinians is only 125 cubic metres while settlers are allocated 1000 cubic metres per capita."

(d) "The Committee calls upon the State Party to undertake the necessary steps to ensure the full legal application of the Covenant within the domestic legal order".[21]

82. One focus of the Committee—on the situation of

Palestinian citizens of Israel—is another radical depature, for it is the first serious attempt by a UN body to deal comprehensively with the discrimination faced by the 850,000 Palestinians living inside the armistice line of 1948, and to examine the impact of this discrimination on their economic, social and cultural rights.

83. Mr. Miloon Kothari, U.N. Representative of Habitat Coalition and the Coordinator of H.I.C. Palestine and Israel National Focus Programme has termed the concluding observations as "historic and primarily it is the first attempt by anybody of the U.N. to get to the structural roots of "racial discrimination" as practised by the Israeli State" (regardless of the Government).

84. In this regard, it is useful to bear in mind the concluding observations of CERD (adopted 18 August, 1994) following an inquiry into the Hebron massacre. These state, in paragraph 6, that: "The Committee regards the Israeli settlements in the occupied territories as not only illegal under international law but also an obstacle to peace and to the enjoyment of human rights by the whole population in the region without distinction as to national or ethnic origin in accordance with the Convention". A central message conveyed by the international human rights instruments and their monitoring bodies is that illegal acts, such as the building of settlements, land confiscations, home demolitions, and the deliberate denial of economic, social and cultural rights to Palestinians must stop.

Respect for the economic, social and cultural rights of the Palestinians, both by Israel and by the Palestinian Authority, is a prerequisite for peace. Indeed, it is the only hope for achieving a solid and long term basis for a liberating and a lasting peace for Palestinians and Jews.

85. In that context it is unfortunate that Israeli Supreme Court of Justice refused to hold the Israeli government accountable for its settlement policies in the Occupied Territories. On August 25, 1993, the Supreme Court rejected a petition filed by Peace Now against government settlement construction in the West Bank and Gaza. Peace Now had presented the petition through Attorney Avigdor Feldman to the Supreme Court on October 13, 1991. The petition's central claim was that "Israeli

settlement in (the Occupied Territories) is illegal according to customary rules of international law".

The Supreme Court ruling accommodated the Government's request. The Court decided that it was not authorised to interfere with Government policy. Furthermore, Supreme Court Justice Eliezer Goddberg, in his concurring opinion, cited a 1978 ruling by former Supreme Court Justice Moshe Landau that the "court should refrain from ruling on the issue of civilian settlements in the administered territories as a matter of international law, because this is a subject of controversy between the Government of Israel and other governments." The Israeli Supreme Court could not be "entrusted with deciding the legality of a political policy" as Peace Now had hoped.[22]

86. It needs no emphasise to say that it is unfortunate that Israel Supreme Court inflicted a self wound by unjustified self restraint and thus failed to apply the logic of housing right jurisprudence so firmly established under International law.

87. As aptly ruled by UN Committee under the International Covenant on Economic, Social and Cultural Rights, each State Party, notwithstanding its level of economic development, has a minimum core obligation to ensure the satisfaction of at the very least minimum essential levels of each of the rights found in this instrument. According to the Committee on Economic, Social and Cultural Rights, a State Party in which any significant number of individuals is deprived of basic shelter and housing is, prima facie, falling to perform its obligations under the Covenant.

88. An independent, impartial and accessible judiciary and the availability of legal assistance are recognised as critical factors in a well functioning legal system where human rights are taken seriously. Legal recourse by its very nature, however, has its limitations and the response of the courts in various jurisdictions has been mixed.

89. Essentially, the role of domestic courts in dealing with housing right cases is also largely one of hesitancy yet with a tendency in some countries more in favour of housing rights than is commonly assumed. With time we may hope that the courts boldness in this field will increase.

2.7 Urban Poor : Victims of Apathy

Facing Gateway of India, Bombay, in the early morning, one can see the sun as a ball of fire emerging from the sea. It is a beautiful sight comparable with anywhere in the rest of the world, with a well-trimmed park and paved roads and cleanliness surrounding the area.

A few kilometres away, one sees a sight which is both ugly and painful. About six lakh pavement-dwellers are spending their lives in the most miserable conditions. This unacceptable situation calls for an answer from both the Central and State governments. The social concern shown to the less-advantaged section of the population in any country is the measure by which the claims of any government that its functioning is poor-oriented and in the interests of the people at large have to be judged.

Surely, it is not suggested that the pavement-dwellers love to live in such horrible conditions. Somehow, a false impression is created as if the pavement-dwellers are unsocial elements, a majority of whom are criminals and unemployed and not interested in work. This is sheer slander. The pavement-dwellers are an important part of the economy of Bombay city. It includes even employees of the Bombay Municipal Corporation.

The Asia Coalition on Housing Rights has found that the poor work for an average of 9.9 hours per day in contrast with 7.3 hours per day by any higher income group. And yet, how cruelly are these people treated becomes apparent in the recent eviction of Subhas Nagar (Bombay) pavement settlement.

It is a small establishment of about 70 households who have been shown in the electoral rolls since 1976 onwards but were uprooted mercilessly without any excuse in November 1993 and without giving any alternative location. My visits to these clusters were a heart-rending experience. Women with children, some in wheel-chairs, old people hardly able to walk but yet earning their livelihood somehow asked in bitterness as to why they were forcibly evicted in such a manner and were they not citizens of this country?

These are questions which need to be answered by those in power, more so when the Central Government's national housing policy has proudly proclaimed that it aims at avoiding forcible relocation or dehousing slum dwellers. How hollow this declaration sounds in the face of the forcible eviction and continuing eviction and brutal firing at Dhulle, Maharashtra, and attacks by the police on peaceful activities of the Narmada Bachao Andolan and the tribal population!

It is true that an average Indian has far more reservoir of being able to take misery than anyone else in the world. But what I saw and heard there leaves me in no doubt that an explosive situation has reached and if necessary correctives are not undertaken an un-imagined explosion of resentment and anger will blow up in the face of the governing class. But one saw no sensitivity to this problem because otherwise how can we explain that, at the same time when these poor people were being rendered homeless, an International City Conference on Management of Urban Settlements was being hosted by the Bombay Municipal Corporation in a five-star hotel at a cost of a minimum of Rs. 30 lakh, an amount which could provide sanitation and water to the slums.

Amongst the basic amenities necessary for survival the following must be listed: (i) housing, (ii) water supply, (iii) sewage and sanitation, and (iv) health care.

It is estimated that there are over three million absolutely homeless households and about 150 lakh Kachcha unserviceable housing stock in urban and rural areas. There are 520 lakh persons living in slums and squatter settlements. Over the Eighth Plan period the required investment is estimated conservatively at Rs. 77,000 crore, but the public investment is fixed at 10 per cent only.

Even this is unrealistic considering the inadequate investments in the past, especially when coupled with false analysis by some market-oriented economists that housing shortage could be partially met by putting pressure on the family to increase its income through house loan schemes. How cruelly insensitive they are considering the fact that 40 per cent of the population of the country spend about 80 per cent of their income on food, fuel and lighting alone.

The enormity of the crisis can be understood when one realises that 45.28 per cent of households have only one room.

On an average, the per capita floor area available to the bottom 40 per cent is 5.68 sq.m.

The present contribution of social housing in meeting the needs of weaker sections is a mere token and was able to contribute only 6.54 per cent of the stock.

Water, sewerage and housing are other critical elements for life, without which there can be neither health nor comfort.

According to one Government estimate, about 57 per cent of the total population is not covered by supply of safe drinking water. The per capita norm for water consumption should be 300 litres per day whereas on an average, the urban population is supplied only 145 litres per capita per day in Class-I cities. As many as 31 per cent of the households have to walk up to 100 feet to collect water and many among the poor—women and children —had to cover the distance not once but several times a day to collect the daily requirements.

The total investment required for water supply is around Rs. 15,000 crore per annum whereas the Seventh Plan outlay for both water supply and sewerage in urban areas was only Rs. 2,935.64 crore.

It is estimated that 31.2 per cent of the urban population is not covered by sanitation services.

A study conducted by the Delhi Development Authority shows that a hut of 2.5 x 3 metres accommodates about four persons. About 50 per cent of the dwellers were using open areas for toilet purposes. Sharing of latrines is quite common among poor households as over 60 per cent among them have shared latrines.

As far back as 1988, the government-appointed National Commission on Urbanisation in its report had thus to say about urban poor: “In this as well, India unhappily is in the forefront. One would have to travel far and wide to find conditions as reprehensible as those existing in our cities.”

How sad that one has to accept, though both in anger and anguish, that these comments continue to be as valid today as they were made years back. So much for the welfare of the poor which is the daily mouthful meal of all political parties!

2.8 Development or Displacement

The Bombay Police Act (Section 68) was conveniently but illegally invoked by the Gujarat Government for detaining for a whole day (August 24 last) human rights activists and preventing them from leaving Baroda to reach Maharashtra's Domkhedi (which is in imminent danger of being submerged), and to show their solidarity with tribals and oustees of the Sardar Sarovar Project (SSP) at a public hearing.

The Narmada Valley Development Project consists of 30 large dams. Two of these are big ones including the Sardar Sarovar (Gujarat). The SSP will submerge 92,500 acres of land in Gujarat, Maharashtra and Madhya Pradesh Conservative estimates place the number of displaced persons at 1,52,000. In addition 1,90,000 farmers are likely to be affected by the canal and irrigation system in a major way.

The Narmada Water Disputes Tribunal Award (1979) specifically directed that "In no event shall any areas in M.P. and Maharashtra be submerged under the Sardar Sarovar unless all arrangements for the rehabilitation of oustees therefrom are made in accordance with directions."

The World Bank, one of the sponsors of the SSP, was criticised Internationally for defying the general comment no. 2 (1990) of the committee constituted under the International Covenant of Economic, Social and Cultural Rights: "International agencies should scrupulously avoid largescale evictions or displacement of persons without the provision of all appropriate protection and compensation."

Consequently, in 1991, the World Bank set up an Independent Review, Morse Commission. Its report (1992) says, "We think that the Sardar Sarovar Projects as they stand are flawed, that resettlement and rehabilitation of all those displaced by the projects is not possible under the prevailing circumstances and that the environmental impacts of the projects have not been properly considered or adequately addressed. As a result, we think that the wisest course would be for the Bank to step back from the projects and consider them afresh. The failure of the Bank's incremental policy should be acknowledged."

Similarly Maharashtra appointed the Tata Institute of Social

Sciences to conduct a study of the SSP. That report summarised the findings reached in 1987-93. It clarified that the report presented the team's perspective on rehabilitation of the displaced based on an analysis of their own data (and was not influenced by the opinions of the Narmada Bachao Andolan or the Government).

It summed up its conclusion: The implementation of the award is far from satisfactory, across both the States (Gujarat and Maharashtra). "The SSP has highlighted one point very clearly: largescale displacement of people from land cannot be sustained. The time has come to look for alternatives to large dams, in order to minimise submergence of land and displacement of people. The Narmada Bachao Andolan has sown the seeds of assertiveness and it has taken firm root in the minds of the affected people."

One would have expected any State Government with even little sympathy for the poor to ponder the continuation of the project without first completing the precondition of resettlement. But such are the vested interests in Gujarat that a near-mania has been created so as to stifle any dissent, calling it anti-national. All kinds of falsehoods continue to be spread. All these actions of the Gujarat Government run counter to the human rights law settled by various international covenants and U.N. resolutions.

The U.N. Sub-Commission on Prevention of Discrimination and Protection of Minorities (1993) reaffirmed that forced eviction constituted a gross violation of the right to adequate housing.

In my report — as a U.N. Special Raporteur (1995) — it has been emphasised that specific attention be paid to any project involving involuntary resettlement of persons from their homes and/or land. This report was accepted by the U.N. Commission on Human Rights.

Further, the U.N. Human Rights Guidelines on Development-based Displacement (1997) reaffirms: "All persons, groups and communities have the right in suitable resettlement which includes the right to alternative land or housing which is safe, secure, accessible, affordable and habitable." The same principle was reiterated in the general comment no. 7 (1997) made by the committee under ICESCR Rights: "Evictions should not result in rendering individuals homeless or vulnerable to the violation of other human rights. Where those affected are unable to provide for themselves, the state party must take all appropriate measures, to the maximum of its available resources, to ensure that adequate alternative housing, resettlement or access to productive land, as the case may be, is available".

But the Gujarat Government, instead of being shaken into taking a fresh look at the project, is persisting with its illegal policy, resulting in vast displacement. A large number of people who will be affected by the project — losing their means of survival — are not counted as displaced or affected, and they do not have the benefit of any rehabilitation policy. For, the definition of displacement considers only those affected by submergence, though other categories may also be losing land.

In Gujarat, resettlement land is being obtained by private purchase of land. In many cases, these lands are held by absentee landlords and are being cultivated by tenant farmers or sharecroppers. Also, many local landless labourers get employment. When these lands are sold for resettlement and occupied by the oustees, the tenant farmers/sharecroppers will be thrown away. The oustee families also normally do not require labour. This situation has resulted in a wave of secondary displacement involving hundreds/thousands of families, and also led to conflicts in many places. In Maharashtra too the allocation of forest land for resettlement has displaced many tribals who were cultivating there earlier.

The irrigation benefits of the SSP are going mainly to influential and rich landlors (which are also politically powerful), though the rationale of the project is to address the needs of the drought-prone areas of Saurashtra and the Kutch.

As per the Gujarat Government, about 8.45 per cent of cultivable lands in Saurashtra are under SSP command. It is 2.4 per cent in the Kutch. Similarly only 20 per cent of the cultivable area of north Gujarat is under the SSP command. Thus, even if all claimed benefits are fully realised, the really water scarce areas will benefit only marginally. Even in the areas where water is supplied, it will be utilised fully only by rich landlords, sugarcane farmers, big industries and elite users for golf courses, five-star tourist centres, etc.

The NBA has brought to the notice of various authorities that the Government does not even had land to offer for community resettlement, and so further work on the dam cannot be justified until reparations are provided to all the affected.

In this context, the Union Government's suggestion, which is supported by experts, that even if the height of the dam is kept at 90 metres, with the construction of an irrigation by-pass tunnel, the same benefits can be obtained by diverting water into the canals already partly constructed, needs favouratble consideration. This plan will drastically reduce submerged and displacement. But the Gujarat Government is indifferent to the misery of the oustees.

Our first Prime Minister, Jawaharlal Nehru, who was for big dams, himself regretted in 1958 that we are suffering from "the disease of gigantism" and expressed himself in favour of small irrigation projects. He recognised the human cost of people moving out and their rehabilitation associated with big projects. This change of thinking was an acceptance of the consistent position taken by Dr. Rammanohar Lohia and the Socialist Party that in an intensively-populated country small dams and small irrigation projects are the only correct alternatives. Nehru wished he could "replace the balance in our thinking, which has shifted too much towards gigantic schemes".

Yet, ironically, the Gujarat Government goes on misusing its machinery to thwart peaceful and constitutional efforts at high-lighting this issue.

2.9 A Housing Policy in the Woods

Atal Bihari Vajpayee Government's announcement of its housing policy, as spelt out in the presidential address, in disappointingly vague when it states that, "Shelter is a basic human necessity. The Government will... facilitate the participation of the private sector in order to ensure that housing for all becomes a reality." A further cause for alarm is the decision to repeal the Urban Land and Ceiling Act. A still more anti-poor and anti-Swadeshi plank is the announcement by Minister for Urban Affairs Ram Jethmalani that he is for allowing foreign direct investment in the housing sector.

In my view, by describing shelter as a human necessity and

not as a human right, the Government is trying to dilute its responsibility which falls on it because of the ratification of the International Covenants, and the decision of the Supreme Court holding that the fundamental right to life, under Article 21, includes the right to housing.

In 1976, a declaration was made by the UN Conference on Human Settlement (Habitat I) that, "Adequate shelter and services are a *basic human right* which places an obligation on governments to ensure their attainment by all people". The global strategy for shelter to the year 2000 has accepted that. "The right to adequate housing is universally recognised by the community of nations..." Agenda 21 (UNCED, 1972) says: "The right to adequate housing as a basic human right is enshrined in the Universal Declaration of Human Rights and the International Covenant on Economic, Social and Cultural Rights".

Throughout the developing world, the urban poor live in life-threatening conditions. In India we have a backlog of 30 million housing unit. Over 45 per cent of households have only one room per capita. Area available to the bottom 40 per cent is 58 sq. ft. Even the Delhi Municipal Corporation prescribes the requirements regarding the minimum size of a habitable room as 60 sq. ft. This backlog cannot be cleared even marginally by the Government if it continues to act as a facilitator for the private sector.

The Copenhagen Programme of Action adopted by the World Summit for Social Development (1995) has stated that "Social progress will not be realised simply through the free interaction of market forces. Public policies are necessary to correct market failures", and that, urban poverty should further be addressed by promoting public and private investments to improve the overall human environment and infrastructure, in particular *housing*.

Experience the world over has shown that the private sector has been unable to look beyond profit and the inherent monetisation and commodification of land and housing. The Economic Commission for Europe has noted: "High levels of squatter housing indicate that the formal land market does not provide affordable residential land for housing."

The National Housing Bank or HUDCO-sponsored schemes and projects for housing the urban poor, stipulate that a minimum of 20 per cent of their income be paid as instalments. This is unrealistic; the urban poor cannot spend above 11 per cent of their income (as savings are negligible). Thus, by their very design, these projects would miss the target group and the benefits would flow to household in the higher consumption bracket, as indeed has been recorded in several studies.

Shortage in housing is often blamed on the inadequacies of the Urban Land and Ceiling Act. This is untrue. Of the estimated 1.66 lakh sq. mtr of land available to the Government, it exempted over 43,000 sq. mtrs and acquired only about 14,000 sq. mtr. Even out of this acquisition, possession was taken of only about 3800 sq. mtr. out of which only 631 sq. mtr has been put to use for housing. It is the lack of political will, not defective legislation, which accounts for land shortage.

The European Parliament wants new provisions to be added to the EU Treaty and insists that, "The fundamental right to decent and affordable housing for all be given operational reality be concrete policies and measures carried out at the appropriate administrative and institutional level".

The Istanbul Declaration on Human Settlements, 1996, (Habitat II) attended by the heads of state says specifically that, "we reaffirm our commitment to full and progressive realisation of the right to adequate housing as provided in the International instruments".

Again, the Commission on Human Settlements as its 16th session, held in June 1997, resolved to promote the realisation of the human right to adequate housing, thus affirming that housing is a human right and not merely a need.

The Indian Government's reluctance to accept the right to adequate housing as a human right is probably owing to the mistaken impression that the Government would have to provide houses at no charge to the entire population, immediately. But this assumption is unwarranted as has been clarified by the UN Special Rapporteur on the Right to adequate Housing, which has also been endorsed by the Commission on Human Rights. It has been clarified that acceptance of housing rights as a human right should not be interpreted to imply inter alia: (a) That the state is required to provide housing to the entire population; (b) that housing is to be provided free of charge by the state to all who ask for it or, (c) that the state must necessarily fulfill as aspects of the right immediately.

The right, however, does imply certain obligations for the state. Among the core areas of the state's role in realising the human right to adequate housing, is the prevention of "illegal and mass evictions, elimination of homelessness". In specific cases, the "state may have to provide direct assistance, including provision of housing units, to the most vulnerable groups of society". A number of such rights that are generally recognised as housing rights are linked to, or derived from other human rights such as equality and non-discrimination, gender equality, property rights, and the right to privacy.

Since any right implies an obligation, and, in the case of housing, governments are the only entities in possession of the resources to face the problem on a large scale, the main responsibility in the implementation of the right to housing is in their hands. It is commonly accepted that social exclusion means obstacles that make it difficult for certain people to play an active part in society, and is usually associated with the related problems of poverty and unemployment. NGOs working with the homeless in Europe insist that all those who are either homeless or poorly housed should be recognised as victims of social exclusion, because having access to decent and affordable housing is an essential condition for full participation in any civilised modern society.

Ms. Anna Lou Dehavenon, Projects Director of Action Research Project on Homelessness, in a lucid report, has made certain recommendations for the homeless in New York. She has prefaced it by emphasising that, "These are based on the presupposition that housing is a human right...".

At present the public expenditure on housing is barely over two per cent. In order to meet the reality of the promise of "Housing for all", a minimum of six per cent of public expenditure is essential. The poor will be watching the BJP-led Government on this aspect when it presents its regular Budget in the coming few weeks.

2.10 The Homeless—Destruction of 5,000 Homes of the Bhimnagar Slum

You are not allowed to bring delegations or morchas here. This is notified forest area, Assistant Conservator of Forests, R.P. Pakade, told retired Chief Justice of the Delhi High Court, Rajendra Sachar, and retired Justice, Hosbet Suresh of the Bombay High Court.

The confrontation took place on Saturday morning, amid the burning ruins of 5000 homes, which formed, till May this year, Bhim Nagar in Kandivli East. Justice Sachar himself put out a fire that had just begun to sparkle under the wooden planks of a demolished hut.

"Why are you bulldozing and burning the remains of these houses?" Justice Sachar asked Pakade. "Why don't you just carry it away so that the people can take them later?"

"There's no need to do that," replied Pakade stonily. "This is forest land. It is a notified national park. These people can't stay here. They are trying to rebuild their huts. We have to demolish them."

Justice Sachar and Suresh, along with retired Justice SM Daud of the Bombay High Court, this morning began hearings on the biggest ever slum demolition drive undertaken in India, ostensibly to save the Sanjay Gandhi National Park. When completed, this drive will have made 60,000 Mumbaiites homeless, who have lived and worked in this city for the last 25 years and more.

The three 70-plus judges, comprising the Indian people's Human Rights Tribunal, took a break from recording the depositions of 500-odd slum dwellers when they were told that the bulldozers had come again. As they trudged up the small hill on which Bhim Nagar once stood, they stepped on not only broken tiles, bricks, cement walls, floors and underground rubber pipes, but also upon children's pillows, disintegrating spongy sofa seats, and coloured rags which indicated the remains of a tailoring shop.

People trying to live out of the rubble of their homes (at one place, all that had remained intact was a cup and saucer stand), showed them correspondence from MTNL and BSES to prove that since they had been provided with these amenities, they could not have been illegal squatters.

Sushma Khope told Justice Sachar that she had sold her mangalsutra to buy her son's SSC books, but the demolition squad had burnt those books.

Earlier, the mother of Chandu Konhale, wept as she deposed before Justice Daud how the police had broken her door and beaten up her two elder sons, the breadwinners of the family of five, and arrested one of them on July 23.

The eldest, Chandu, was admitted to Bhagwati hospital the day after the beating, and died there. The family did not know if any post-mortem had taken place. The January 22 to 23 demolition took place despite a state government notification staying demolitions till September 30.

In an exclusive interview with ***Sunday Mid-Day,*** Justice Sachar described what he had seen as "Barbaric, savage. It's as if a bomb has fallen here. Seeing the spot as it is," he added, "there is no question of it ever becoming part of any national park. For 30 years it's been stone and cement. These are all pre-95 structures, which are protected by government policy. At any rate, after the demolition, the people have a right to carry away the remains of their homes. Or the authorities can carry them away and dump them somewhere. But here they are burning them. That's illegal. I am going to advise the concerned groups to ask for remedies from the forest department."

"The demolition may be under court orders, but no court has ordered or can order that the remains of the demolished homes be burnt. They have not received any notice, warning them that the remains of their belongings will be burnt if they don't remove them."

Justice Sachar expressed the hope that the Bombay High Court would come to the spot and take a "personal look" at the manner in which the demolition was taking place. "I'm sure then this inhumanity won't be allowed to continue."

References

1. Oppenhein's International Law (9th Edn.) Vol. I, p. 31.
2. Brierly's contribution to International Law - By Sir Hersch

Lauterpacht, Q.C., LL.D., F.B.A. P.XV at XXI.
3. International Law in a Divided World - Antonio Cassese - Clarendonpress, Oxford, p.148.
4. *Ibid* (1), p. 54.
5. Theory and Practices of European Convention on Human Rights by Professor Van Dijk and Van Hoof.
6. Craig Scott and Patrick Macklem in University of Pennsylvania Law Review, Vol. 141, No. 1, 1992, p. 28.
7. Wade and Forsyth in The Administrative Law (7thEdn.)
8. Maxwell on Interpretation of Statutes.
9. *Concocraft Ltd.* vs. *American Airways*: (1969) 1 AER p. 80.
10. The right to a home, the right to a future - The Third report of the European Observatory on Home lessness, 1994 by Mary Daly.
11. Homeless in Europe-The Newsletter of FEANTSA, Issue 3, Spring 1998, p.7.
12. *Jolly George Varghese* v. *Bank of Cochin* : (1980) 2 Supreme Court Cases 360.
13. *Olaga Tellis* vs. *Bombay Municipal Corpn.* : (1985) 3 SCC 545.
14. *Chameli Singh* vs. *State of U.P.* : (1996) 2, SCC 549.
15. *Shantistar Builders* vs. *Narayan Khimalal Totane*: (1990) 1 SCC 520.
16. *People's Union for Civil Liberties* vs. *UOI*: (1997) 1 SCC 301.
17. General Command No. 4 (E/1992/23-E/C-12/1991/4, Annex. III).
18. U.N. Year Book 1991.
19. U.N. Year Book 1995.
20. The Right to Adequate Housing : Report of the Special Rapporteur Mr. Rajindar Sachar, United Nations, New York and Geneva, 1996.
21. Committee on Economic, Social and Cultural Rights General-Unedited version E/C.12/1Add. 27 dated 4th December, 1998.
22. Clever Concealment - Jewish Settlement in the Occupied Territories Under the Rabin Government:August 1992 September 1993. Palestine Human Rights, Information Centre, Jerusalem, February 1994.

Act.

The Act — now repealed — was brought into force in 1987, originally for four years and continued to be extended notwithstanding the fact that it seriously violated one of the most prized human rights of an accused, namely, that the court would not entertain the evidence of anonymous witnesses, and even when the denial of opportunity to cross-examine those witnesses had been held by the European Court of Human Rights denial of the right to a fair trial. The press did not expose the inertia of the members of Parliament who showed almost no concern for human rights — as is clear from the fact that the duration of Parliamentary discussions varied between one hour and 10 minutes in 1993 and a maximum of eight hours in 1985 and that the participation of the number of MPs varied from eight to a maximum of 34. Nor did the media emphases the gross misuse of the TADA Act which was evident from the largescale detentions in Punjab (14,451), while 14,049 persons were detained in a recognisably peaceful State Gujarat, Where it was used against tribals, trade unionists and student activitist. Here, the media regrettably failed the nation.

It however, woke up later when a famous young filmstar of Mumbai was detained under the TADA Act (a totally illegal and motivated act). Possibly because it was a story appealing to millions of film fans — here the commercial interest won: the media had forgotten the warning of philosopher Solon of Athens. Asked how people could most effectively be delivered from committing injustice, he said, "If those who are not injured feel as much indignation as those who are".

Governments conveniently invoke the sensitive ground of national security to silence the media from reporting human rights violations in affected areas. Unfortunately, the media, by and large has a tendency to accept this gratuitous advice without much demur. But this kind of yielding is totally counter to the spirit and confidence with which our Constitution gave the free press the protection it needed to fulfil its essential democratic role. The media needs to bear in kind the caution given by U.S. Supreme Court in the well-known case of *The New York Times* in "Pentagon papers" where it said about the First Amendment, which guarantees free press. "The word 'security' is a broad,

3
Violation of Human Rights

3.1 Human Rights Bill Seriously Flawed

The proverb about a mountain of labour producing a mouse is the only way of describing the National Human Rights Commission Bill, 1993 which was introduced in the Lok Sabha on the last day of the budget session. The Bill is such an anti-climax that I doubt very much whether any sitting or retired or retired Judge of the Supreme Court would agree to head it.

The pre-requisite for any Commission is its acceptability as an independent body which is free from the influence of the executive. The Bill is seriously flawed. The proposed commission will consist of eight members. Though the bill talks of persons being selected as those having concern for human rights, it says that at least one member each will be from the IAS and IPS, and legal affairs ministry who have held the office at the level of Secretary. This hardly inspires confidence. The members belonging to the fraternity are unfortunately the most suspect in the matter of violation of human rights.

The commission is to be so composed that it will become docile and dominated by the Government. Surprisingly, the personnel for selection include neither the nominee of the Chief Justice of India nor the Press, the Editors Guild, both of which are the main bulwark for the protection of human rights. Also, as the Commission is to have an all-India jurisdiction, it should also include one Chief Minister from States ruled by the opposition.

The functions of the Commission on paper are broadly well-defined. I am surprised however to find that the power of the commission to visit the jails to study the living conditions therein is subject to obtaining the prior approval of the State Government. This is insulting. At present Sessions Judges have control over jails, and their inspections are part of their normal duty. In face of this to provide that such a high powered Commission does not have an independent right to inspect jails is to make a mockery of its stature.

Another principle laid down is that the Commission should be empowered to investigate the conduct of the police, the paramilitary forces. And in order to effectively do this, the Commission should have more facilities to conduct thorough investigation, independent of the police and other security forces whose conduct it will be called upon to inquire. This independent agency for investigation should also be empowered to award compensation, which is the essential basis on which an independent human rights commission can function. But all these essential requisites are absent in the Bill.

Section 14 only empowers the Commission to utilise the services of any agency whether of Centre or State, but only with the concurrence of the State Government. This is like the power of the Vigilance Enquiry Officer. That is made clear by Section 18, because even when the Commission finds a prima facie viotation of human rights it is only empowered to recommended to the concerned Governments for initiation of any action. It has no independent power to award interim compensation and for this also it has to request the concerned Governments which may or may not honour its recommendations.

It cannot inspire confidence among the people if the Commission is to function like a fact finding body, as the Bill envisages. To be effective in should be empowered to prosecute or direct prosecution where it detects violation of human rights, and not be dependent on the whims of the State Governments.

A very undesirable feature is the manner of dealing with violations committed by the armed forces which in terms of definition will include not only the regular Army, Navy and Air Force personnel, but also Border Security Force (BSF), as is clear form Section 4 of BSF Act 1968.

It is well documented that the overwhelming mass of

violations are committed not by the regular armed forced but by other forces like the BSF and CRPF. To keep them out of the purview of enquiry by the Commission is to play a legal fraud on the real concept of the Human Rights Commission. The whole procedure in this aspect is farcical. The Bill provides that in case of the armed forces, the Commission is only empowered to seek information from the Government and on receipt of a report it might either drop its complaint or make its recommendations to the Government. This in reality means that all violations of human rights by the security forces will be immune from independent scrutiny by the Commission. The futility of such an exercise and the cynicism it will spread amongst the victims is quite patent.

Another undesirable innovation introduced in the Bill is the need for the Commission to enquire into human right violations by terrorists, which has the same meaning as given in Terrorist Act (TADA). Violation by terrorists is condemned by all human rights organisations. But this strange procedure of enquiry by the Commission is unintelligible. It is impossible for a Commission to hold an enquiry into the alleged terrorists acts. Obviously it cannot enforce the presence of terrorists. In reality what is there to enquire when terrorist kills, kidnaps or extorts. His act are all criminal offences punishable by law. The police has full authority and duty to proceed against such acts by the terrorists. It does not need any authorisation from the Commission.

In my view this weird innovation is only a crude attempt by the Government to deflect public scrutiny of human rights violations committed by it. The unspoken premises seem to dull people into accepting the pernicious doctrine that to meet the menace of terrorism, State agencies should not be faulted for violating human rights. State as custodian of rule of law can never violate the law under any circumstances.

These are all matters requiring indepth study. The Bill should not be passed in its present form. It is to be hoped that there will be serious debate by the members of Parliament, Human Rights organisations and social activists, before giving it a final shape.

3.2 Devaluing the Human Rights Commission

Ansal Plaza incident has pitchforked National Human Rights

Commission (the Commission) into the forefront of uncalled for controversy. Its critics have seized the opportunity not only to attack the jurisdiction of commission - some have even gone to abusing it by calling it a National Commission for Terrorists, which who has only the welfare of terrorists as its agenda. This is slander, such criticism goes against the very core of our constitution which enshrines the Fundamental Rights to Life.

It may be sobering especially for the young critics to inform themselves of the compelling international pressure which forced the Central Government to legislate Protection of Human Rights Act, 1993, notwithstanding the reservation of the Executive and the bureaucracy.

In a background note on the imperative need for setting up NHRC Government of India itself emphasized "that National and international organizations in this field have been highlighting alleged violations of Human Rights by various Government functionaries. There is a growing feeling that the Government is not serious about such violations and excesses and bringing the guilty persons to book. Against this background, any impression of Government's lack of seriousness on the issue of Human Rights is a matter of serious concern and needs to be dispelled."

Notwithstanding the above the Government of India and State Governments of all political hues continue to be indifferent to remedy the deficiencies which have been found in the effective working of the Commission. To remedy this Chief Justice Venakatchaliah, the then Chairperson of NHRC, constituted a Committee of some of us under the Chairmanship of former Chief Justice Ahmadi. Based on the report of the Committee, the Commission sent its recommendations to the Ministry of Home Affairs on 7.3.2000 and which if considers absolutely essential if the purpose of the Commission to safeguard the Human Rights is to be served.

In the present Act Armed Forces have been defined to include all Armed Forces of the Union which would includes all the security agencies, i.e., BSF and CRPF. Section 19 permits the Commission only to send its report with regard to the Armed Forces to Central Government but cannot on its own take any action. This is a big drawback considering that most of the Human Rights violations are done by these security agencies. The recommendations, therefore, suggests that Armed Forces should only mean the Naval, Military and Air Force thus striking a balance between the felt need to keep the Armed Forces outside the public controversy and the people rights (though some of us would want to include the armed forces too within the Commissions jurisdiction). It may be noted that the present provision excluding para-military forces is the subject of adverse comment which affects seriously the credibility of NHRC and commitment to Human Rights on the part of Government of India.

At present the only qualification for appointing 2 members from the public to the Commission are only as having knowledge or practical experience in mater relating to the Human Rights. This is too vague. Amendment suggests that they should be person who are working or had worked in the field of Human Rights so as to make certain that the composition of Commission shall ensure that it reflects the pluralist character of society. Another important amendment suggested is that the Chairperson who is at present kept out of the selection of the members must be a member of the selection committee when selecting members.

Section 11 sought to be amended by providing that the staff which is made available shall be done with the concurrence of the Commission, to focus on the autonomous position of the Commission. The present provision that the Commission can visit a jail after intimation to the State Government is sought to be deleted as it is neither in keeping with the authority of the Commission nor is capable of ensuring the element of surprise over the visit. Power is sought to be given to the Commission to recommend to the Government for grant of interim relief to the victim during the pendency of the enquiry where the enquiry discloses a prima facie case thus giving much needed relief to the victim - the absence of which is a great hardship to the victim. At present Section 19 only requires the Central Government to inform the Commission of the action taken on its report. In order to give more teeth to the Report of Commission it is proposed that if the Central Government does not accept the recommendations of the Commission, it shall communicate the reasons for its inability to the Commission within a period of three months and that the Commission shall consider the same and make such final recommendations. The annual reports of the Commission are to be laid down before the Parliament by the Central Governments. But the Parliament has unfortunately not yet even discussed the report submitted for period ending March 2000. As Commission can only publish its report after it has been discussed in the Parliament, amendment is suggested that the Central Government shall within a period of 3 months from the date of report, cause it to be laid before the Parliament with the action taken on the recommendations and where such a report is not laid before the Parliament within that period it shall be open for the Commission to publish that report. This amendment flows from the principle of fundamental right to know of a every citizen of public affairs. Shockingly even after a lapse of two years the Central Government continues to maintain studied silence and the work of the Commission continues to suffer.

The Commission consists of Chairperson who is a retired Chief Justice of India and 4 members - one member who has been to be a Judge of the Supreme Court and one member who is or has been a Chief Justice of the High Court and 2 from persons having knowledge in matters relating to Human Rights. The appointments are to be made by the President after obtaining the recommendations of the Committee consisting of the Prime Minister, Speaker of the House of People, Minister Incharge of the Home Affairs in Government of India, Leaders of the Opposition in the House of People, and in the Council of State and Deputy Chairman of the Council of States.

But such is the total indifference of the Central Government to the functioning of the Commission that even its full strength is not maintained. Thus one of its members Mr. Sudarshan Aggarwal retired about 2 years back and another member Mr. Justice Ramaswamy retired on July, 2002. Both these posts are still unfilled. Considering that Selection Committee is a small one and a high powered one will it be rash if one suggests that the Government is deliberately not wanting to fill up the posts so as to slow down the process of the working of the Commission.. But it is distressing that the Leaders of the Opposition in the

House of People and the Council of States who are also appointing authority should not have taken up this matter which touches the Human Rights of the common person. But then the opposition at the Centre has its Government in various States and as figures reveal, in the matter of violations of Human Rights, Governments of various political hues are equally guilty. The total number of complaints registered in the Commission in 1999-2000 was 50,634, - state of Uttar Pradesh accounted for the largest number of complaints, being 56.5 per cent Bihar followed with 4,409 complaints, and Delhi was third, with 3,077 complaints.

As far as custodial deaths, they were 1093 in 1999-2000. Maharasthra was highest (30 deaths in police custody) followed by West Bengal (19).

The calculatingly indifferent attitude of Central Government is further highlighted by the fact that the present Chairperson Justice Verma is to retire by 18th January, 2003, and yet there is no announcement of the successor. Considering that as per the Act choice is limited from available three retired Chief Justice, this delay seems deliberate attempt to devalue the institution of the Commission. A sad commentary on the present state of political morality.

3.3 Government Circulars—Violation of Rights

The Rejection summarily by the Supreme Court, without giving any reasons, of the writ petition challenging the circulars of the Central Government by which prior approval is to be obtained from the Ministry of Home Affairs in regard to international conferences to be organised by Indian NGOs, associations, universities, even with regard to subjects of human rights, and worse, from the Ministry of External Affairs also if the participants are from Bangladesh, Sri Lanka and Pakistan may be considered by the Government's apologists as a shot in its arms. But it has also revived the debate about the effectiveness of the Judiciary in safeguarding the fundamental right of freedom of speech guaranteed to the citizens of the country and has occasioned the caustic comment that while legislatures are one generation behind public opinion, the Judiciary is one generation behind the legislature.

For some time, the alleged judicial activism was being projected as a repudiation of the charge of the courts being conservative. But that was due more to the concern over alleged environmental pollutions, as obsession of the affluent, while the misery of hundreds of thousands of slum-dwellers and oustees of projects such as Narmada has not received similar response.

The Government would be mistaken if it assumes the challenge to such patently illegal circulars has ended. The reason is that the Supreme Court in several decisions has ruled that dismissal of a petition at the preliminary hearing without giving reasons is neither a *res judicata* nor binding as a precedent under Article 141 of the Constitution, and could be challenged in fresh proceedings before the High Courts or Supreme Court.

The continuance of the Government order flouts the decision of the Supreme Court in its earlier judgment in the Secretary, Cricket Association of Bengal (1995) case affirming that "under Article 19 (1) (a) every citizen has a right to impart and receive information as part of his fundamental right to speech and expression". And that the Government is under an obligation to ensure conditions under which this right can be meaningfully and effectively enjoyed. And further that "freedom of speech and expression carries with it the right to gather information, and to exchange thoughts and ideas with others not only in India but also outside".

An equally forceful mandate was expressed in Article 13 of Universal Declaration of Human Rights, 1948. But the real embarrassment to the Central Government is that the circulars violate Article 19 of the International Covenant on Civil and Political Rights (ICCPR), 1966, and which has been ratified by the Central Government in 1979. Article 19 of the ICCPR reads "everyone shall have the right to freedom of expression; this right shall include freedom to seek, receive and impart information and ideas of all kinds, regardless of frontiers". A similar right of the citizen is recognised in Article 10 of European Convention on Human Rights. Should India be the only defaulter amongst the democratic nations?

It is well settled that this fundamental right can be limited only by reasonable restrictions under a law made for the purposes mentioned in Article 19 (2). And further that the burden is on the state to justify the restrictions. Government circulars undoubtedly have no statutory basis and that is why it is legally inform as the Kharak Singh case (1963) has categorically held that "if any regulation constitutes in infringement of any of the freedoms guaranteed to him by the Constitution then the only manner in which this violation of the fundamental right can be defended is by justifying the impugned action taken by reference to a valid law i.e., be it a stature, a statutory rule or a statutory regulation".

This precondition is essential otherwise it will also violate Article 14, because as said in Satwant case (1967) "While in the case of enacted law one knows where he stands, in the case of unchallenged arbitrary discretion, discrimination is writ large on the face of it. Such a discretion patently violates the doctrine of equality, for the differences in the treatment of persons rests solely on the arbitrary selection of the Executives. The arguments that the said discretionary power of the state is a political or a diplomatic one does not make it anytheless an executive power". The Government circulars also run foul of the fundamental right of Article 21 of the Constitution, because as said by the Supreme Court in the Reliance Ltd. case (1988), "Right to know is a basic right which citizens of a free country aspire in the broader horizon of the right to live in this age in our land under Article 21 of our Constitution". That right has reached new dimensions and urgency.

The Government cannot claim immunity by merely calling circulars a matter of procedure, as Article 21 mandates a "procedure established by law " which means an enacted law or statutory order, and not executive circulars as in the present case. It is well settled that procedure can only be followed if there is a statutory provision. Absent that, the present order is null and void. Also, "Procedure which deals with the modalities of regulating, restricting or even rejecting a fundamental right falling within Article 21 has to be fair, not foolish and must rule out anything arbitrary, freakish or bizarre. A valuable constitutional right can be canalized only by civilised process".

Why this suspicion about public bodies? The danger of foreign invitees being in fact saboteurs does injustice to the responsible individuals, NGO, universities. Such an approach shows greater confidence in the ability and patriotism of small officials rather than top academicians and public men.

If the circulars continue, we may have the indignity of the organisers (who includes Supreme Court judges) of the International Law Association, who are holding a conference at Delhi to be presided over by the Chief Justice of India having to obtain prior approval for holding the conference (to be attended by foreign judges, law professors) from the minions of the Ministry, not withstanding that all foreign visitors have to obtain Indian visas in any case.

Comical if not a tragic paradox that while seeking to improve good relations with our neighbouring countries especially Pakistan by even opening sensitive borders, the circulars should so insult their citizens that if the participants from these countries are attending a meet on even an innocent subject such as international arbitration law, clearance has to be taken from both the Ministry of Home Affairs and the Ministry of External Affairs ,which is not needed if the participants were from other countries of Asia-Europe.

It is in that context that one recapitulates with nostalgia the anguished but determined rap given by Chief Justice Patanjali Sastri to the highest of political leaders such as Pandit Nehru, who were visibly upset at some earlier judgments of the Supreme Court striking down legislation because it violated fundamental rights of citizens by firmly stating "that we think it right to point out what is sometimes overlooked that our Constitution contains express provision for judicial review of legislation, as to its conformity with the Constitution. If then, the Courts in this country face up to such important and none too easy task, it is not out of any desire to tilt at legislative authority in crusader's spirit, but in discharge of a duty plainly laid upon them by the Constitution. This is especially true as regards the fundamental rights, as to which this Court has been assigned the role of a sentinel on the *qui vive*—and that while the Court naturally attaches great weight to the legislative judgment, it cannot desert its own duty to determine finally the constitutionality of an impugned statute". Wise and strong words which still continue to act as a beacon light to the legal fraternity."

3.4 Punjab and Human Rights

Prime Minister Mr. Narasimha Rao deserves credit for his

consistency in going ahead with his decision to have the Punjab election in February, notwithstanding the opposition to it from various quarters including from within the Congress party. But all this is being nullified by some of the negative working methods before the announcement and subsequently. For a full month, it was given out that the Central Government would announce its decision on some of the important measures like (a) transfer of Chandigarh to Punjab (b) reference of water dispute to Supreme Court and (c) taking legal action against the politicians involved in the 1984 Delhi riots. Every sensible person felt that decisions on these points, apart from being justified on the ground of justice, would also help the wavering and pusillanimous Akali leadership to break away from the fear of militants and participate in the elections.

But having created this atmosphere, the Central Government developed cold feet. It involved Mr Bhajan Lal and out went the Punjab package. The Akali leadership, craven as it is, clutched at this and announced the boycott. Now, the bungling by Central Government does not in any manner justify the Akali party's response. It rather shows that the Akali leadership has become irrelevant to Punjab and especially to Sikh politics. Because there is an announcement of elections, any party or group which claims the support of the masses would immediately welcome this chance to come to power and then negotiate or even force the Central Government to concede the just demands of Punjab including the ones mentioned above. After all, the major criticism against the Central Government is the denial of democratic aspirations of Punjab.

But when a chance was offered, it was shunned. I would still appeal to the Akali leadership to call off the boycott and participate in the coming Punjab elections. Boycott by Akalis means playing into the hands of the Congress. It would be a real tragedy if the Akalis refused to appreciate that the Congress is interested in increasing its parliamentary majority and boycott by Akalis will only help it in its half-concealed game plan in the Punjab elections.

I also feel that boycott by Akalis will deprive Punjab of a very badly needed healing touch of a non-Congress government. The next worse thing in not holding elections would be a Congress or a Congress-supported government in Punjab. Boycott by Akalis is thus fraught in what serious consequences. Will the Akali leadership fail Punjab at this juncture?

However, no credit can be given to the Prime Minister for his approach to the observance of human rights, as is shown by his uncalled for slander against human rights organizations at the recent meeting of National Integration Council.

It appears as if a deliberate effort is being made to try to project the human rights organizations in a false colour. That would appear to be the only explanation for the recent editorial of a weekly paper, which, following Mr. Rao's example, has gone to the length of calling human rights activists as fifth columnists, a language totally undeserving mention in a paper which calls itself responsible. And this consent from an Editor who, when he was proceeded against for defamation by a Chief Minister of a State for having allegedly written a defamatory article against him, was given India-wide support from various human rights organizations, journalists and liberals I knew at that time — he obtained fully the support of human rights organizations which upheld the right of the Editor to say even the nastiest of things against a public person, of course, subject to its being true and in public interest. This support was given to him in an unstinted manner. It is a different matter that all these bodies and supporters of the editorial freedom were let down badly by the Editor when he unreservedly withdrew these allegations unilaterally accepting thereby that it was more sensationalism than pursuit of truth which had motivated him to write the article.

This onslaught on human rights does not seem to be a sudden affair. One had apprehensions about it when the Prime Minister Mr. Narasimha Rao had gone to attend the Harare meeting (summit) of commonwealth countries. It would be remembered that at Harare, a question had arisen whether financial aid to the countries should be linked with their record of upholding of human rights. Mr. Rao had taken a hawkish attitude against linking foreign aid to human rights record of the country. Of course, so far as the British Government wanted to include good governance in that packet, the suggestion was unacceptable because good governance in that packet, the suggestion was unacceptable because good governance is a relative term and could be misused against any country to suit the political expediency of some countries.

Thus, it could even be urged that there is no good governance in England because of the many excesses committed by British security forces against the Irish Revolutionary Army in Northern Ireland. It could also be said that there is no good governance in USA because of its unsatisfactory record in the treatment towards Blacks. But it would be wrong to say that England and America are not democracies.

In my view, insistence on observance of human rights is essential because in that way, the minimum of free periodical elections, representative government, freedom of speech and independent judiciary will at best be assured in all countries desirous of seeking aid. In my opinion, any country seeking aid must at least ensure these minimum standards of human rights. The Commonwealth Secretary himself lamented that half of the 30 commonwealth countries are not democracies.

I see no reason why aid, limited as it is, should be given to boost up countries which violate human rights. Present these minimum requirements, aid should not be withheld on the ground of any particular political or economic policies being pursued by any country. To do so would be plainly discriminatory. But to insist that aid should be given even to non-democratic governments is really to deny the purpose of aid, such aid will not be used for upliftment of the masses for whom it is meant, but will be hijacked by the non-democratic rulers.

In that context, I feet that Mr. Rao's insistence of not linking aid with observance of human rights was unfortunate. He seems to fall in the fallacy of thinking as if there is conflict between observance of human rights and development. He seems to accept that development can take place even when there are no human rights. This is the same kind of fallacy which finds a conflict between economic or political rights and seeks to treat either right as superior to another, depending on one's objective preference. But this is muddled thinking. Bread and freedom are two sides of the same coin and deprivation of either will destroy the democratic fabric of the society.

Similarly, democracy and human rights are not antithetical to development. Rather, development and growth are in direct proportion to the observance of democracy and the pursuit of social justice by the State.

3.5 Curbing Human Rights in Tamil Nadu

The Human Rights issue in the country is not showing any improvement. Normally the violations that get publicised in the Indian Press and more in the international Press relate to areas like Punjab, Kashmir or some parts of North East where the activities of armed forces and paramilitary units controlled by the Central Government operate. It is generally assumed that violations take place because of security and defence needs and this sometimes is put forth as a usual defence even by decent people.

But a look around the country will show that Human Rights violations on a vast scale are taking place in State in which there is supposed to be normal functioning. In that context the case of Tamil Nadu is an illustration of the most blatant violation of the Human Rights. The Government of Tamil Nadu has already shown scant respect for the freedom of Press and the individual by arresting journalists and starting false cases against them. The intolerance of the government is increasing so much that it revived the pre-independence draconian enactment like the Prevention of Seditious Meetings Act 1911.

It is ironic that the Government of Tamil Nadu which is the biggest supporter of the Congress government at the Centre should choose to revive this unconstitutional act against which decades back in 1921, the great Mr. C.R. Das had protested and called it a violation of the rights of the people. It is amazing how the present government wants to hide its inefficiency by resorting to the repressive measures promulgated by the Britishers. Not only that, the Government of Tamil Nadu has recently (June 1992) promulgated the Ordinance amending the Tamil Nadu Open Places (Prevention of Disfigurement) Act, 1959, prohibiting pasting of posters in Madras and other places in the State. The annual conference of the Peoples Union for Civil Liberties (PUCL) held at Madras in June strongly condemned these repressive measures. It felt that the ordinance is aimed at curbing the rights of citizens and political groups/parties to free expression and to dissemination of ideas and opinions. That such a legislation is meant to curb the opponents is clear from the fact that even two days later after the promulgation of this ordinance I saw in Madras, while attending the PUCL conference, large number of posters with pictures of the Chief Minister Ms Jayalalitha put on the whole city of Madras. It appears that these laws are meant to snuff out all kinds of opposition. The right even to small parties and groups to give their views by inexpensive measures like posters is also being taken away.

The result of this suppression of these individual freedoms is that the police has become totally irresponsible and answerable to none except perhaps to the Chief Minister herself. Thus even a case where a poor woman was sexually assaulted in police custody and in spite of public protests has not moved the woman Chief Minister. There is no justification not to have arrested the police officer once a statement had been made by the woman. As a matter of fact so much brazenness is to be found in the bureaucracy, no doubt encouraged by the attitude of the Chief Minister that the DG, Police, has the temerity to say that their inquiry revealed that both the police officer and the woman have misbehaved with each other. I cannot imagine a more shameful approach of the highest police officer in the State. But then what can you expect when a murder takes place, properties are destroyed, houses are burnt and yet not even a Judicial enquiry is ordered.

After having interacted with a large number of people the impression that I go was that the distinction between the State and the party in power is fast receding in the State of Tamil Nadu.

It may be recalled that there was an unfortunate tragedy at Kumbakonam during Maha Maham. The Government announced compensation of Rs. one lakh. It included an amount of Rs. 30,000 said to have been given by the AIADMK party. Now whether the party gives any particular sum, no one can object but the Government cannot in its announcement of Rs. 1 lakh include in it a sum of Rs. 30,000 which is said to be given by the party for the obvious reason that Government and political party are two separate entities.

Any mixup of these two is dangerous to democracy. It is

because this difference is not being kept, that most serious violations take place on the rights of the citizens. The Tamil Nadu Government celebrated its one year at Madurai. From Press reports it appears that patrol pumps around the area had been closed on account of alleged security risks.

The jamboree of procession deprived the citizens of Madurai of normal facility to move about. The total sycophancy of the ordinary politicians was again in the forefront when about 80 cut-outs (barring a few of MGR's) of the Chief Minister were spread over the city.

I am told each cut-out of 100 to 150 ft. costs about Rupees one lakh and a half and there were about 80 of them. Such wastage of money when the State is deficient even of the normal facility of drinking water and cleanliness. But such is our lack of public opinion and public consciousness, that these misuse of State machinery and public expense instead of being frowned upon is being taken as a sign of popularity of the Chief Minister. No wonder a State where the MLAs and other political leaders publicly tatoo their arms with the name of the Chief Minister and get themselves photographed without any embarrassment can hardly throw up a healthy criticism of such like acts.

3.6 An Opportunity Missed to end Phone Tapping

Irrespective of the Supreme Court's recent judgment in the *PUCL* vs *Union of India* case, where it held telephone tapping as a serious invasion of an individual's privacy, the continued misuse of such power is unlikely to end.

Though there is no specific provision in our Constitution guaranting the right of privacy, the judgment has categorically ruled that "right to privacy" is part of the right to "life and personal liberty" enshrined under Article 21 of the Constitution, and that telephone tapping unless it comes within the grounds of restrictions provided under Article 19 (1) would also violate Article 19(1) (a) of the Constitution.

But the judgment has not provided any firm and satisfactory safeguards against the continued misuse of telephone tapping. The PUCL had filed a writ petition in the wake of report on "tapping of politicians' phones" by the Central Bureau of

Investigation. Its plea that no telephone tapping be permitted without obtaining prior ex-parte judicial authorisation has not been accepted. Instead, interception has been permitted by Home Secretaries, whose order is subject to review by a committee consisting of Cabinet Secretary at the Centre, Chief Secretary in States, along with some other secretaries.

This is unfortunate because even earlier reports of interception were sent regularly to the Cabinet and Home Secretaries, and yet the CBI report is frank enough to admit that its enquiries had revealed unjustified interceptions of telephones of a large number of journalists, members of Parliament, Chief Ministers, and even some Central Ministers. In fact, the CBI had recommended that with regard to members of Parliament the proposal should have the approval of the Prime Minister who may consult the Speaker and Chairman of Rajya Sabha.

Even this innocent suggestion has not been incorporated in the judgment. Provision in the judgment for the review committee is equally toothless as it would be an appeal from Caesar to Caesar, all within the intimate obliging circle of the bureaucracy. This touching, though misplaced, faith in the bureaucracy is a serious flaw in the judgment, especially in view of courts' own finding that several lapses had occurred in the execution of the order passed under the Act.

Even the moderate recommendation of the Second Press Commission that the original order should emanate in writing from the Minister and that it should come up for approval before a board constituted on the lines prescribed under the Preventive Detention Law, was not accepted.

I am of the view that the court should have laid down the procedure for prior judicial scrutiny. In this regard it had the precedence of American legislation giving details on the procedure for such scrutiny. Instead the court seems to have drawn its inspiration though not adequately from Britain's Interception of Communications Act, 1985. Under the British law, the home secretary alone is authorised to permit telephone tapping. A tribunal consisting of a senior judge can review the order. Not only this, a judicial review by courts is also permitted.

None of these have been provided for in the judgment.

As it is, the efficacy of the UK legislation has been seriously criticised by Helen Fenwick who has commented that "the main criticism of this scheme is that there is no judicial scrutiny of the warrant procedure at any time and that the balance created at present between this interest of security and that of protecting privacy is unsatisfactory in a democratic society". Another study entitled "Civil Liberties in conflict" edited by Larry Gostin has commented that "the scope of the legislation was, however, described as an act of 'dumb insolence' to the European Court. It contained no provision for judicial approval to be sought before a warrant for interception would be issued".

The court seems to have imposed unnecessary self limitations in the matter of civil liberties, unlike those in the matter of environmental degradation. The alleged spectre of inconvenience and danger to security, trumpeted by Union of India, in case prior judicial scrutiny was mandated seems misconceived. The investigation of criminal activity has long involved imparting sensitive information to judicial officers who have respected the confidentialities involved. Judges may be counted upon to be especially conscious of security requirements in national security cases.

The US Supreme Court (1972) caustically repelled as untenable similar arguments on the plea of national security, when it held that "we cannot accept the Government's argument that internal security matters are too subtle and complex for judicial evaluation". Courts regularly deal with the most difficult issues of our society. There is no reason to believe that judges will be insensitive to or uncomprehending of the issues involved in domestic security cases. Certainly courts can recognise that domestic security surveillance involves different considerations from the surveillance of ordinary crime. If the threat is too subtle or complex for our senior law enforcement officers to convey its significance to a court, one may question whether there is probable cause for surveillance.

The judgement while laying down the procedure specially mentioned that it was doing so till the Central Government lays down a fair and reasonable procedure. Here is an opportunity for Parliament to prove that it is more active and concerned with safeguarding the rights of individuals than the courts. Will the MPs translate their rhetoric into reality by providing for prior judicial scrutiny in case of telephone tapping. The ball is in their court now.

3.7 National Human Rights Commission

Government of India held a Seminar on setting up N.H.R.C. in Delhi of the 11th of November, 1992.

Most of the non-official invitees were of the view that, unless certain basic conditions were fulfilled, even prior to the constitution of the Commission, the doubt about the motives of the Government in forming the Commission will not fade. Thus, the view was that the withdrawal of TADA and similar draconian laws and also amending the Evidence Law to provide for presumption of guilt of police officer in case of any death or injury in the custody of the police, should be immediately implemented.

In intend to however to deal only with one legal aspect, namely whether the Commission should have investigative powers and its own investigating machinery or only make use of the machinery of the various State Governments. In my view unless the Commission has its own investigating machinery, it would remain a lame duck and the criticism will be well made that to ask the government agencies to investigate human rights violations is like asking the violator to give judgment on his own misdeed.

Some well meaning participants, though agreeing with this principle expressed anxiety that conferring power of investigation on the Commission might amount to trespass on the States exclusive power of legislation, and hence the Parliament will not be competent to legislate and also further the States will never agree to yield such power to the Centre.

In my view the apprehension is misplaced, under the Constitution parliament has full legislative competence to pass an Act constituting the Commission and also conferring investigative powers on the Commission itself without violating any of the States rights.

In this connection it will be proper to appreciate the background and the object for the formation of N.H.R.C. The

Universal Declaration of Human Rights which was adopted and proclaimed by the General Assembly of the United Nations on 10th December, 1948 set up as a common standard of achievement for all peoples and all Nations. This Declaration has become thus a yardstick by which to measure the degree of respect for and compliance with International Human Rights Standards. The two most important International Covenants adopted by General Assembly of U.N. are the International Covenant on Economic, Social and Cultural Rights (1966) and the International Covenant on Civil and Political Rights (1966). The Government of India has ratified this Convention, though belatedly in 1978-79. Article 28 of the convenient on Economic Rights and Art. 50 of the Civil Covenant specifically provide that the provision of the Covenant shall extend to all parts of Federal States without any limitation or exception. Similarly Art 16 of the Economic Rights Covenant and Article 40 of the Civil Covenant mandate the State parties to undertake to submit Reports on the measures which they have adopted and which give effect to the Rights recognised in these Covenants and on the progress made in observance of the achieving and enjoyment of those rights.

In Government of India is sincere in its explanation for constituting N.H.R.C., namely that it has a legitimate concern in preventing human rights violation, and to provide for a machinery to see that such violations do not take place or that if they do, then, proper effective remedial measures could be taken by N.H.R.C. I can see no hurdle in the way of Parliamentary legislation conferring such powers of investigation on N.H.R.C.

Chapter-I of Part XI of Indian Constitution deals with distribution of legislative powers. Thus Parliament has the exclusive power to legislate on matters mentioned in List I (Union List) and the States have similar exclusive power with respect to the matters in List II (State List). Both Parliament and the States have power to legislate on List III (Concurrent), with the provison that if State legislation is repregnant to the law passed by Parliament, the later law shall prevail.

The apprehension expressed is that giving power of investigation to the Commission might conflict with matter mentioned in List II, like it item I (Public order), item 2 (Police).

This misgiving is misplaced. Reference may be made to Article 253 of the Constitution which provides "that Parliament has power to make any laws, for the whole or any party of the Territory of India for implementing any Treaty, Agreement or Convention... or decision made at any International Conference association of other bodies, notwithstanding anything contained in the foregoing provisions of Chapter XI. This provision thus authorises in specified circumstances to legislate on matters even if enumerated in State List II. The Supreme Court in the Rann of Kutch Case (1969) has clearly held that "effect of Art 253 is" that if a Treaty of Convention deals with the subject within the competence of the State Legislature, the Parliament alone has, notwithstanding Article 246 (3) (which deals with the power of the State to legislate on List II), " the power to make Laws to implement the Convention for any decision made at any International Conference. In terms, Article deals with the Legislative power, thereby power is conferred upon the Parliament which it may not otherwise passes". In the present case the implementation and effectuation of the Covenants would be a complete answer to any challenge made to the competency of the Parliament to make Law conferring investigative powers on the Commission.

But this would necessarily mean that N.H.R.C. must be entrusted to deal with violations of rights mentioned in both Economic and Civil Covenants as against the suggestion of Union Government of limit the Commissions function only to the violation of rights mentioned in Civil Covenant.

That apart, it should also be noted that the Entry II Concurrent List (List III) Criminal Procedure including all matters included in Cr.P.C. which means that both the Centre and the State can legislate on this aspect .Parliament can thus legally modify chapter XII of Cr. P.C. (Powers of Investigation) by providing that any complaint made to the Commission on human right violation will be investigated only under its supervision and by its own investigating agency, and not by State police officer. Thus there is no lack of legislative competency. It is only political will and genuineness to form independent Commission that is required.

4
Human Rights : The Political Morality

4.1 Some Rights are Sacred

Every government when overwhelmed by crisis in its functioning seeks to find any easy way out by looking for scapegoats. It would appear that the present government of Mr. Narasimha Rao is no exception. (I say this because though Mr. Rao is projected by the media to be a suave, soft-spoken person his outburst against human rights organizations in the recent meeting of National Integration Council held to discuss Kashmir and Punjab would show that even a mild-mannered Prime Minister when overwhelmed with problems he cannot solve, wants an easy way out by putting the blame on others.) I am referring to Mr. Rao's statement, where-he apparently showed his sympathy for those massacred at Ludhiana and commented that the human rights organizations had not talked about the human right of the victims and that from their conduct it appears that only terrorists have human rights and not those who have been killed by them.

This ourburst is unfair against human rights organisations and to the person working in them. Giving Mr. Rao the benefit of sincerity it seems he has been ill-served by his Information Advisers. I do not know who advised Mr. Rao to take on the responsibility of saying that "human rights" organizations have not condemned the violence and the crimes committed by the terrorists/ militants. This allegation is totally contrary to record. Human Rights Organisation like PUCL, have consistently, as a matter of policy, condemned violence in public life whether committed by private individuals or by Right terrorist groups.

Right

Every human rights organization accepts the right of the Governments both at the centre and in the States of deal with terrorism and related crimes with full resoluteness and firmness. Human rights organizations are on record that the cruelty and violence on the part of the militants, whether in Punjab or in Kashmir, must be condemned unreservedly. In fact a report on the Kashmir situation submitted in March 1990 by the PUCL stated unequivocally that the kidnappings and killing of innocent persons like Prof. Haque, Vice-Chancellor of the Kashmir University, and Mr. Khera must be denounced by all. The view was openly expressed that the militants by their violent activities are depriving the innocent person of their human rights. Criticism was made that the militants are responsible by their actions in strengthening the repressive machinery of the state and are providing justification to the Government for assuming more and more arbitrary powers.

Violence

As a matter of fact human rights organizations firmly believe that by indulging in violence the militants clearly violate the human right of the individuals in the society. But this does not mean that unlawful excesses by the State agencies are justified or can be condoned, even though one appreciates the strains and risks under which these agencies operate. Any such condonation will destroy the fabric of democratic institutions.

In any democratic society whenever such things happen it is the duty of an alert citizenry to protest, and of any responsible democratic government to take note of it. In fact in my view refusal of the governments to own up such excesses only creates a credibility gap between the government and the masses.

If the people had assurance that any such reports of violation of the rights of individuals would be honestly and impartially inquired into and guilty officials suitably punished, they would be more readily inclined to accept the government version of the incidents. But it is this faith which gets shattered by such statements of the Prime Minister and others. This is all the more surprising because Mr. Rao apparently when questioned at Harare about alleged violations of human rights in Kashmir agreed to even allow access to international observers to visit the Valley. In that context is it not ironic that Mr. Rao should so unfairly accuse Indian human rights organizations of pointing out the lapses in the matter of observance of human rights? And especially when the reports give factual details of the incidents and the government has not been able to contradict the veracity of such reports.

It should now even be more embarrassing for the Prime Minister to receive publicly gratuitous advice from visiting British Foreign Secretary Douglas Hurd to the effect that "India should show greater openness whether through Amnesty International or in some comparable way in dealing with allegations of human rights violations." This, Mr. Hurd opined, was necessary so that terrorists cannot hide behind the 'cloak' of human rights violations by security forces. In fact when a similar sentiment was expressed to me by US Congressman Stephen Solarz, on his visit last year to Delhi, I had told him that while we support the demand that Amnesty International should be allowed to operate in India, becasue we as an open and democratic society should have no objection to any international body seeing the functioning of democracy in our country, I would resent the suggestion if it was founded on the ground that in the absence of Amnesty, there were no human rights organisations which were capable of monitoring and giving an objective and impartial reportage on human rights violations in India.

Question

It was a question of self-respect and faith in my fellow Indians and their capacity and commitment to human rights. But obviously Mr. Rao could not answer back by confidently stating that India was proud of objective reporting by various human rights organizations in the country when he himself had tried to erode their credibility by his outburst. Compare with the responsiveness of the British Government to Amnesty in its latest report by 1991 has condemned the British Government and its security forces for human rights violations when dealing with the armed Irish Republicatio. Army and expressed concern to the British Government about disputed killings in Northern Ireland. It is this lack of sensitivity on the part of governments, both at Centre and in the States, to the violation of human rights that needs to be exposed at all costs.

Action

It further needs emphasizing that human rights violation do not relate only to state action in the disturbed areas. Deaths in police custody in Delhi or Bombay, the misuse of detention laws by which about 10,000 trade unionists are detained in Gujarat alone and the horrible exploitation of child labour are clear cases of deprivation of human rights with which we are involved. Those who would keep quite in such times need to be reminded of what the great poet Dante said "The hottest places in hell are reserved for those, who in times of great moral crisis maintain their neutrality." Everyone should remember that human rights are not a gift from the government nor a bounty, which any government in its discretion may choose to distribute or withdraw at its whim. Acceptances of human rights are essential prerequisites of a civilized and a democratic country. It is only such civilized conduct that distinguishes democracy from totalitarianism.

Any government which claims to respect human rights must proceed on the recognition of the inherent dignity and of the equal and inalienable rights of all it citizens even those who are dissenters to the then existing government, and its regime. This basic principle is many a time ignored by those who happen to be in power at a particular time – and this weakness is shared by all political parties, notwithstanding their protestations to the countrary.

4.2 Political Morality Need of the Hour

Recent trends in the political behaviour are greatly disturbing. I find that politics is becoming more and more fictionalized, well established principles and norms which one may expect from all political parties, as the barest minimum on which there should be no controversy, are nowhere to be found.

We are having a situation where for narrow party ends, different standards and norms are being applied. Take the cases of Bhilai firing. The Madhya Pradesh Government is rightly being condemned for ordering firing on un-armed workers resulting in at least of 20 deaths. This top on a group of workers who have been peacefully agitating for their demands for several years, without any results. It is amazing that in spite of the fact that when the employers are refusing to even join conciliation proceedings being held by State Conciliation Officer, the State Government did not even take the next logical step of at least referring the matter to Industrial Adjudication (not that it would have satisfied the workers, but at least it would have shown somehow the minimum confide requirements of the State Government). Human Right Organizations like Peoples Union for Civil Liberties (PUCL), trade unions and other parties have rightly called for resignation of Patwa Government.

The Congress not to be left behind is taking deep interest in the matter and its official spokesman has also called for the dismissal of Patwa Government As a political party they are entitled to give their views and express their indignation, and this can be accepted as legitimate response. But as against this consider the reaction of the Congress to what has happened in Gujarat. As a result of communal incidents and police action, a number of deaths, stabbing has taken place there. The situation calls for a Judicial enquiry at the minimum. Should not in such a situation as many Human Rights Organizations especially PUCL who have always maintained that whenever deaths takes place in police firing, the minimum democratic response must be the resignation of the Minister who happens to hold the Home porfolio and if it happens to be the Chief Minister himself, it must be the resignation of the Government. But no such response has come from the Congress because Mr. Patel, C.M.Gujarat has now formally been accepted as a close companion in the Congress fold.

Consider again the latest report of the Amnesty International which has stated that about 25000 political prisoners are being detained in India. Even the Government of India and Punjab Government have admitted having detained 10000 persons in Punjab alone. It was stated that cases are being screened to see how many of them can be released. It is a matter of shame that even after so many months of Beant Singh Government screening process has not yet been completed in Punjab. Each day's illegal detention of an innocent person is a blot on the democratic functioning of the State and the gross violation of human rights.

Now this eligibility is only possible because of the unholy nexus between the bureaucracy and political leadership, with the result that politicians are able to get away with their excesses, which it would not be possible if only the bureaucracy was to act within the Rules. The bureaucracy does this in the hope of basking in political favour. But this is a short-term approach. Soon the bureaucracy finds that having fed the massive ego and power lust of the politicians against the common citizen, a day soon comes when the bureaucrat is at the receiving and then at that time there is no one to support him because he has in league with politicians destroyed the strength of public opinion. The recent example of acid throwing on an IAS women officer Ms. Chandralekha belonging to the Tamil Nadu Cadre is very eloquent. It is commonly known that she as the chair-person of a State Public Undertaking had refused to oblige the Chief Minister of Tamil Nadu in the matter of opting out of purchase of certain shares, which would have benefited private promoter unless she was given written orders by Government. The Chief Minister was obviously so much interested that written orders were given, the result of which was to cause loss of about 30 crores to the State Exchequer. But the political mafia did not forget - so we have acid thrown on the lady officer. The shock to the bureaucracy was so tremendous that at long last the proverbial worm stirred and moved. The IAS officers Association of Tamil Nadu has in a defiant public gesture strongly condemned this acid attack on Ms Chandralekha and demanded the immediate apprehension of the culprit and to provide protection to all officials in the State. But the irony was that this appeal has been issued on behalf of the Secretary of the IAS Association who happens to be the present Home Secretary of T. N. Government itself. What low level the Administration would have reached where the police is not making full efforts to bring the culprit to book. Police has naturally denied the charge. But the real point of concern arises in the fact that a situation has arisen where the highest Administrative Officers feel that none of them are safe from the hoodlums, when they take a position against a politician. Such a situation can only spell a doom for the proper democratic functioning of the State.

Custodial deaths are the most aggravated form of the violation of human rights. From the investigations done by some of the Human Rights Organizations, custody deaths have taken place even in the capital of India. Thus there were 11 deaths in police custody in 1991 and 34 people died in Tihar Jail. Though, under the law, a Magisterial Enquiry has to be held, but this does not serves any purpose because they are more or less a cover up of the police excesses by the Executive. In my view, there should be a law when death in policy custody or in jail takes place the onus should rest with the custodian to show that it is a natural death. The law needs to be amended in this regard, in my view, if death takes place in custody, Judicial enquiry at least by a retired Judge of the High Court must be ordered. Compensation of rupees one lakh must also be automatically given to the family irrespective of the findings of the Judicial Enquiry because un-natural death in police custody can never be tolerated in a civilized society. Pressure must be mounted on Parliamentarians to pass this Law immediately.

4.3 On Preserving Human Rights — One Universal Standard Needed

The recent visit of Mr. Stephen Solaraz, U.S. Congressman who is the chairperson of the U.S. House Foreign Relations Subcommittee on Asia/ Pacific Affairs to India on a fact finding mission bring out the various nuances and subtle differences on emphasis between the two approaches.

Mr. Solaraz had come from Pakistan; Pakistan occupied Kashmir and has some linking of Pakistan thinking. He met various shades of opinion including the small on of Human Rights activists of various organizations.

Kashmir was the natural topic of discussion of those weedings. Difficult aspects needed to be clarified and understood.

Apart from Government of India's version at almost all private meetings Mr. Solaraz was left in on doubt that the question of any Government agreeing to hold a plebiscite which would permit Kashmir to opt out of India was impossible to contemplate. Kashmir and its people were so much a part of India that rest of the country would suffer irreversible emotional strain even to contemplate it being out of India. In addition it was also emphasized that condition precedent to holding plebiscite was the vacation of Pakistan occupied Kashmir (POK) portion, the withdrawal of Pakistan army from those areas and the returns of normalcy. Sometimes the foreign visitors would stress that the demand in Kashmir was for 'Azadi' independence and not so much for governing Pakistan. This impression, unreal as it was in no longer even arguable because Pakistan Prime Minister Benazir Bhutto has categorically stated that Kashmir has only two options India or Pakistan and not independence. And it also must be recognized that though J & K Liberation Front talks of independent Kashmir, Mujabbedin group, which by all standards has a sizable following (and we found this out on our visit to Kashmir in March) is openly for Pakistan.

Mr. Solaraz recognized this and accepted that in his visit to POK he came across people who were openly advocating only one option for Kashmir – namely accession to Pakistan. It is no longer in dispute to any unbiased observer that Pak held to the militants is on the considerable scale. This recombination must explain the soft mental attitude of countries to the US in this matter.

Another aspect which comes up in discussion with foreign leaders like Mr. Solaraz is the role of security agencies, some of the excesses committed, the response to these by human right organizations to the PUCL and the attitude of Central Government to all these.

Now it would be meaningless to deny that excesses have been committed by the security agencies and that they are not only deplored and condemned by all right thinking people. But from that it does not follow that it is Central Government policy to engage in illegal acts and as some of the western apologists of Pakistan case try to present. At a meeting I was asked how was it that if Government Policy was to avoid any use of unnecessary or excessive force, security personnel engaged in killing innocent people by reckless firing. One of the obvious answers is that our security agencies are not trained to meet the type of situation as existed in Kashmir. It need not also be denied that there may be some individual acts of barbaric behaviour (of course for which even a responsive and responsible Government must own responsibility and take proper adequate step's to check it) but it does not mean that these barbaric acts are the policy of Government of India. When pressed for an explanation I said that it was Vietnamis Syndrome. What I mean is that American army engaged in the most cruel, inhuman and barbaric massacre of countless South Vietnam civilians. American army was responsible for the savage act of chemical spraying. All this is condemnable. And yet it would be unfair to say that these barbaric acts were the result of deliberate American Government Policy. Recently we have heard of Moguire Seven cases, wherein a family of 7 persons was convicted for having a bomb factory at home and sentenced for 14 years. Only a few days back, after the matter had been reopened the Government of British has conceded that the conviction was unsafe and that it should be set aside. Newspaper accounts show how police put up false evidence, concealed evidence which was favourable to the accused. A Newspaper also carries stories of torture committed by the police on women and small children. Reputation as a fair and competent Judge of Lord Donaldson (the present Master of Rolls and who was the trial Judge at the time) has also been seriously questioned. And yet it would be unfair to say that British Government and Judiciary deliberately inflicted these wrongs – the correct analysis is that investigating and security agencies many in time indulge in these excesses as a part of their own internal and compulsive syndrome. If that be the way west wishes to be judged, why the double standard should be applied to Asia especially to India which has a fine record of open society as any western democracy can boast of. Take even the record of institutions in Kashmir even in the existing situation Jammu & Kashmir High Court granted stay of a detention order issued by Government against an alleged terrorist. High court even issued an order directing the state government how to regulate hours of curfew. The Government only took the legal steps of appealing against those orders to the Supreme Court. No action was taken against the Judges or Lawyers. The constraints of democratic functioning were fully respected. It is in this connection that American Governments threat to withhold economic aid to India unless it allowed Amnesty International was allowed entry must be viewed with concern. Now so far as entry of Amnesty International is concerned, I believe that there should be no objection. After all we are an open society. We should be prepared to have our action seen by any one. We have no skeletons to hide. As a matter of fact PUCL. has for a very long time written to Government of India to permit all genuine organizations including Amnesty to visit India. But what annoys and exasperates is the suggestion that in the absence of Amnesty, full facts concerning the violation of human rights in Punjab and Kashmir are not being brought out in open. It is this western attitude that one finds unacceptable. Any fair minded person can see the number of reports by various organisations on Punjab and Kashmir retouching the violations and serious breaches of human rights – Report on Kashmir by PUCL. being the latest. The facimile assumption that respect for human rights is firmly established feature in countries of the UK. and American conflicts with the actual facts refers the latest reports of Commissioner for Right to Equality for 1989 (U.K.) points to the serious racial discrimination against blacks and Asians prevailing in England. West and especially American must accept that Indian democracy is firmly established that efforts for preservation of human rights is the serious concern of majority of Indians and that institutional safeguards and human rights organizations are ever alert on this sensitive issue. A friendly suggestion, even advise may be welcome, but a superior attitude, a reminder of, a colonial era is most certainly not acceptable. Armed attack by US. forces on Panamas even in purported exercise to check narcotic trafficking) is not an example of respect for human rights. Just as there are universal Human Rights - let there be one universal standard to judge the respect given to the preservation of human rights by each country. Judged by any standards India may have some matter to explain (like all other countries) but it can hold its head high in its respect for upholding human rights.

4.4 Fundamental Rights for Children

On 20th of Nov. 1989, the 44th Session of U.N. General Assembly unanimously adopted the Convention on the Rights of Child. The original of adoptation of this convention is a climax of large number of organizations engaged in human rights especially amongst children and their voice to have this Convention on the Rights of child adopted by General Assembly. Logically, the origins of this Convention could be traced loosely to the five basic principles for child welfare and protection set out in the "Declaration of Geneva" which was promulgated in 1924 to "Save the Children Fund International Union".

This first attempt to codify in one text the fundamental

conditions to which children had a right was endorsed by the League of Nations the same year. It was revised and amplified in 1948 and the resulting text formed the basis of the ten-point Declaration on the Rights of the Child adopted unanimously by the General Assembly of the United Nation on 20th November 1959.

Universal Declaration of Human Rights adopted in 1943 lent a great fillip to the urgency of matter to take steps for to meet the challenge of vulnerable needs and situation of the children. Though there was wide range of instruments under ILO, Convention, the Civil and Political Rights, it was felt that these texts have been drawn up separately over the last 50 years and without specific reference to the children's global needs. After all it may not be forgotten that Children Rights are an integral part of human rights.

In this back-ground the Polish authorizations launched their proposal for a Convention on the Rights of the Child on the eve of the International Year of the Child 1979. This initiative was greatly welcome as it provided an opportunity to define more clearly and to harmonise human rights standards for children to fill in the many gaps identified in current provisions and to set the results of this indepth reassessment exercise within the context of a single binding international instrument. It is necessary to emphasize that the Convention on the Rights of Child is supplemental to the previous Universal Declaration of Human Rights. It was, of course, easy task and the working group, which was set up by UN Commission on Human Rights in 1979, went into the various aspects and there were many debates with responses from various organizations and NGO's. The NGO's adhoc group has been most helpful in giving this move for Convention of Child Rights a further fillip. Various texts were adopted trying to reconcile the various points of view. Many of those associated with it were in the course of period feeling disappointed that the Convention was not being finalized. Some of those involved in it, therefore decided that 1989 be taken as the target date for completion and adoption of the text of Convention. The major reason for choosing 1989 was the symbolic importance of that year, it marked the 10th anniversary of the International Years of the Child and therefore of the start of the drafting process it was also the 30th anniversary of the adoption of the Declaration on the Rights of the Child.

In India also a great deal of efforts were necessary to make the people and various organizations conscious of working towards this Convention. The Declaration was signed on 14th Jan. 1988 by Smt. Kamaladevi Chattopadhayay who devoted her later years towards this and some other Human Rights Activists urging the Government and the public to take prompt and decisive action and to participate effectively in the delayed processes of shaping national law in defence of children and right to equal opportunity to develop. The Declaration alerted the public conscience, opinion and policy into urgently restoring to every child the birthright to develop in freedom and creativity. Such social action cannot wait in fairness either to children in their own right or to the future of the human race. The right of the child are therefore a priority for adult responsibility. The human costs of this running neglect are hazardous. Nothing abnormal and more preventable than infants and children dying, yet thousands of them each day are denied the rights to life. Many more go without love, without food they need to grow or the opportunity for them to learn and develop. The 1959 UN Declaration of the Rights of the Child represents the sensitive core of the Universal Declaration of Human Rights adopted by the UN General Assembly four decades ago. It was therefore a welcome step when the 44th Session finally adopted Convention on the Rights of Child.

Of course no one should have any illusions about 1989 convention itself changing the situation of children automatically. Simultaneous steps have to be taken to reshape national laws and structures to provide adequate resources to self-reliant communities and to enhance public awareness to the point of change in culture. An International Conference on Protection and Promotion of Child Rights sponsored by UNICEF and China Law Society was held in Beijing on 20-21 November 1989. I was one of delegates to the Conference. While the conference was in session the 44th U.N. General Assembly unanimously adopted the convention on the Rights of the Child. At the conclusion of the conference all the participants proposed and passed an appeal to all the State, Social Organizations and people concerned to pay attention to Child Rights. The Conference further in view of the great importance and protection of the child rights to peace and development of human beings and the fact that of the children are the future of mankind and in consideration of the sacred duty of adults the World over to the upbringing growth and development of children unanimously appealed to all States, Social Organizations and concerned individual to implement the Convention on Rights of Child through laws and policies consistent with the Convention to embody in various form the spirit of Convention in their legislation.

The Conference made a strong appeal to all nations to take expeditions measures to *sign, ratify* (Emphasis Supplied) and implement the Convention.

It is one thing for International Convention to be passed. It is however a very different matters to have it implemented amongst the nations. The Convention on Child Rights is meeting with the same kind of lethergy and ambiguous sounds for various quarters.

It is well known that India, together with China account for a third of Worlds Children and a for higher proportion of those in need. It is self evident thatnotwithstanding the adoption by General Assembly the Convention on Rights of Child, it cannot make much headway unless China and India implement. It promptly.

Personally I was and am of the view that politically and socially such a step of implementation would begin a new phase in the admittedly slow progress towards realizing basic human rights. India which is already a signatory to the convenant on Civil and Political Rights and the Covenant on Economic, Social and Cultural Rights, under the Universal Declaration of Human Rights, can officially have no inhibition in ratifying the new Convention on the Rights of the Child.

Being of this view I, on behalf of Peoples Union for Civil Liberties wrote in January, 1990 to the then Prime Minister Shri V.P. Singh suggesting that in view of the special position of India, it would be apt for Government of India to promptyl ratify the Convention and give a lead to the world. I also addressed a similar plea to the Minister for External Affairs. I did receive, acknowledgements of my letters. But as far as some concrete steps are concerned there has been no intimation of ratification (even with some reservations – though personally it would be most deplorable) if India with its democratic traditions was not to accept the full Convention Completely).

It is also ironic, rather tragic that China which took the lead in calling upon other nations of the world to immediately ratify the Convention continues to be default. The embarrassment to Asian prestige in the comity of nations by this unpardonable delay on the part of India and China to ratify the Convention can be readily appreciated more especially when we pride ourselves on excelling in sense of compassion and sympathy and spirituality as against the alleged materialism of the west. Our organization has again recently written to the Mr. Chander Shekhar, the Prime Minister requesting him that India immediately ratify the Convention.

The enormity of human neglect in the case of 300 million children of our country is a deep festering wound in our body politic – one out of every ten to die in the first year; half the number of primary school age children are not able to attend school because of extreme poverty.

Many a time I wonder how deep and genuine our commitment to Human Rights can be, if this large, sensitive future of India is ignored and neglected in the present in such a cruel manner. After all we cannot forget that the country has a social responsibility to children to assure them their rights to face development.

It is unnecessary to specify various principles and the Rights of Child mentioned in the Convention. Time for that will come after India has ratified the convention. It may be noted that to our shame as well as of China, already 39 nations have ratified the convention and it is now an internationally binding legal document. How long can we avoid the social compulsion to ratify this Convention?

I would therefore call upon all political parties, voluntary associations to take up this item of getting ratification of the Convention by Government of India as a priority item on their agenda of action – because the fight for the ratification and implementation of the Convention is to fight for the assertion of one of the most important aspect of Human Rights.

4.5 Gender Equality and Dignity

The uniform civil code issue has been blown out of proportion. I do not see how it is so very urgent. There are far more intractable problems, which have to be addressed to. To make it as if the country's integrity is at stake, due to different personal laws, is, I think, not tenable.

But, I do feel that the important aspect involved here is gender justice — the discrimination against women. Members from all communities should look into this aspect of their respective personal laws. It is not as if it is peculiar to the Muslims alone. As far as rights are concerned, the basis should be gender equality and dignity.

Gender inequality is a social problem. Even among Hindus, the daughter is not a part of a Hindu joint family. She has no right to succeed or inherit property. On the other hand, the fact is that Islam has been one of the most progressive religions. Almost 1200 years ago, Islam was the first religion, which recognized the right of women to remarry.

The marriage between a girl and her maternal uncle, which has been medically known to be harmful, is prohibited in Islam. Conversely, such marriages are not prohibited among Hindus in some parts like Andhra Pradesh. Similarly, marriage among cousins is permitted by all other religions except Hinduism. It only goes to show that all religions have some good elements and some bad elements in their personal laws.

Even on the misunderstood right of polygamy in Islam, the Prophet had stipulated that all four wives has to be given fair and equal treatment. When that was not possible, polygamy was strictly prohibited, polygamy was strictly prohibited. It is for the Muslim community to ponder over the issue and see if the violation of the command by the Prophets himself is fair to the women from their own community. Or is it a deliberate distortion to suit certain elements?

But, the caveat is that the introspection and remedies have to come forth form within the Muslim community itself. I do not think that it is necessary for non-Muslims to make all this into an issue.

Muslims have similar laws all over the country whereas Hindus have different laws in various parts of the country. Let the people calling for a uniform civil code, first formulate a common law for the Hindus that will be applicable to them right across the country.

I think that typecasting of religious groups has more to do with the conscious and unconscious minds of people and not with facts. For example, I call myself a modern man, but I do not eat beef because I have been brought up in an atmosphere where beef was considered something prohibited. So also, I do not eat pork because a close relative of mine developed a cyst, which was considered a direct result of eating pork. From then on, I also associated pork with something harmful. So, to argue that only the Muslim community is prey to such a phenomenon will be wrong and is surely not true.

I think that the reform of personal laws of any community is a question of gender justice and not of religion. It is more social than religious. Some people are trying to introduce the religious aspect in an issue which has very little to do with religion. It is more a question of empowerment of women.

Even when the Hindu laws were codified in 1956, it was not as if there was no opposition from the Hindus. No less a person than President Rajendra Prasad fought against the codification. Fortunately, we had other people how had a more progressive vision and the laws were codified.

Why do we assume that the Muslims are not capable of realizing the urgency of what the society needs? Forcing the issue can only weaken the hands of the progressive and young elements among the Muslims.

Let the Muslims brothers and sisters come out and clarify what they want. Because a party identified with a particular community has taken up the uniform civil code issue, there is a natural reaction among Muslims to oppose it, with the result that the intellectuals among the Muslims are reluctant to come forward.

I think it is utterly wrong and dangerous to our society if these Hindu parties go on making the uniform civil code an issue for the elections.

I do not think that politicization of the issue for electoral gains is permissible. If these parties are so concerned about women's empowerment, they should decide to give at least 30 per cent of their own party's tickets to women in the coming elections.

Somebody told me of an interesting episode in Bangladesh where one of the women's groups called an all–religious meeting for changing some of the personal laws.

The Hindus protested saying that the changes would be endangering and destroying the Shastras and the traditions that they followed. Mind you, they were seeking the traditional laws to remain, while were in India, which is overwhelmingly composed of Hindus, have discarded since 1956.

It is more to do with psychology. In Bangladesh, a Hindu is a minority and there to it is seen as an attack on one's identity.

There is a story that after a king won a war he went to the Prophet and asked him about how he should rule. The Prophet asked him to follow the Koran and if it had nothing to offer, refer to the Sunna. The king against asked if the latter too also did not offer any solution then what should he do. In reply to this, the Prophet said that in such a situation, he should rule as the time and circumstances demanded. The point is that even the Prophet conceded that the modification of any law or practise was inevitable as and when the changed circumstances so demanded.

But, then in order things like the rituals, each community has the right to follow its own practices.

If the Muslims believe in performing namaz five times a day, let them do it. For me, it is the end of the matter; they simply have the right to do so. There is no question of an argument.

4.6 Stop Defections-Misuse of Article 356

A constitutional crisis was averted by the sagacious exercise of power by the President under Article 74 of the Constitution, introduced in 1978, in sending back for reconsideration the untenable recommendation of the Central Cabinet to dissolve the UP Assembly and dismiss the BJP Government, and the sensible response of the Cabinet in withdrawing rather than in repeating the recommendation which would have left no option to the President but to accept it however unwillingly.

The 1978 amendment introduced by the Janata Government was to undo the 1976 amendment in the wake of criticism of President Fakhruddin Ali Ahmed's decision to impose the Emergency in 1975 when he could have asked the Cabinet to reconsider its advice, especially when its was known that the cabinet had not seen the proclamation. But power by it self is no guarantee that it will be wisely used. Thus, when in October 1996 Governor Romesh Bhandari extended President's Rule in UP beyond one year as permitted by the Constitution, and endorsed by the Dev Gowda Government, it did not elicit advice for reconsideration by President Shankar Dayal Sharma, who was by all standards a gentlemen.

Even a broad reading of the judgment in the Bommai case would leave no one in doubt that the course adopted by the Governor was wrong. His reference to horsetrading which may apparently appeal to the average person has been negatived in the Bommai case where the Supreme Court held the "even assuming that horsetrading is going on the proper course for the Governor to adopt is to await the test on the floor of the House." The court warned that "the assessment of the strength of the ministry is not a matter of private opinion of any individual, be he the Governor or the President. It is capable of being demonstrated and ascertained publicly in the House."

It is not understood why if the Cabinet had genuine reasons to believe that the confidence vote was vitiated, it should not have recommended that Kalyan Singh be asked to seek another vote of confidence. I have no doubt that if such a recommendation had been made, even persons like me who are opposed to the BJP ideology might have, though hesitatingly,, gone along with it. But this course wan not adopted presumably becasue the Cabinet apprehended that the voting margin may be bigger.

It is no longer a mystery that the Cabinet decided against the above course because of the pressure of Mulayam Singh Yadav and Sitaram Kesri who though minitially were excited over the withdrawal of support by the BSP unfortunately suffered in setback when suddenly there were large- scale defection from the Congress and other groups.

Such pressure also made the Cabinet recommend the dissolution, rather than suspension, of the House, notwithstanding that in the Bommai case it was said that the President has no power to dissolve the Assembly till the proclamation is approved by both Houses of Parliament. Had the Attorney General's advice been heeded, as was done by the President, the Cabinet may have avoided the subsequent public embarrassment.

No doubt violent incidents inside the Assembly call for severe condemnation. But in this all are equally blameworthy. As such this could hardly be a ground for the Governor recommending dissolution, more so when at the end of it all, the majority supported Kalyan Singh. The continuous refrain of the Congress of horsetrading is amusing considering that the Congress is supporting the Vaghela and now Parikh group in Gujarat, which broke away from the BJP. Kansi Ram and Mulayam Singh Yadav who were publicly abusing each other are now seeking to combine on no ground other than their alleged opposition to the NJP. In his quest for power, Mulayam Singh Yadav had even gone to the length of announcing that if he came to power in UP, he will withdraw the Scheduled Caste Act while Ms. Mayawati had apparently broken away from Kalyan Singh on the grounds that he was not genuinely implementing the Act.

Of course, there is no denying that the BJP has thrown out of the window all standards of morality by offering ministerial posts to each and every Congressman and members of the other defecting group. But then such absence of moral standards afflicts all political parties. The answer to this is not the Governor's partisan action; but the anger of voters. In all this drama the only "consistency" is that of Kanshi Ram. He proclaims unabashedly that he is a political opportunist and a manipulator who is ready to make alliance with any one if he thinks he can get political power. If these are the so-called ideologies of the alliance, one wonders, what is opportunism.

It is well known that all the defections as in the present case are occasioned by the lure of the ministership or chairmanship of public sector corporations. I therefore, feel that more effective alternative would be to amend the Constitutions to provide that any MLA who defects even if he avoids the sweep of the antidefection act will not be eligible for appointment as a minister or to public corporations during the life of that legislature unless he resigns and gets re-elected. If this is done. It may act as a check on the evil of floor-crossing.

4.7 Where are we Heading?

The full effect of Sonia Gandhi opting out of the political scene at least for the time being is going to have contradictory impacts on the working of the present government. This is irrespective of the results of the by-elections which, in any event, are marginal. So long as Sonia did not give out her mind, Narasimha Rao had, alway a lurking suspicion of his being displaced from the prime ministership because the induction of Sonia Gandhi could not have been as a mere MP.

The split in the Congress would have been vertically down because the highest post in the government, namely prime minister, would have been the price demanded by supporters of Sonia Gandhi. Now Rao is going to feel less isolated in the Congress party and will. I am afraid, commit the mistake of not worrying about keeping his links with the opposition to develop a consensual politics.

In my view, this will be an unfortunate development for the country because I continue to believe that in the crisis that India is passing through, it political parties (may be, minus the BJP, if it does not give up its strident call on Mandir- Masjid issue) should participate in the government, of course, on the basis of concrete minimum programme. But I feel it does not seem possible now because of the lack of pressure on the prime minister. But there is going to be the other adverse effect which will multiply in times to come.

The prime minister is going to depend more and more within the groupings in the Congress, with the result that the government at the Centre may function more as separate fiefdom, unmindful of the impact it may have on the other ministries. Immediately, one thinks of the disaster in which we find our foreign policy has landed us. I have never been able to understand what prompted Rao to allot external affairs portfolio to Solanki who, by all standards, is totally innocent of any knowledge of international affairs and who does not even claim to have a working knowledge of the present day trends in international affairs. The only claim to fame of Solanki may perhaps be his discover or, rather invention, of 'Kham formula a small–time manoeuvre to an approach which can bring India recognition in international fora.

Thus we have the disaster of abortive SAARC summit at Colombo. Whatever the explanation the present government may give, it is clear to everyone that India has come out the worst in the SAARC controversy. The clumsy manner in which India went about to abort the summit showed the skill of short-term political manouvring of small-time politician. But it was totally cut of place in sensitive matter like SAARC. This aspect has also given rise to the charge made by neighours of India, especially Pakistan, that India does not wish to treat its neighbours as equals but rather be-have as a big-time bully.

Another serious and disastrous matter in which possibly the foreign minister may not be responsible is the sudden raise of visa fees, five to 10 times more, by all countries, especially the UK. It is well know that when the visa fees were substantially reduced in the UK, there was great jubilation and a sense of relief among thousands of Indian families mostly by the Sikhs whose families come over to India quite often. This was accepted as a gesture of not trying to keep the Sikh families from visiting their place in Punjab.

In this connection, if it was a question of savings, it may be mentioned that in early 1990, the then high commission to the UK had recommended to the government a largescale pruning and reduction in expenses in the establishment of the high commission in London. Had the government accepted our mission's proposals then, it would have made a saving of one million pounds a year at least. But the influence of the bureaucracy seems to be so strong that Solanki has yielded to the pressure because the former would have lost expensive perks if the pruning had been carried out.

It is rumoured that there is going to be a reshuffling of the cabinet soon after Parliament meets. One can only hope that prime minister will appreciate that keeping the present in-cumbent in the external affairs ministry will only make laughing stock of our foreign policy. Another ministry which needs immediate attention of the prime minister is the ministry of the law, headed by the gentle but ineffective Bhaskar Reddy and the garrulous Kumaramangalam. It is a common knowledge that decisions by the law ministry are ad hoc in nature and under ground pressure. Lawyers in Delhi are on strike for months because promise by both ministers to them have given contrary signals.

Inefficiency has been accentuated by moving one set of amended legislation while ignoring the other, whereas combined legislation would have salvaged the whole matter. It is surprising that courts in Delhi are not functioning for the last several months and yet the law ministry seems to be treating it as if this is a normal trend.

Another serious paralysis of the decision-making by the law ministry is evident in its inability to name the solicitor general of India. The reason obviously is because of the pressure by various groups within the ruling Congress party. Surely, the ministry should be able to decide one way or the other, even by succumbing to either group. This is the first time that the post-independent India has had no solicitor general for such a long period. Prime Minister Rao needs a replacement for this ministry immediately. There is no dearth of competent personnel in the Congress and who have had very long successful career both at the bar and the bench and who could pre-eminently fill this post. Of course, for this the prime minister would have to look for talent and not be overwhelmed by group loyalties.

The knee-jerk functioning of the government has been exposed in the manner of calling an all-party meeting on Kashmir. Apart from propaganda in the press, it was a futile effort because it was composed of person whose credibility in the valley is almost non-existent. Not only these so-called leaders' mutual mistrust was well known, but their views as well. The cosmic nature of this meeting was shown by the fact that none of them, though not belonging to any political party by mere knowledgeable and have fair amount of public recognition and acceptability even among the militants in Kashmir, was not called.

Thus, one found that the undoubted, competent, knowledgeable Kashmir specialists. Balraj Puri or other well-known editors in the valley like Ved Bhasin, were not associated with it. The most sensitive topic of Article 370 was just swept under the carpet when a little study would show that Parliament is incompetent to abrogate Article 370 and all talks by BJP and similar groups to abrogate Article 370 is sheer propaganda because constitutionally and legally parliament of India cannot modify it at all.

4.8 Back to the Strategy of Shilanyas

There is an old and cynical saying that advises one to "join them, if you cannot beat them". This must have weighed with the Congress Working Committee when it passed a resolution claiming that India's secular credentials had been maintained because of Hinduism. By this game of one-upmanship, the Congress has eroded opposition to the *Hindutva* line which is the sheet-anchor of the BJP's political programme. This stance lends credence to the charge of the Congress being only psuedo-secular.

To seek to give an exclusive role to Hinduism as the sheet-anchor of secularism is to offer a gratuitous insult to other religions. How can the role be denied to God, similar to that of the Bhagwat Gita and the Koranic axiom that all the created ones belong to the family of God? In what manner is the compassion even for one's tormentors, in the line "Forgive them for they know not what they do" which is the core of message of Christ, any less of contribution to the development of the Indian ethos?

That Hinduism has had its core of tolerance owed a good deal to its origin in the rich Indus valley thousands of years ago. There were then no other rival religions to contend against and Hinduism had exclusively a big area like the Indian subcontinent where peaceful coexistence could naturally blossom. These favourable circumstances were denied to Christianity which had to struggle hard to establish itself against the butchery and desolation by the pagan Roman Empire and to Islam with its origin in the arid Arab land and also facing the challenge of religious crusades of the Middle Ages. Though not in any way diluting the noble teachings of Islam and Christianity, these circumstances did create a climate of some rigidity and exclusivity.

It is not as if Hinduism has remained in its pristine purity for all these thousands of years. Ritualism, casteism and obscurantism had to be continuously fought by great souls like the Buddha, Mahavira, Nanak, Vivekananda and Swamy Dayanand.

Congress spokespersons accept that, grammatically speaking, the *Hindutva* of the BJP and Hinduism as put forth by the Congress means the same thing. But in a politically obtuse manner, the Congress claims that the BJP offers a distorted version of *Hindutva* while it is going to present Hinduism in the right perspective. Pray, are we having a theological debate about the core and essence of Hinduism in a religious conference?

The reality is that the Congress is going back to the old strategy of *shilanyas* (1989) – of appeasing the conservative Hindu voted-bank by claiming to the better Hindus than the BJP. What else can explain Sonia's crowded itinerary of visits to religious places like Tirupati, Hardwar and mutts in a Kerala?

More quixotic was the statement of P.A. Sangma that Sonia was not a practising Christian? Why this unnecessary reference to her faith? There is nothing wrong in Sonia being a devout Christian. Those who oppose her becoming the Prime Minister do so not because she is a Christian but on the ground that she is not an India–born citizen (the same prohibition as in the USA) or that it will encourage dynastic rule (they may or may not be right). But certainly no one can be ruled out from aspiring to the highest political office in India only on the ground of religion. That would be repugnant to our Constitution. How differently President Kennedy reacted when his being a Catholic was made an issue in his election. He said that he was not a Catholic President but a "President who happens to be a Catholic". The same apporach applies to all political offices in our country and for members of all religions. The Congress, by the change in its stance, has seriously damaged the secular fabirc.

In India, whether under a Hindu or a Muslim rule, the secular authority was never subordinate to religious authority and neither of the two religions claimed that the sacred was superior to the secular. Unfortunately, with Sonia Gandhi now launching on a journey of religious pilgrimages, the BJP's emphasis of *Hindutva* is likely to get a more respectable acceptance.

That the Congress is not prepared to collide with the obscurantist ranks in Hinduism is clear from the fact that Sonia did not, rather the Congress did not protest and demand the end of the practice at the Tirupati temple of asking for a declaration of faith in Hinduism before being allowed to visit it. In my view, such obsurantism breeds discord and is the antithesis of the basic philosophy of Hinduism—that Truth is only one, though there are many paths that lead to it. Gandhiji had shown his protest by refusing to enter a temple where Dalits were not allowed entry: the abodes of God cannot be the monopoly of any particular religion or caste.

This surrender by the Congress to invoke religiosity in the political field is doubly dangerous, when the country is already undergoing a trauma of minority witch-hunt and killings of Christian missionaries.

That good governance must have a foundation of secularism was realised by Jinnah who played the communal card skilfully to create Pakistan. He was far too intelligent and responsible not to realise that mixing of religion with politics would spell disaster. That is what made him proclaim at the inaugural session (1947) of Pakistan's Constituent Assembly (and I had the good fortune to hear it personally):

> You are free, you are free to go to your temples. You are free to go to your mosques or other places of worship in this state of Pakistan. You may belong to any religion or caste or creed—that has nothing to do with the business of the state.

It is a pity that Pakistan lost the guiding hand of Jinnah soon thereafter, and the loss encouraged religious bigotry. That is why this effort of the Congress to outdo the *Sangh Parivar* in the race for capturing the obscurantist and fundamentalist trend in Hinduism is a matter of deep concern and bodes ill for the development of a healthy, secular political agenda.

Surely politics is not to be reduced to showing off avowed knowledge about such subjects as the real essence of Hindusim. Politics, one would have thought, was about the removal of poverty and inequality, for the establishment of a secular and socialist republic as mandated by the Constitution. But then; probably, the Congress wants us to unlearn the lessons learnt during the freedom struggle. The Indian masses, however, will not surrender to communalism notwithstanding the political parties' antics.

4.9 Beware of the Danger Ahead

The BJP is working on a planned, deeply thought out divisive strategy for the next state and parliamentary elections. This is highlighted by the call that Hindutva is a way of life and not a religion.

Every spiritual soul in each religion having reached the height of communion with Universal Soul has the same message of universal love, common humanity and the acceptance that same divine power runs through all human beings though outwardly professing different religion and practices.

Thus Hinduism's "Vasudhaiva – Kutumbakam" (world is one family) is equally reciprocated in the Quran which says, "All the created ones belong to the family of God … so, an Arab has no precedence over a non-Arab, a White over a Black". And Christ said succinctly, "All are children of God."

Evidently, all great souls and prophets have the same vision of God. There is that indissoluble unity of thinking that no religion whether Hinduism or Islam can claim to be the sole interpreter of God's Vision. Their paths to reach God may differ, but the goal is the same – mainly how to obtain God's mercy and blessings.

Another not-so-clever slogan being projected by the BJP is by seeking to equate Hindutva with Bharatiya. This is utterly unwarranted. I can accept that all people of whatever religion living in this country are Bharatiya – that is resident of Bharat, because our Constitution under Article 1(I) says "India, that is Bharat"- the later has a connotation to territory stretching back thousands of years even before the advent of Islam or Christianity. But if I were a Muslim or Christian I would certainly resent being called Hindu because it amounts to denying me the identity of my religion.

No, the BJP cannot be allowed to get away with the unacceptable formulation of equating Hindutva with Bharatiya. Yes, we are all Indians and Bharatiya and proud of it, and also equally proud of being Hindus, Muslims, Christians, Sikhs, et al. As it is, it is more apt to call Indians as Bharatiya because of the policies of globalization there is conflict of India vs Bharat – the former represents the elite and the minority of the privileged few while Bharat represents the overwhelming poverty–ridden masses. This is not a clitche. It is a reality.

According to the Human Development Report, a country in which the capacity of each individual to spend is limited to US $ two per day is passing through a situation of below poverty level and if $ 1 per day is below extreme poverty level. The per capita income of India is $ 480 annually. It is quite clear that barring few privileged, the overwhelming millions of residents are living below extreme poverty level. Thus, this is the real conflict between India vs Bharat.

One of the tragedies of our narrow outlook is that though some of most crucial and important parts of respective religions are similar, they are not known to the other side.

Many non–Muslims are not familiar with the fact that pre-Islam society in Arab land worshipped as many idols as are worshipped in India today. Prophet Mohammed's movement was a revolt against idolatry and a call for belief and faith in one universal God. Similar onslaught was initiated by Swami Dayanand in the 19th century who was the bitterest opponent of idolatry. He maintained that there is not a single verse in the Vedas to sanction the invocation of the Deity, and likewise there is nothing to indicate that it is right to invoke idols.

He said, "Idol worship is a sin." His remedy, in his own words: "Under a righteous government these lovers of idols (priest) would have been compelled to earn their living by breaking stones, making bricks and carrying materials for building purposes or doing the like work."

The BJP government, which invoked reverentially the name of Swami Dayanand in the Gujarat elections, may consider acting on his advice.

In its quest for power the BJP is totally indifferent to the damage it may do to one of the still surviving institutions – judiciary. I am referring to its application to the Supreme Court for the release of acquired undisputed land in Ayodhya to be given to the VHP for building a Ram Temple. I am surprised that because the BJP has a set of talented lawyers, including the Law Minister, whom it had given impartial advice would have certainly advised them that it is not possible to persuade the Supreme Court to accede to this request when the matter of mosque is pending in the High Court.

The VHP still maintains that it will have the sanctum sanctorum (Garbh Griha) of the future Ram temple at the very site of the masjid. Thus the court is being asked to predetermine the decision of the suit. There is no way the Supreme Court can accept such a request unless the VHP publicly gives up its claim to the masjid site and the case before the High Court is withdrawn.

As a matter of fact, the Supreme Court had positively ruled in 1994 that handing over the so-called undisputed area can only be done after implementation and in terms of final adjudication in the suit. Knowing full well this situation, the only motive of the BJP is to do public relations exercise with its Parivar and then innocently turn round to blame the court for want of honouring the Hindutva sentiment. Must cynicism and political morality fall so low.

It is now quite evident that in the fight for secularism the Congress will not be playing the leading role as is clear from its falling a victim to the issue of cow slaughter raised by the BJP, considering that the slaughter of cows and she-calves is already prohibited in the whole of India excepting Kerala and the North-East.

The talk of cultural nationalism is phoney. The persons living in Punjab have more cultural closeness in the matter of folklore, marriage customs and eating habits with the Punjabi Muslims in Pakistan. The Hindus and Muslims in the South have common dress and food habits and social manners far different from the Hindus and Muslims in the North. The effort of the BJP to split the Hindus, Muslims and others religious groups into separate categories is doomed to failure because it is contrary to commonly shared history, culture and philosophy for centuries.

4.10 Can Coalition Work

A suggestion that it is absolutely essential for the nation that the three political groups, namely, JD/NF, CPI and CPM and Congress must jointly take on the responsibility of running the Central Government is likely to generate different and shrill reactions. The BJP for obvious reasons and because of its open anti-minority stand, strident and rigid stand on Article 370 vis-à-vis Kashmir and its fundamentalist call to distort the universalism and tolerance of Hindu religion to the parochial shrill Cry of Hindutva, obviously rules it out for sharing power at the Centre.

The suggestion for the coalition politics at the Centre immediately provokes the question about he platform or programme for this coalition Government. No doubt some broad programme will be agreed to. But this controversy on ideological question is not so relevant, in the conditions prevailing in the country, as it was in 1953-54, when the overwhelming members of the Socialist Party led by Dr Lohia repudiated the 14-point programme formulated by the Nehru–JP talks. Whether that decision was correct or not is immaterial now. The basic difference then and now is that at that time we had a functioning democratic State which was not in danger of collapsing in the absence of coalitions. That situation no longer exists. The Indian state is on the edge of the precipice. The ground realities have to be taken seriously.

Foreign Debt

We have a foreign debt of Rs. 140,000 crore, our deficit for April 90-91 is said to be Rs. 10,770 crore. But such is the partisan discussion that the Congress would put this blame on either Chandra Shekhar Government or the V.P. Singh Government. The reality, however, is that while this deficit was Rs. 1,715 crore in 80-81, and it had risen Rs. 5,580 crore in 85-86 and during the Rajiv Gandhi period 1985-89 had risen to Rs. 12,000 crore.

For violence in the elections each party blames only the other. Election violence takes place in the State like Andhra Pradesh, Bihar, Bengal, Tripura, but condemnation by these parties is selectively partisan only against the other party Government, not against its own.

Such is the partisanship that though each of these group makes the harshest of criticism against Mr. Seshan, the Chief

Election Commissioner, for his arbitrary orders concerning each one of them, they in the same breath laud him for passing similar whimsical orders against the other groups; what a pity. Because here is a fit case where these parties should have started a common onslaught against Mr. Seshan for his disgraceful conduct in all these matters which has tarnished the high office of the Chief Election Commissioner. In fact these parties should really have combined to take steps to start impeachment proceedings for Mr. Seshan's removal. But, alas, we find no agreed pattern amongst them. How can this jaundiced approach restore the nation's confidence in the free electoral system.

Poverty Levels

Admittedly 40 per cent of the population is below the poverty line. The disparities in wealth/ income in our society are horrendous. Five per cent of our top in society enjoy 33 per cent of the national wealth as against the bottom who own only .001 per cent wealth, similarly 20 per cent of the bottom population share seven per cent of the national income against 10 per cent of the top population which shares 34 per cent. One-fourth of the villages have no driking water supply and three-fourths no all-weather roads, even in Punjab, the pride of Green Revolution, 40 per cent of those working in agriculture own less than seven per cent of the land. Each of them owns less that one hectare of land which has no marketable surplus.

According to the survey, marginal farmers, landless labourers, artisan's constitute more than 50 per cent of the rural population of the land. Sixty per cent of the rural household in India hold 10 per cent of the land, while top two per cent hold 20 per cent of the land. The disparities of consumption are a standing fester on our body politik. The share of consumption of top 10 per cent rose from 20 per cent in 1950 to 60 per cent in 1980. Our democracy cannot live with this humiliating poverty, the deprivation of human rights and the prevention of social relations. But to bring a change requires hard political choices to be made high—level of taxation, a strong curb on conspicuous consumption by the affluent sections of society.

We have consciously to decide whether we are to build a society – a State where 100-150 million people will enjoy European standard of living or we will so utilize our resources as to uplift 800 millions of our countrymen to a respectable human existence. In my view, the latter can only be done if both social justice and equity become an integral part of the growth strategy. As Prof. Gunnar Myrdal, the Swedish economist has said in ***Asian Drama*** that "it is possible to point out to a number of conditions that suggest that there (in developing countries) more than Western countries, an increase in equality would help rather than hinder development."

It is a specious argument that urges that poverty is a long – term problem and that current deficits are short-term emergency —that poverty can wait but deficits cannot. This is muddle-headed thinking. To reduce and eliminate massive absolute poverty line at the very core of development itself. It is critical to the survival of any decent society.

Problems

How can any Government meet these problems unless it is seen to be determined and one which would last for a full period of five years. This public credibility gap cannot be closed by any of the two groupings. The group left out will still have a fairly large electoral base. So in order to be effective the triangle must be complete—without it the inculcation of work culture and work ethic in all segments of the working population will not be possible. It is now accepted that mere public ownership is no guarantee of full production. Take the example of generation of electricity. Our average generation capacity is 50 per cent of our installed capacity. Experts have concluded that a mere 15-20 per cent extra generation of electricity would meet the full demand in the country. The loss is in hundreds of crores of rupees every year.

In Marxist-ruled West Bengal the average generation of electricity is 45-50 per cent lower that the all India average. This would show that change in property relations does not by itself remove all the negative features of human relationship that have accumulated over the centuries. A corrective must be made to bring in real economic democracy by the elimination of over-bloated bureaucracy which stifles and undermines the initiative of the masses and shackles creative thinking. Private enterprise has also much to answer for. Hundreds of crores of rupees are locked up in private sick units. It has been found that

that the cause of sickness of 52 per cent of such units is due to faulty management.

Economy

At present, we are facing one of the worst ever periods in economy, social tension and human relations. Violence and open defiance's of law seem to highlight the total ineffectiveness of the State. All political philosophers define State to be the ultimate repository of force.and authority. No State can exist or command respect unless every individual or any group or combination of groups in the country recognizes that the State is more powerful than any group or combination of groups. It is this confidence which is fast receding in the face of large-scale violence, massive Government corruption and a totally pulverized public service. To meet this challenge requires a complete stop to competitive politics.

There is a slight risk in this course. It may be said that combination fo major political parties will weaken the strength of masses outside. Class organizations like trade unions, kisan organizations, the vast number of human rights organizations, women's organizations, the students' organizations can redouble their activities and act as vigilant sentinels on the functioning of the Government and prevent it from acting as a colossus to the neglect of the needs of the average citizens.

It is an unchartered course. But then circumstances prevailing in the country leave no choice but to adopt this new method and thinking to build a prosperous, equitable and stable India.

4.11 Secrecy is Central to Voting

In the next sessions of parliament, anti-democratic legislations is likely to be moved by the government. Unfortunately, it has the support of all the opposition parties. My reference is to the government's move to amend the Constitution and also the Representation of People Act, 1951, so as to make two vital changes in our election law; to amend Article 80(4) of the Constitution and Section 3 of the 1951 Act which provide that a person shall not be qualified to be chosen as a representative of any state in the Council of States (Rajya Sabha) unless he is an elector for a parliamentary constituency in that state and secondly that the voting for the elections of the Council of States should be by show of hand or open and not by secret balloting, as mandated by Section 94 of the 1951 Act.

This change, if carried out, will only strengthen the hold of party bosses to pick up their favorites. At present, even the most autocratic party leader has to pay consideration to the local sentiment. But with the proposed change, centralization will increase and cronyism will become the rule resulting in nominating persons whose activities or business or profession may be limited hundreds of miles away from the state which he or she is supposed to represent.

Arguments that many able people are not accommodated because of the present restriction is an insult to the large number of capable persons in each state. This argument seems to assume that it is only within the coterie of the top party leadership and their hangers on at Delhi that capable people are found. This also goes against the principle of federalism which demands that the states must have an effective voice in all functions at the Centre and it obviously cannot be done by a person in the Rajya Sabha purportedly representing a state whose language he is not able to understand. He may also not be familiar with its culture and may never have interacted with the people of the State whom he is supposed to be representing. What an ironic situation!

In the US, for both the House of Representatives (our Lok Sabha) and the Senate (our Rajya Sabha), the constitution provides that no person will be qualified to be Representative or Senator who shall not, when elected, be an inhabitant of the state for which he shall be chosen.

Secrecy of ballot can be appropriately styled as a postulate of constitutional democracy. It subserves a very vital public interest in that an elector or a voter should be absolutely free in the exercise of his franchise untrammeled by any constraint, which includes constraint as to disclosure. A remote or distinct possibility that at some point a voter may under a compulsion of law be forced to disclose for whom he has voted would act as a positive constraint and check on his freedom to exercise his franchise in the manner he freely chooses to exercise.

The only argument given is that the party bosses have found

that many of their candidates have been defeated because in the secrecy of voting some legislation sell their votes for money. How sad! I should have thought that this evil, which is certainly there, would force political parties to make an earnest effort to find ways of checking it rather that destroy the fundamental basis of secrecy of voting and thus weaken parliamentary democracy. This amoral attitude reminds one of the famous advice given by cynics that "if you cannot fight thieves, join them." Of course, no one put it better than in the piercing satire by novelist Oscar Wilde, namely, "the best way to resist temptation is to yield to it".

I fear that this kind of thinking may lead to the suggestion of denying secret ballot in Assembly polling on the ground that buying of voters takes place in some slums and bustees.

Nowhere in the world where democracy prevails will one find a law which profanes the sacred principle of secrecy of voting. Parliament would be making a laughing stock of sanctity of free and fair elections if these amendments are passed.

4.12 Agenda for the Central Government

It is time that the Prime Minister, Mr. I.K. Gujral, told the Congress (1) president, Mr. Sitaram Kesri, that enough was enough. The continuous threatening and alternately patronising tone of his speeches, coupled with an arrogant resolution of the Congress Working Committee can only demoralise the functioning of the Government.

It is a pity that the United Front steering committee swallowed this insult and refused to react. Even when it is well-known that notwithstanding his professions to the contrary. Mr. Kesri will withdraw support to the United Front Government, the moment he finds the election game plan suitable for the Congress.

Maybe in the initial period. Mr. Gujral was somewhat overwhelmed by the apprehension of the system collapsing if he did not try to carry along with him as much of the political spectrum as possible. That stage is now over. With wise restraint and transparency of functioning, he has now worked his way to a firmer footing.

Mr. Gujral is right in his enunciation that being in authority does not mean becoming authoritarian. But it does require Mr. Gujral to cease thinking of himself as a mere consensus Prime Minister — he must act and lay down priorities and agenda which is his right and duty as an elected Prime Minister. He must create a national constituency which is outside the beaten track of caste and regional orientation.

Mr. Gujral's strength will have to be based on his prioritising vital issues of administration and forcing the other political grouping to go along with him, failing which those groups will be in danger of being isolated in public if they were to attempt to destabilise the government. This course is necessary to make issues of national concern firmly entrenched in political life so that irrespective of whosoever is the Prime Minister, the public pressure will not permit anyone to backtrack on these issues.

Consider what ridicule and abuses were thrown on Mr. V.P. Singh by the Congress and the BJP in the beginning, but now these very parties are the most enthusiastic about the Mandal formulation. Mr. Gujral must therefore, chalk out his own independent course based on programmes which are people-oriented.

In this fight, the support of women, constituting half of the population, is absolutely essential. The proposal to empower women by providing them with representation in the legislature has got stuck because of the contrary and hypocritical stands taken by different political groupings. In my view, Mr. Gujral should take a decision on the empowerment of women as the first agenda, irrespective of the opposition from even within the Janata Dal—this slogan and action will release much more powerful political and social forces than were released in the wake of the empowerment of the backward castes through the Mandal formulation.

It may be that the percentage of reservation which women groups are at present asking may have to be diluted to some extent—but beyond that there should be no compromise. Rather, Mr. Gujral should go round the country creating public support on this issue. The political groups opposed to it need to be exposed for their anti-women attitude. The argument that this measure will empower only urban women is a deliberate distortion. It can readily be accepted that some of the priorities of urban woman may be different from that of rural women. But that is no argument why women's reservation in legislature should be stalled.

The argument that in elections only the urban women will get representation against the rural women is utterly futile. As it is, men belonging to the backward classes get elected in many constituencies not because they are the best candidates but because of the caste configurations; why should not the same advantage be made available to the backward caste women against urban women? As it is, a number of candidates belonging to both the forward and backward castes even with criminal record manage to get elected. In that context, I can only visualise an improvement of public life by providing reservation to women in the legislatures.

Another immediate agenda is elimination of the nexus between politicians and criminals. This would necessitate the immediate passing of the Lokpal Bill in the next Parliament session and a law debarring convicts from participating in elections.

Mr. Gujral also needs to keep in check those groups which are projecting privatisation and the market economy as a panacea for meeting the challenge of poverty.

That this approach of unchecked liberalisation is not the answer is recognised in the recent World Bank report in regard to the so-called East Asian Tiger economies of Indonesia and Malaysia wherein it has said, "that after three decades of even rapid growth, inequality is becoming more widespread". This, coupled with a currency crisis in these countries, must force us to realize the danger of over-liberalisation and the wisdom of following a policy declared in the preamble to the Constitution, namely, of economic and social justice.

In finalising the environmental policy, the Gujral Government must do so in the context of the social justice awareness that there is no worse environmental degradation than the environment of pauperisation, and of mass unemployment.

No one disputes the importance of a clean environment. But the developed world is motivatedly utilising the WTO (World

Trade Organisation) platform and insisting on environmental laws which are disproportionate to the economic growth of the developing countries. Principle 11 of the 1992 Rio Declaration on Environment and Development calls it inequitable, and has said "Standards applied by some countries may be inappropriate and of unwarranted economic and social cost to other countries, in particular developing countries."

The Gujral Government must a show greater awareness of the mischief practised by the developed countries to deliberately link environmental laws with international trade.

The brazenness of this concern by the developed nations is again highlighted by the latest guidelines finalised by the Japanese Government for its policy to be made effective from 1998, namely nations seeking the Japanese Official Development Assistance (ODA) for environmental and anti-pollution projects will now have to make obligatory purchases of goods and services from Tokyo.

That environmental insistence is a neat way of trade advancement is clear from the fact that the Japanese Government plans to limit the "tied ODA loans" to projects related to anti-pollution and other environmental protection projects and measures. Environmental concern of the West in fact is in aid of its biggest environmental manufacturing industry.

The Prime Minister must deflate the arrogance of the Congress by immediately releasing the Jain Commission report. Whatever the Congress motives, publication of enquiry reports is a right of the citizens and part of the culture of democratic governance. This is all the more necessary as passing of the Right to Information Act has been promised by the Prime Minister. As a matter of fact, this demand of the Congress should be an occasion to make public some other equally important reports.

Indira Gandhi's assassination was tragic. Mr. Justice M.P. Thakar of the Supreme Court, who held an inquiry into it, is said to have expressed an apprehension of foreign power conspiracy with support from some of the close confidants of Indira Gandhi. Are not the public entitled to know the truth about the motives for her assassination, the same way about the killing of Rajiv Gandhi.

We, then, have the debacle of the 1962 Chinese invasion, which caused such anguish to our nation and the great leader Jawaharlal Nehru. The General Henderson Brooks Report still continues to be under wraps for which there is no justification.

People are also strenuously demanding full information on the Bofors and the connected material which were recently made available by the Swiss Government. In my view, there is no legal bar to placing the said material before Parliament because in any case it has to be produced in court. It is to be hoped that the Congress will expand its demand for releasing all the above said reports.

I know the course suggested above can have some political pitfalls. But then I also believe that Mr. Gujral genuinely subscribes to and accepts the well-known moral philosophical principle that while a politician looks to the next election, a statesman looks to the future generations — Mr. Gujral, I have no doubt ,would want to be remembered as a statesman.

4.13 Dead and Buried

The Babri Masjid Dispute Drags on only because of the Weakness of Political Will

An Extensive debate has ensued on the significance of the Lucknow Bench of the Allhabad High Court directing the excavation of the area near the Babri masjid site. Some have raised the question about the competency and even impartiality of the Archaeological Survey of India to carry out the excavations. Some have pointed out that there could be many conflicting and uncertain interpretations of the finds and this exercise may turn out to be a futility.

I am not competent to comment on these technical formulations. But I have no doubt that the high court will duly take note of these warnings. It should, however, be noted that one of the issues before the high court is whether or not the Babri masjid was built after a temple was demolished. Large evidence of historical literature and circulars from the Mughal court have been – and are being – produced by both conflicting parties in support of their respective stand. I can, therefore, see no extraneous motive behind high court order per se.

But then there is genuine apprehension and I can appreciate

the fear of this precedent being used for divisive and mischievous purposes by the Sangh Parivar in its attempts to reopen the question of other mosques at Varanasi and Mathura. I concede that there is some danger in taking such a course. But it can be resisted successfully provided the non-BJP parties look inward and do not repeat their prevarication as in the past which has allowed the situation to develop to such present dangerous proportions.

It is well-known that the RSS's communal ideologues manufactured the question of Babri masjid in 1948. We had leaders like Jawaharlal Nehru and G.B. Pant (the chief minister of Uttar Pradesh). But somehow they allowed the matter to remain in limbo by virtue of a magistrate's order, assuming it was the best option – presumably under the stress of post-Partition India. But I feel the seed of future trouble was planted when it was decided to skirt the issue rather than face it squarely.

The matter remained dormant for about 40 years. But then the older leadership was gone, and we had, on the one hand, the central government which sought to reap benefits through the shilanyas ceremony and, on the other, a weak and divided opposition unable to react strongly. This led to the deterioration of the situation.

In July 1991, the Congress government at the Centre still refused to take a principled stand on the Ayodhya issue. It compromised its position by passing the Places of Worship (Special Provisions) Act, 1991, plausibly to foreclose any controversy in respect of any place of worship defined as temple, mosque or church. Section 4 declared that the religious character of a place of worship existing on August 15, 1947, shall continue to be the same as it existed on that day.

While this was a worthwhile legislation (though it would have been more reassuring if this act was incorporated as constitutional amendment), the pusillanimous conduct of political parties came to the fore when the act stated that since the case relating to the place commonly called 'Ram Janmabhoomi-Babri masjid' forms a classes by itself, it was necessary to exempt it entirely from the operation of the act. Had the secular force been strong, no such exemption would have been incorporated as it went against the grain of the Constitution that accords equal status and respect to all religions.

This passivity of the non-BJP political groups encouraged elements of the Sangh parivar to commit the dastardly act of the Babri masjid demolition on December 6, 1992. Even that tragedy did not spur these groups to take the only correct stand—that is, state that since the RSS had committed the unforgivable sin of demolishing a place of worship, it would not be allowed to reap any benefits. In common law, if a heir kills his ancestor, he forfeits his inheritance. In the Ayodhya case too, there was 'murder most foul, and the only response should have been that the exemption clause be deleted and the Babri masjid restored to its original Muslim owners.

But that did not happen. Various alternatives started being put forward by well-meaning but politically weak people. The easy way of letting the matter be deciding by the court was taken. The Sangh parivar purportedly claimbed down from its proclamation of the Babri masjid site being where Lord Ram was born – a claim that was a non-issue right from the start as there was no way such an ancient event could be proved. So it made a further dilution – namely, that a temple existed which was destroyed to build the Babri mosque. Had the strong, this plea should have been rejected outright and the cowardly goons who had demolished the masjid shown the boot.

Muslims, in a measure of accommodation, conceded that if it was found that the masjid was built on the site of temple. They would give up their claim because the Koran forbids Muslim to build a mosque by demolishing any other religious place. That is the issue that the court is to decided and it is in that context that the present order has been passed.

It is somewhat curious that the non-BJP parties are still not prepared to suggest the only honourable course: that the demolition of the masjid was an act of sacrilege and no such dispute can be raised in a civilized State. Once the digging is permitted, it is near impossible to stop anyone from demanding excavations to find out whether a particular Hindu temple was built on an old Jain or Buddhist temple.

History teaches us that people who continue to look backward learn no lessons. Rather, the correct and impartial reading of history will show us the people who can learn to look forward need not be condemned to relive the past. Consequently, they learn to live with each other harmoniously.

Legally, the Sangh parivar has no case even if a temple had been demolished to build the Babri masjid. (It is a different matter that Muslims on their own may not like to persist with their claim if that is the case, as it would be against the injunctions of the Koran.)

I say this in view of the precedent of the case of Masjid Shahid Ganj in Lahore decided by the Privy Council in 1940. Muslims failed to win back the masjid built in 1200 and converted into a gurdwara in 1760 as the 12-year period for reclamation had long passed. Whatever the nature of the title of the site under the mosque, by the very fact that the Babri masjid had existed for over 400 years, the VHP/ RSS cannot claim any title to the contentious site in Ayodhya.

The legal position is clear. It is only the weakness of political will that is responsible for the Ayodhya imbroglio to continue as one of the bitter disputes within the country. By keeping the Ayodhya issue alive, the country has been kept from addressing its most urgent task – how to meet the challenge of the growing pauperization of the masses. And that includes both Hindus and Muslims.

5
Forced Eviction : Violation of Human Rights

5.1 Shelter and Development—National Policy and the International Commitments

1. In the aftermath of Second World War nations recognised that war would have been fought in vain if basic Human Rights were not incorporated in various covenants so that they could form an agenda for action for the international community. Universal Declaration of Human Rights 1948 enumerated a number of such Rights. The measure of sucess of any society can only be to the extent to which its policies, programmes approximate, to various items of Declaration.

2. Somehow the "Right of Shelter" or the "Right to Housing" as an aspect of Human Right has not formed the agenda for action by various state governments. This is a surprising omission because the "Right to Housing" has been recognised as one of the basic rights in various international documents.

3. The right of housing is not a new human right. Article 25 (1) of the Universal Declaration of Human Rights 1948, states that:

> Everyone has the right to a standard of living adequate for the health and well-being of himself and of his family, including food, clothing, *housing*...

The most significant placement of the "Right to adequate Housing" under international law is found within the Covenant on Economic, Social and Cultural Rights 1966 which is currently binding on 99 states, and which in Article 11(1) provides:

> The States Parties to the present Covenant recognize the right of everyone to an adequate standard of living for himself and his family, including *Housing,* and to the continuous improvement of living conditions....

The "Right to Housing" is also enshrined in Article 5 (e) of the International Convention on the Elimination of All Forms of Racial Discrimination (CERD), the UN Vancouver Declaration on Human Settlements (1976), as well as within the Convention on the Elimination of All Forms of Discrimination Against Women (Art. 14) and ILO Recommendation No. 115 on Worker's Housing.

4. All these legal instruments speak of the recognition of housing as a right, but, how far is our modern society from accomplishing even the minimum housing conditions for a growing high percentage of the world's population.

5. Now Shelter is thus fundamental human need, the same as food and clothing. The lack of either of these deprives the human being to live a dignified life. Physical and psychological health and even life itself depend on the possibility of individuals and families to use and enjoyment of a shelter.

Since a shelter is a fundamental requirement related to a primary human need, its lack must be seen as an injustice. And it is a structural injustice which is part of the unequal distribution of income and consequently of goods and services within and among the nations.

6. Thus the struggle for a place to live is a fundamental one. The sense of security, of belonging gained from being able to retain a home is essential to begin and sustain any other struggles — for education, for gender equality. Second that individuals and communities want to live a life that allows scope for assertions of identity, skills and culture. Essential to their assertions is the right to a safe, secure and adequate dwelling reality that demands the resources of land, building materials, fuel, fodder, water as well as civic services and finance.

7. In generic terms housing should become, an organising principle of state policy and the following be accepted as the maxim for housing in the plan: 'A democratic state must guarantee conditions where all women and men may gain and

retain adequate housing and where they and their children live with security and dignity .... Housing must be send not simply as the provision of houses but primarily as an instrument for the promotion of Justice, equality and peace; for the expression of diverse cultures; for the self-determination of individuals and communities; for the fight against discrimination and for the regeneration of a ravaged environment, within the perspective of the living earth as a home for us all. In all this we must recognize the role of women in the struggle for change towards a better place to live. The right to a secure place to live is a fundamental one. The sense of security, privacy and community gained from being able to retain a home is an essential prerequisite for the pursuit and exercise of a variety of other human rights, including the right to choose one's residence, the right to vote, the right to popular participation, the right to health, the right to a safe environment, and others.

8. While all human rights are clearly indivisible and interdependent, the right to housing is a right that everyone is involved with directly and confronts and experiences everyday.

9. The right to housing applies everywhere to everyone, without any political, social economic gender, religious, racial or other form of discrimination, wherever he or she may live. This right refers to habitat as a whole, in its cultural, historical and territorial implications it means nothing if the people are excluded from the process of making the specific rights which make up the right to housing.

10. For decades the United Nations has consistently re-affirmed the inter-dependent nature of civil and political rights (CP) on the one hand, and economic, social and cultural rights (ESC) on the other. Despite recent strides towards giving greater and more substantial attention to ESC rights by various organs within the UN however, a large gap still remains between actual action on CP rights as contrasted to ESC rights. How ironic it is that over 100 million people live in conditions of absolute homelessness, with the numbers increasing annually, despite the recognition of the human right to adequate housing within the 1948 Universal Declaration of Human Rights and other international laws binding to varying degrees on all nations.

11. Any historical analysis of human rights (particularly

economic, social and cultural rights, including the right to housing) reveals how rarely the state has been the leader in giving clarity, substance and strength to human rights norms. In many contexts states gladly accept international obligations in order to improve their global image, and after ratifying a treaty will conveniently do little to carry out these legal duties. So, while the United Nations continually emphasizes the interdependence and equal value of all Human Rights, state practice has certainly been lax in actually fulfilling housing rights.

12. Thus we learn that according to UN Statistics, over one billion persons throughout the world remain either ill-housed or homeless. Within the UN's Global Shelter Strategy to the Year 2000 (GSS), adopted by the General Assembly in 1988, it is stated that "no nation can claim to have fulfilled the housing needs of all of its citizens". This constitutes an extremely serious situation, and one which remains far from being either solved or adequately addressed. In fact, the magnitude of violations taking place concerning this right are not even recognized as issues of human rights by most actors involved. All indications point to the prevalence of homelessness and inhuman living conditions increasing, rather than being on the decline. In spite of this recurring social reality in all States, recognition of the notion of housing constituting a human rights concern, remains wholly insufficient. Even though some 30 States have enshrined the right to housing within their national Constitutions, most persons are either unaware that they possess housing rights or of the remedies available for enforcing them. However, in concrete terms, the great majority of humanity remain unable to enjoy or exercise the right to housing as found in international human rights law.

13. It is however somewhat gratifying that in response to the UN sponsored International Year of Shelter for the Homeless (IYSH) held in 1987, a variety of generally worded resolutions on "the realization of the right to adequate housing" were adopted by the UN Commission on Human Rights, ECOSOC and the General Assembly, between 1986-1988.

14. Further it must also be recognised that the issue of housing rights has begun receiving increased consideration within the UN system. The UN Committee on Economic, Social and

Cultural Rights has placed increasing emphasis on the right to housing during its first five sessions (1987-1990). The Committee held a day-long "general discussion" on the right to housing during its fourth session. During its fifth session, an entirely new set of "guidelines for States Reports" were adopted, which include a three page long series of questions to states concerning legislative and policy measures they have taken to fulfil obligations surrounding the right to housing. The new guidelines represent a substantial and meaningful improvement over the previous set of guidelines. Also during the fifth session of the Committee, held in December 1990, this body declared the Dominican Republic to be in violation of the right to housing due to this governments policy of supporting large-scale forced evictions. This action by the Committee constitutes the first time this body had formally declared a State Party to the Covenant on Economic Social and Cultural Rights to be in violation of the legal duties it contains, thus setting a crucial precedence in the arena of housing rights, and economic, social and cultural rights across the board.

15. All these actions were however isolated, uncordinated. No single document programme or activity of the UN has housing Rights as its Central focus. Fortunately support for action on housing Rights as a right in itself within the UN human rights bodies has been clearly recognized. The First Progress Report (E/CN.4/Sub.2/1990/19, pp. 38-42) of the UN Social and Cultural Rights, Mr. Danilo Turk, dealt with housing rights in a comparatively extensive manner. In this report the Special Rapporteur stated:

The need for greater precision and enforceability of housing rights and for adopting further standards clearly exists. Virtually no analytical work has been carried out within the human rights organs of the United Nations directly concerning housing rights. (p. 38).

16. We must realize that this right to housing will not be attained automatically, simply by issuing this declaration nor by enshrining it into the national constitutions. Rather, it will be attained primarily through the collective efforts of governments, politicians, people's representatives, public and private sectors, non-governmental and community-based organizations,

international and multi-lateral agencies, and above all, by people themselves. International institutions must take the housing rights obligations of States into account then formulating development policies, especially in view of the fact that less than 5 per cent of such international co-operation has been directed to human settlements.

17. The pursuit of the right to housing empowers communities to make their own decisions about social, economic and ecological relations, and to be able to pursue freedoms which can reduce what may have become crippling dependencies on authorities and government.

18. One of the areas, often ignored as such, but one which is used by governments to create segregation discrimination and which often benefits one social group at the expense of another is housing. Housing embodies social harmony or disharmony, social integration or disintegration.

19. Governments have the obligation to create the conditions necessary to satisfy the right to housing.

20. A particular problem facing developing countries is posed by the large number of homeless and of those living in extremely poor shelter and unhealthy neigbourhoods, whether in urban slums and squatter areas or in poor rural areas".

21. Most of the people affected of course live in Third World countries where they represent one-third of their whole population, but now more than a million people in Western Europe are without homes and for the most powerful country, the United States, it has been estimated by one NGO, the National Coalition for the Homeless, that between 3 and 5 million per night are without permanent homes.

22. The number of homeless in the United States has been increasing since the 1981-1982 recession, but also the characteristics of homelessness is changing. More and more families, mostly female-headed and their children, are among homeless. In many locations their proportion has shifted from one third to more than half of the homeless.

23. A housing Rights campaign in the United Kingdom initiated in 1987 has been struggling against any type of

discrimination on housing provision, for the government to increase and maintain the housing stock and to campaign for a housing right act.

24. More than three years ago a campaign for housing rights was started in India which as a first step is promoting an amendment to the constitution declaring housing as a fundamental right. Recently, nearly 150 organizations and individuals submitted a people's petition on housing rights, which in itself represents a very comprehensive and concrete document.

25. Progressive achievement of the full enjoyment of the right to housing implies two aspects: (a) the progressive development and protection of the right itself and of its component parts : (b) the progressive improvement in the quality of housing and related infrastructures and services in the context of a safe and healthy environment. Recent studies in India indicate the following, largely unrecognised, facts.

(i) The share of formal housing agencies (including government, public sector and large, private developers) is less than 15 per cent of the total addition to housing stock since 1951.

(ii) The formal sector contributes 10 to 12 per cent of total housing activity in the country. The commercial private sector contributes 18 to 25 per cent. The remaining 65-70 per cent takes place in the community sector (the variation is 85-90 per cent in rural areas and 45-50 per cent in urban areas).

(iii) The bulk of the housing activity in the community sector is directly dependent on local materials (mud, thatch, palmyra, bamboo, secondary timber, tiles) and supporting resources (fuel, fodder, water). This activity functions in what is called a biomass-based gathering economy ranging from being non-monetised to partially monetised.

(iv) The bulk of the building activity in rural areas comprises self-built efforts: housing in biomass materials, artisan-built housing (self-supervised with a master meson or carpenter) or by small contractors. The situation in urban areas is not significantly different. The bulk of construction activity is undertaken by owners (that is, owner-supervised artisan constructed). According to NSSO round 34 (1979-80) computations, this was true of even class I cities, and the all-India average for cities was as high as 83 per cent.

26. In rural areas during the 1971-1991 period there was a 45 per cent in-crease in houses made with biomass roofs and biomass walls — this is known as the lowest performance segment. Over the next few decades incomes of the poor are not expected to rise to the extent that will decrease dependency on gathering biomass for meeting dwelling needs.

The right to housing, including the right to access to resources (material and non-material) necessary for ordering an adequate living environment, offers an alternate inherently participatory vision. This calls for the vesting of control over the production, distribution and regeneration of necessary dwelling resources in local, popular democratic processes, and for the recognition and creation of responsibilities at local levels to order priorities for a sustainable lifestyles.

27. Since any right implies an obligation and, in the case of housing, governments are the only entities in possession of the resources to face the problem on a large scale, the main responsibility in the implementation of the right to housing is in their hands.

28. International organizations, ranging from political bodies, multi-lateral aid agencies, international non-governmental organizations, housing and other human rights a bodies must defend the right to housing and create the corresponding international development policies to fulfill it.

29. Although the emphasis that UNCHS has placed on the rights side of the broader issue of human settlements has been relatively minor, their recognition of housing as a right has certainly been apparent. For instance, in the Global Strategy for Shelter to the Year 2000 (GSS) which evolved out of the International Year of Shelter for the Homeless (IYSH) in 1987, UNCHS states that:

> "The right to adequate shelter is recognized universally, and all nations, without exception, have accepted some form of obligation to meet the shelter needs of their

people. To address this obligation effectively, Governments must make basic changes to their existing policies on shelter...."

30. WHO could also play an extremely useful role in developing additional, concrete legal instruments relating to the right to housing. Its programme "Environmental Health in Rural and Urban Development in Housing" has direct implications to issues relating to housing rights. WHO has recognized the health threats and problems associated with inadequate housing conditions for decades. The Global Programme on AIDS (GPA) of WHO could help to develop the right to housing on the basis inter alia, of the work they carry out or sponsor on the multitude of housing problems faced by people with HIV or AIDS. Finally, the work of WHO is in the fields of water, sanitation in the area of social indicators in general, and in the evaluation of the Health For All by the year 2000 Programme, would also be of the utmost importance, towards this end.

31. ILO also maintains a mandate relevant to housing rights. In addition to the Building, Civil Engineering and Public Works Committee, ILO Recommendation No. 115 on Worker's Housing (1961) remains one of the most detailed international instruments dealing with housing and other related issues. The preamble of No. 115 states that "Whereas the Constitution of ILO provides that the Organization shall promote the objects set forth in the Declaration of Philadelphia, which recognizes the solemn obligation of ILO to further among the nations of the world programmes which will achieve the provision of adequate housing". In the three decades which have passed since the adoption of this instrument substantial changes have taken place in many perspectives concerning housing, and housing rights. It is for these reasons that a resolution adopted in 1987 by ILO's Governing Body recommended the revision of Recommendation No. 115.

32. A variety of issues, principles and perspectives not traditionally dealt with by human rights bodies will need to find recognition within any future international instrument on housing rights.

33. In this connection a very encouraging development took place when at its forty-third Session held at Geneva in August

1991, U.N. Sub-Commission on Prevention of Discrimination and Protection of Minorities passed a Resolution 1991/26 on the subject of promoting the realization of the Right to adequate housing and entrusted his author (who is a member of the sub-commission) to submit copy; the working paper to the Sub-Commission, at its forty-fourth session, for its examination of, inter alia, how most effectively to proceed on issues concerning the human right to adequate housing.

The Resolution welcomed the increased attention paid to this right by the Committee on Economic, Social and Cultural Rights, at its 1990 sessions and the recently adopted revised guidelines regarding the form and contents of reports to be submitted by States parties under Articles 16 and 17 of the International Covenant on Economic, Social and Cultural Rights.

The Sub-Commission also was *Deeply concerned* that over one billion people do not enjoy their right to adequate housing and that in many States the number of homeless and inadequately housed people is increasing.

The Sub-Commission was also *Concerned* that both the obligations and the entitlements inherent in the right to adequate housing remain unclear and unspecified in terms of the law.

The Sub-Commission expressed its awareness that no State can claim to have fully realized the right to adequate housing for all its inhabitants.

The Sub-Commission therefore affirmed the need for additional human rights activities leading towards the full realization of the right to adequate housing for everyone; and it has also urged all States to pursue effective policies and adopt legislation aimed at ensuring the realization of the right to adequate housing of the entire population, concentrating on those currently homeless or inadequately housed.

34. The Sub-Commission has required the present writer to examine, in the working paper, the utility of donating an international declaration or convention on the right to adequate housing, and also to examine the specific contents of this right: (A copy of the said Resolution 1991/26 is annexed to this article).

35. It is to be hoped that this development will give a fillip and support to the movements and organisations who are engaged

in concretising, codifying and effectuating one of the most important Human Rights belonging to an individual, namely) the Right to adequate housing.

36. The short term outlook for the one-fifth of the world's population, the poorest of the poor living in cities with no capital resources or productive land is bleak. These people have little choice but to live in crowded cramped housing conditions.

37. In these cramped habitats this year if 15 million children under the age of five die—99 per cent of these will be from the developing world. In countries such as Switzerland and Japan the average life expectancy is 77 years, 35 years more than in Afghanistan or Sierre Leone.

38. In makeshift settlements that lack readily available water and sewerage facilities, garbage collection and primary health care services, every season people in slums in the Indian cities die of Diarrhoea, dysentery, typhoid, intestinal parasites and food poisoning.

39. Everybody must realise that the problem is too horrendous and urgent to brook and delay at remedying this evil.

5.2 Forced Evictions Against Human Rights

Does a ailing but socially conscious former Prime Minister of India (Sh. V.P. Singh) have to endanger his life and spend a night with over a lakh of jhuggi slum dwellers of Wazirpur to prevent their being wantonly thrown out like a garbage — what kind of democratic conscience does the society project.

The facile explanation by government that the Wazirpur colony was on Railway land and hence they were unauthorized occupants and were being justifiably evicted is hollow and in violation of internationally recognized Human Right against forcible eviction.

The callous indifference of people in general to the plight of these slum dwellers is borne out of colossal ignorance of the phenomenon of Slum creation. Somehow a false impression is created as if the pavement dwellers are unsocial elements, a majority of whom are criminals and unemployed and not interested in work. This is sheer slander. The pavement dwellers are an important part of the daily economy of city life. They are in reality the victims of unjust social order.

The compulsions of why these squatter colonies exist was highlighted by Economic Commission of Europe, which said: "High levels of squatter housing indicate that the formal land market does not provide affordable residential land for housing, forcing households to occupy land illegally. High levels of this indicator also suggest that eviction may not be a realistic option, but rather calls for policies and programmes which lead to strengthening tenure security in squatter settlements, thus facilitating higher levels of housing investment".

Even World Bank whose policies in the past have been responsible for forcible eviction of at least 3 to 4 million, has under pressure from Human Right activists revised its guidelines and now insists as a precondition to assistance to any Bank funded project on the rehabilitation of affected persons. In the wake of that policy, World Bank has made resettlement of the evicted people from near the Railway Tracks in Mumbai a condition precedent for giving aid for Metropolitan Railway Project.

Is it not ironic that slum dweller should be given protection by the World Bank (no sympathizer of the poor), against the evictions ordered by the regime of Mamta Bannerjee, a self-proclaimed "messiah" of the poor. This notwithstanding 1976 Declaration made by the UN Conference on Human Settlement (Habitat-I) that, "Adequate shelter and services are a basic human right which places an obligation on governments to ensure their attainment by all people" — the same has been reiterated in Istanbul Declaration of 1996. (Habitat II) to which India is a signatory.

India has a backlog of 30 million housing units over 45 per cent of households have only one room. Per Capita area available to the bottom 40 per cent is 58 sq. ft. — a shame as even Delhi Municipal Corporation prescribes the minimum size of a habitable room as 60 sq. ft.

The National Housing Bank or HUDCO sponsored schemes and projects for housing the urban poor, stipulate that a minimum of 20 per cent of their income be paid as instalments. This is unrealistic; the urban poor can only spend about 11 per cent of their income (as saving are negligible). Thus, by their very design, these projects would miss the target group and the benefits would flow to household in the higher consumption bracket, as indeed has been recorded in several studies.

That demolition and forced eviction like that proposed in Wazirpura should still form a part of government policy or that any court could give such a direction is amazing and illegal, because of the Supreme Court decision that the right to life "would take within its sweep the right to .... a reasonable accommodation to live in ....." and that "Eviction of the petitioners from their dwellings would result in the deprivation of their livelihood".

Such forced evictions also violate the guidelines laid down by the Expert Committee on Forced Evictions formed by U.N. Human Right Commissioner for Human Rights.The Committee has recognized that forced evictions intensify social conflict and inequality and invariably affect the poorest, most socially and economically vulnerable sectors of society, specifically women, children and indigenous peoples, and that further Forced evictions constitute prima facie violations of wide range of internationally recognized human rights and can only be carried out under exceptional circumstances and in full accordance with the present guidelines and relevant provisions of international human rights law, and have laid down as under:

(a) States should ensure that no persons, groups or communities are rendered homeless or are exposed to the violation of any other human rights as a consequences of a forced eviction.

(b) States should fully explore all possible alternatives to any act involving forced eviction.

(c) All persons have a right to security of tenure which provides sufficient legal protection from forced eviction from one's home or land.

(d) The present guidelines shall apply to all persons, groups and communities irrespective of their tenure status.

It is well to remind the Government of warning given in General Comment No. 7 of Committee appointed under

International Covenant on Economic, Social and Cultural Right 1966, wherein it has categorically said (16th session 1997) "evictions should not result in individuals being rendered homeless or vulnerable to the violation of other human rights. Where those affected are unable to provide for themselves, the State Party must take all appropriate measures, to the maximum of its available resources, to ensure that adequate alternative housing, resettlement or access to productive land, as the case may be, is available".

The state must unhesitatingly accept its obligations considering that there is a inextricable connection between the free enjoyment of the right to adequate housing and certain civil and political rights. A wide range of civil and political rights of the slum dwellers like the right to equal protection and benefit of the law, the right to gender equality, the right to be free from discrimination, the right to property will be seriously compromised in the absence of measures geared towards respecting, protecting and ensuring the human right against forcible eviction.

No Government can be permitted to violate its international obligation in the field of Human Rights. Are slums the ugly sights and the environmental pollutants as the upper middle class of the cities would like us to view them or are they not in reality, a blot on the governance of any administration and the reflection of the insensitivity of a few privileged to the plight of the disadvantaged slums jhuggies dwellers. It needs to be emphasized that this segment of population is the dry tinder which if continued to be ignored by the affluent sections under the illusions of Globalisation, can be in danger of catching fire and blazing everything in its way in its blind fury.

5.3 Narmada Valley Dam : A Human Right Issue

The judgement in Narmada Bachao Andolan (N.B.A.) case by the Supreme Court has understandably sharpened the debate about the real content of the "Right to development", namely whether the bureaucratic decisions without prior consultation with affected disadvantaged section and by just parroting the refrain that a price has to be paid is a sufficient answer but without answering as to why the sacrifice must always be paid by the disadvantaged and the tribals and the benefits go only to the powerful ones political as well as moneyed.

No doubt judgement of the Supreme Court has disappointed the Human Right activists who were hoping for a more incisive examination of the rationale of project and a greater sensitivity to the cry of the suffering project affected families (PAF). But at the same time the pro dam lobby has no reason to indulge in the vulgar dance of victory and fire crackers that the Gujarat Government indulged in. Has sensitivity gone so low that the undoubted displacement and suffering of lakhs (which even the Supreme Court accepts) leaves the government cold — this was not a football match between Government and N.B.A. — the later was only highlighting the Human Right aspect of the concerned people and demanding a recognition of their right to live with dignity guaranteed by the Constitution.

The prayer of N.B.A. that because of wrong data and actual experience the Court should appoint Expert Committee to re-examine the project regarding its cost effectiveness and till then further construction beyond 85 mtr be kept in abeyance, has not been accepted. But on environmental aspect the Court split 2:1.

The environmental clearance to the project was given by the then Prime Minister Mr. Rajiv Gandhi in1987. The minority judgment of Bharucha J expressed his anguish that the requisite data for assessment of the environmental impact of the Project was not available when the environmental clearance thereof was granted..." and that further in May, 1992 the Secretary, Environment took the view that the conditions of the project were not yet met and failing such compliance, a formal notification may be issued revoking the earlier clearance.

Bharucha J, therefore, directed that "until environmental clearance to the Project is accorded by a Committee of experts to be appointed by the Ministry *further construction work on the dam shall cease*". (emphasis supplied). But the majority (Chief Justice & Kirpal J) on the same material however, came to the contrary opinion thus highlighting the oft repeated dictum that the highest Court is not necessarily right—it is only right because it is the last Court.

The majority surprisingly adopted a technical approach in not applying the requirement and conditions of Environment Act, 1994, on the ground that clearance had been given in 1987. No such exclusionary rule to Environmental considerations has been entertained by the Court as it has treated environmental considerations as broad fundamentals arising out of Article 21, namely the right to life. That is why it issued relocation of industries outside Delhi, even when such industries had been established decades back, and when no environment clearance was required in law. The plea of labour that this would and in fact has resulted in unemployment of over a lakh of workers families proved of no avail.

Similar was the response of the Court to evictions of immigrant population of 150,000 who had settled on the border of Sanjay Gandhi National Park — a forest reserve on the outskirts of the Mumbai city, as far back as 20 years when even no alternative location had been earmarked for them. The oustees continue to live exposed to the sky and without a shred of shelter. Besides slum dwellers, the evictions involve the removal of nearly 2,500 adivasi' or tribal families — whose hamlets occupied parts of the forest even before the area was declared a national park in 1982.

The majority seems to have taken it for granted that the construction of big dam will improves the living standard of oustees. One regrets that the majority was not made aware of the misery suffered by the oustees because of Chambal Dam (MP). A sensitive officer who dealt with these oustees even now feels a pang of guilt when remembering the fate of Rampur Town that was totally submerged throwing away 30,000 families to start life afresh.

Further raising of height, as permitted would result in forest area Hoshangabad (MP) to be completely destroyed, when Narmada Sagar Dam is built.

The Court has accepted that the States are lagging behind in the matter of identification and acquisition of land upon which oustees are to be resettled, Bharucha J has given direction that each of the Grievance Redressal Authorities of the states of Gujarat, Madhya Pradesh and Maharashtra should after inspection certify, before further work on the further construction of the dam can begin; that all those ousted by reason of the increase in the height of the dam by 5 mtrs from the present level have already been satisfactorily rehabilitated, and also that suitable vacant land for rehabilitating all those who will be ousted by the increase in the height of the dam by another 5 metres is already in the possession of the respective States. This process shall be repeated for every successive proposed 5 metre increase in the dam height.

The majority, however has permitted the construction of dam to be continued. But it has recognized the possibility of environmental lapses by directing that the Government of India at each stage of the construction of the dam will give environmental clearance before further construction beyond 90 mtrs. can be undertaken. The majority has also directed that further raising of height beyond 90 metres will be only pari passu with the R & R Relief and Rehabilitation (R & R) and on the clearance by (R & R) Sub Group which it will give after consulting the three Grievance Redressal Authorities.

The majority, while accepting the legal position that the International Treaties and Covenants can be read into the domestic laws of the country, has nevertheless permitted further construction notwithstanding the categorical assertion by the Chief Minister (MP), even after the judgement, that he has no land for oustees. As a matter of fact, the oustees of Bargi Dam (near Jabalpur) built years back have not yet been properly rehabilitated because of non availability of land in M.P. Such a situation is violative of the guidelines laid down in UN Comprehensive Guidelines, 1997, which mandates that "all persons, groups, and communities have the right to suitable resettlement which includes the right to alternative land and housing which is safe, secure available and habitable"

Though this judgment may apparently seem a setback of N.B.A. and its supporters, but they need not throw up their hands and become demoralized. A direction of the Court that the further raising of the height be made on getting clearance from all authorities including the Grievance Redressal Authority which are headed by former Chief Justice will enable the organizers to keep this issue alive and also in the meanwhile to sensitize public opinion and political parties to the human suffering and to compel the Government of India to have an impartial examination of the issue. This is not a partisan issue but a Human Right issue, and must be seen in that context.

The direction by the majority that in case of disputes matter will be decided by Prime Minister whose decision will be binding and final raises an important jurisprudential issue. Directions by the Court can be given to statutory bodies or the Grievance authority, a body created by the Court itself. But by a Court order to provide for reference to Prime Minister in his individual capacity and which will pre-empt the rights of the parties to seek remedy according to law, is to say with respect, rather unusual. This direction might also embarrass the Prime Minister, who understandably may wish to keep away from this dispute in which different states have conflicting perceptions, and also belong to rival political parties, and any such involvement by him could become a political issue, and introduce unnecessary complexities in the issue which are already complicated enough.

5.4 The Sub-Commission on Prevention of Discrimination and Protection of Minorities

Welcoming the analysis of the situation with respect to the right to adequate housing contained in the progress report of the Special Rapporteur on the realization of economic, social and cultural rights (E/CN.4/Sub.2/1990/19).

Welcoming also the increased attention paid to this right by the committee on Economic, Social and Cultural Rights, at its 1990 sessions and the recently adopted revised guidelines regarding the form and contents of reports to be submitted by States parties under articles 16 and 17 of the International Covenant on Economic, Social and Cultural Rights (see E/1991/23), which now much more effectively address the issue of the right to adequate housing.

Deeply concerned that over one billion people do not enjoy their right to adequate housing and that in many states the number of homeless and inadequately housed people is increasing.

Considering that in spite of the numerous international instruments including the Universal Declaration of Human Rights and the Covenant on Economic, Social and Cultural Rights. Virtually no analytical work has been carried out on the right to adequate housing by United Nations human rights bodies.

Concerned that both the obligations and the entitlements

inherent in the right to adequate housing remain unclear and unspecified in terms of the law.

Recalling General Assembly resolutions 41/146/ of 4 December 1986 and 42/146 of 7 December 1987. Economic and Social Council resolutions 1986/41 of 23 May 1986 and 1987/62 of 29 May 1987, and commission on Human Rights resolution 1986/36 of 12 March 1986, 1987/22 of 10 March 1987 and 1988/24 of 7 March 1988, each entitled "Realization of the right to adequate housing".

Considering that the Committee on Economic, Social and Cultural Rights, at its fourth session, expressly stated that housing rights could be subject to violation, especially in the context of evictions (E/1990/23, para. 285 (i)).

Aware that no State can claim to have fully realized the right to adequate housing for all its inhabitants.

Recognizing that non-government and community-based organizations have made a useful contribution in the field of housing rights.

Aware of the many national and local campaigns for housing rights in countries throughout the world.

Convinced that it can play a useful and constructive role in promoting the recognition of the right to adequate housing.

1. Affirms the need for additional human rights activities leading towards the full realization of the right to adequate housing for everyone:
2. Urges all States to pursue effective policies and adopt legislation aimed at ensuring the realization of the right to adequate housing of the entire population, concentrating on those currently homeless or inadequately housed:
3. Requests the United Nations Centre for Human Rights to compile and publish a "Human rights fact sheet" on the right to adequate housing;
4. Entrusts with producing, without financial implications, a working paper on the right to adequate housing, with a view to determining how best to further both the recognition and the enforcement of this right;
5. Requests to examine, in the working paper, the utility

of adopting an international declaration or convention on the right to adequate housing, and also to examine the specific contents of this right.

6. Encourages to consult and use the widest possible variety of sources in the preparation of this working paper, in particular non-governmental organizations working in the area, including those currently not in consultative status with the Economic and Social Council;
7. Requests to submit the working paper to the Sub Commission, at its forty-fourth session, for its examination of, inter alia, how most effectively to proceed on issues concerning the human right to adequate housing.

6

Human Rights, Individual Liberty and Poto

6.1 A Necessary for Civilised and Human Existence

Overwhelmed by the misery and the almost total rout of all civilized and humane existence both within and inter nations, the General Assembly of the United Nations in recognition of the inherent dignity of the individual proclaimed the Universal Declaration of Human Rights (U.D.H.R.) on 10.12.1948. This document is a foundation which emphasized the place of human rights as being essential for the development of individual and society. Article 19 of the declaration mandates that every one has the right of freedom of opinion and expression; *and to receive and impart information and ideas through any media* (emphasis supplied).

A step towards concretising of these human rights was effected when the United Nations Assembly on 16th Dec. 1966 unanimously adopted the International Covenant on Economic, Social and Cultural Rights (I.C.C.P.R.) and the International Covenant on Civil and Political Rights and the Optional protocol to the latter. Article 19 (2) of I.C.C.P.R. highlighted similarly the right of a citizen to receive information through any media of his choice.

Our founding fathers and mothers who framed the Constitution showed similar concern by incorporating Article 19 (1) of the Constitution which guarantees to all citizens the right to freedom of speech and expression. Though formally the right of free press was not mentioned in Article 19 (1) (a) ther has never been any doubt that the freedom of the press is comprehended within the right of freedom of speech guaranteed under Article 19 (1) (a) and it has been so emphasised by various Supreme Court Judgements which have said that the freedom of press is the foundation of the free Government and the free people.

During the period of cold war human rights unfortunately became a political football being used by the Western and the Eastern block. To impartial observers it was a painful sight to watch the ringing declaration of (U.D.H.R.) being used in arena of the World diplomacy by various governments helped regretfully be their own media by purporting to pose an artificial choice between political or Economic rights or Bread versus Freedom. Fortunately this myth of conflict was exploded when representatives of 171 states adopted by consent Vienna Declaration and Programme Action at the World Conference on Human Rights (1993) and emphasised that the UDHR which constitutes the common standard of achievement for all people in all nations is the source of inspiration. The Vienna Declaration affirmed that human rights are the birth rights of all human beings and their protection and promotion is the first responsibility of the government and that all human rights are universal, indivisible, and interrelated.

The Vienna Declaration rightly recognised role of the press as emphasised in para 39 as under :-

> "Underlining the importance of objective, responsible and impartial information about human rights, and human itarian issues, the World Conference on Human Rights encourages the increased involvement of the media, for whom freedom and protection should be guaranteed within the framework of national law".

The role of Indian Press in the earlier period in the matter of safeguarding human is a mixed one. Though individual cases of police excesses of the poor, slum dwellers were no doubt reported, but not in the context of human right violation, but as an individual police official's aberration. This attitude was disappointingly reflected in the passive, even more as negative role the media played when dealing with the working of Terrorists and Destructive Activities Act (TADA).

The said Act was brought in force in 1987 originally for 4 years and continued to be extended (though now repealed), notwithstanding that it violated seriously one of the most prized human right of an accused, namely, that the court will not entertain evidence of anonymous witness, and even when denial of opportunity to cross examine that witness had been held by European Court to Human Rights as a denial of the right to a fair trial. The press instead of lambasting and exposing inertia of the Member of Parliament who, showed almost no concern as is clear from the fact that from 1985 to 1993 the discussion in Parliament varied between one hour and ten minutes in 1993 to maximum eight hours in 1985 and participation of the MPs varied from 8 MPs to maximum 34. Nor did the Media emphasise the gross misuses of TADA which was evident in that detentions in Punjab were 14,451 while 14,049 were detained in a recognizable peaceful State, Gujarat and in the later it was used against tribals, trade unionist, and students activists. Here, the media, one has to regretfully say, failed the nation. It however woke up later when a young famous filmstar of Bombay was detained under TADA (totally illegal and motivated act), possibly because it was a story appealing to millions of film fans — here the commercial interest won: the media had forgotten the warning of Philosopher Solon of Athens, who asked how men could most effectively be delivered from committing injustice replied "If those who are not injured feel as much indignation as those who are".

Government conveniently invoke the sensitive ground of national security to silence the media from reporting Human Right violations in affected area. Unfortunately the media by and large have a tendency to accept this gratuitous advice without much demur. But this yielding is totally counter to the spirit and the confidence with which our constitution gave the free press the protection it needed to fulfill its essential role in our democracy. Our media needs to bear the caution given by U.S. Supreme Court in well known case of *New York Times* in "Pentagon papers" where it said about first amendment, which guarantees free press. "The word "security" is a broad, vague generality whose contours should not be invoked to abrogate the fundamental law embodied in the First Amendment. The guarding of military and diplomatic secrets at the expense of informed representative government provides no real security for our Republic ... For this reason, it is perhaps here that a press that is alert, aware, and free most vitally serves the basic purpose of the First Amendment. For without an informed and free press there cannot be an enlightened people".

A good percentage of press has also gone along with the vicious propaganda by the Executive that Human Right organizations, are more concerned with the rights of terrorists, rather than of victims of terrorism. This is a untrue, considering that established Human Right bodies have unequivocally condemned the killings and taking of hostages by terrorists, whether in J & K or North East. The painful part is that even while publishing the statements of the N.G.Os, condemning the killings by terrorists of Sanjay Ghosh, a Human Right activist in Assam, the prejudice against Human Right organization continues to persist in the media.

India has ratified the Convention on the Rights of child though after a delay of years. Abolition of child labour mandated by it did not get the backing from the majority of the media which bought the untenable suggestion that abolition of child labour could pose problem for the poor. Media needs to remedy its remissness and launch a crusade against this evil which span on a conservative estimate 20 to 30 million child labour.

Admittedly women face discrimination and marginalization in subtle as well as in flagrant ways. Women constitute 70 per cent of the world's poor. The media needs to take seriously the lament of platform for action adopted by Fourth World Conference of Women held at Beijing, China (1995), wherein it pulled up media by pointing out that "the lack of gender sensitivity in the media is evidenced by the failure to eliminate the gender based stereotyping that can be found in public and private local, national and international media organizations".

Taking into account the ground reality that in a developing like ours where the impact of public opinion is weak and the manoeuvering by the politician - criminal bureaucracy nexus continues to be a very strong, both the media and the NGOs have a common stake in preservation of human rights.

I believed strongly that just as Human Rights cannot be safeguarded unless there is a free press, and a strong public opinion reflected by NGOs be a free press, NGO feeling if human rights of the majority continue to be violated, because then there will be no democracy and which alone is a condition precedent to preserving both.

6.2 Why Security at the Cost of Freedom POTO and Media

When a joint session of Parliament passed the Prevention of Terrorism Ordinance (POTO), the government did not win; nor was the Opposition defeated — it was the nation which lost temporarily, the battle for civil liberties. But the BJP seemed to be riding a high horse. It was sue of its numbers in the joint session and presumably also keen to obtain approval from the US State Department (as its spokesperson has publicly stated) — the patronising comments come all from the USA which is a strong ally of Israeli terrorism in the current Israeli-Palestine conflict surely irony will not be lost on the public.

Considering that the entire Opposition had shown rare unanimous opposition, it would have been an act of grace and correct parliamentary convention if the government had withdrawn this controversial Bill. After all, the supposed justification of fighting terrorism is not a partisan programme, the Central government cannot claim to have a monopoly of patriotism — such self-patting will hardly pass muster. The whole purpose of such a law gets defeated when the Congress governments in the majority of states vehemently deny the need for it (of course, there is an element of false bluster because Madhya Pradesh and Maharashtra have a law similar to POTO). Such is the partisanship that the Congress-ruled Maharashtra has even taken the embarrassment of withdrawing the POTO case against Afroz, whose arrest had been trotted by the government as the height of efficiency of the state police and even a foreign government had been warned of a plot that Afroz was said to be engaged in—boowing up the House of Commons (UK). Now that the government says that POTO should not have been applied—the result is that in the one-upmanship game between the Centre and the Maharashtra government, the credibility and efficiency of Indian investigating agencies has taken a dip.

The apparent urgency to pass POTO, attributed by Mr. L.K. Advani to the compulsion of Resolution No. 1373 (2001) passed by the Security Council is misplaced.

The Central government's invocation of the USA Patriot Act is inapposite. It applies to non-citizens. "This law is based on the faulty assumption that safety must come at the expense of civil liberties," says the ACLU's Washington National Council for Civil Liberties. It adds: "The anti-terrorism laws in this country have led to some of the worst human rights abuses in this country over the last 30 years, contributed to miscarriages of justice".

POTO is modelled on TADA, which remained in force from 1987 to 1995, and yet militancy remained at the highest in the country. Even the government concedes that acts of terrorism have come down in the last half a decade.

The apprehension of misuse of POTA has a strong basis considering the history of its predecessor TADA. The Supreme Court, while reluctantly upholding TADA ,was constrained to observe: "It is heart-rending to note that day in and day out we come across with the news of blood-curdling incidents of police brutality and atrocities, alleged to have been committed in utter disregard and in all breaches of humanitarian law and universal human rights as well as in total negation of the constitutional guarantees and human decency..."

How with the ancestry could anyone assure that POTA will not be misused — this boast has been belied even before the ink has dried on this legislation. Witness the Gujarat government shamelessly making partisan arrests under POTA of minorities, when, according to all credible reports, they have suffered the maximum; also the National Conference hypocritically abstaining in the Rajya Sabha but soon thereafter arresting Yasin Malik, a JKLF leader, with the sole purpose of muddying a Kashmir settlement and sabotaging chances of holding peaceful and free forthcoming Kashmir elections.

A confession made before the police is made admissible under Section 32 of POTA even when two out of the five Judges of the

Supreme Court had described a similar provisions of Section 15 of TADA is "unfair, unjust and unconstitutional, offending Articles 14 and 21 of the Constitution."

One of the most objectionable features in Section 30 of the Act, which empowers the court to issue directions that the identity of witnesses be not disclosed to the accused. This would mean that the right of the accused to show his innocence through a cross-examination of the witness will be denied. Dr. Ambedkar, the father of the Indian Constitution, could not even contemplate such a situation and said that it was not necessary to have a provision specifically providing for cross examination because such a right cannot be taken away "unless the provincial government goes absolutely stark mad..." This provision is also a denial of fair trial. All regional and international human right instruments recognised the right of fair trial to the accused.

The question whether evidence of anonymous witnesses denies the accused a right to fair trial has been answered in the affirmative by the European Court of Human Rights, which said: "Being unaware of (the witnesses) identity, the defence was confronted with an almost insurmountable handicap : it was deprived of the necessary information permitting it to test the witnesses credibility or cast doubt on this credibility". The court held that a domestic court may not rely on the evidence obtained from anonymous sources whom the defendant has not had the opportunity to challenge.

Section 48 of the Act dealing with bail is a serious inroad on liberty of the citizen. Thus, the reversal of burden of proof for bail for a period of one year and before the filing of a charge-sheet is contrary to a basic principle of cirminal jurisprudence, apart from the unfair requirement that the accused should prove that he is not guilty.

Section 18 of POTA empowers the government to declare an organisation as a terrorist organisation. Significantly, this provision has been included against the recommendation of the Law Commission, which had categorically stated that "we have not suggested herein any amendments providing for banning of unlawful organisations and for confiscation of their assets in as much as there is already an enactment of force viz, the Unlawful

Activities (Prevention) Act, which deals with the said aspects". Thus Section 18 is not innocent but has a mischievous intent.

The government efforts to mollify the Press by purporting to delete Section 3 (8), is eyewash because as journalist will still continue to be covered by Section 14 of the Act.

Meeting the challenge of terrorism requires determination, proper utilisation of intelligence information and support of the public and not these draconian laws, violating the human rights of citizens.

The loud noise that POTA, even if it denies civil rights, is necessary for protecting freedom can be dismissed in the words of Mr. Muggeridge, a former Editor of *Punch*, when he warned: "The choice for us is between security and freedom. And if we ever ceased to prefer the later, we should soon find that we had nothing of any worth left to secure anyway".

Any government shaky about its credibility has to conjure up a sense of panic in order to survive. That alone can explain the BJP government rushing through with POTA in spite of its universal condemnation.

Over whelmed by the misery and the almost total rout of all civilised and humane existence in various nations, the General Assembly of the United Nations proclaimed the Universal Declaration of Human Rights (UDHR) on December 10, 1984 in recognition of the inherent dignity of the individual. This document is a foundation which emphasised the place of human rights as being essential for the development of the individual and society. Article 19 of the declaration mandates that everyone has the right of freedom of opinion and expression: and *to receive and impart information and ideas through any media* (emphasis added).

A step towards concretising these human rights was taken when the U.N. Assembly on December 16, 1966 unanimously adopted the International Covenant on Economic, Social and Cultural Rights (ICCPR) and the International Covenant on Civil and Political Rights and the Optional Protocol to the latter. Article 19 (2) of ICCPR highlighted similarly the right of a citizen to receive information through any media of his choice.

Our Constitution makers showed similar concern by incorporating Article 19 (1) (a) which guarantees to all citizens the right to freedom of speech and expression. Though the right of free press was not formally mentioned in the Article, there has never been any doubt that press freedom is comprehended within the right of freedom of speech guaranteed under the Article and it has been so emphasised by various Supreme Court judgments.

During the Cold War, human rights unfortunately became a political football used by the Western and Eastern blocs. It was painful for impartial observers to watch the ringing declaration of the UDHR being used in the arena of world diplomacy by various governments helped regretfully by their own media purporting to pose a artificial choice between political and economic rights or bread versus freedom. Fortunately, this myth of conflict was exploded when representatives of 171 states adopted by consent the Vienna Declaration and Programme Action at the World Conference on Human Rights (1993) and emphasised that the UDHR, which constitutes the common standard of achievement for all people in all nations, was the source of inspiration. The Vienna Declaration affirmed that human right were the birthrights of all human beings and their protection and promotion was the first responsibility of governments and that all human rights were universal. indivisible and interrelated.

The Vienna Declaration rightly recognised the role of the press as emphasised in para 39: "Underlining the importance of objective, responsible and impartial information about human rights, and humanitarian issues, the World Conference of Human Rights encourages the increased involvement of the media, for whom freedom and protection should be guaranteed within the framework of national law".

The role of the Indian press earlier in safeguarding human rights is a mixed one. Individual cases of police excesses against the poor, slum-dwellers were reported, as an individual police official's aberration, but not in the context of human rights violation. This attitude was disappointingly reflected in the passive, even negative, role the media played when dealing with the working of the Terrorist and Disruptive Activities (Prevention)

Act.

The Act — now repealed — was brought into force in 1987 originally for four years and continued to be extended, notwithstanding the fact that it seriously violated one of the most prized human rights of an accused, namely, that the court would not entertain the evidence of anonymous witnesses, and even when the denial of opportunity to cross-examine those witnesses had been held by the European Court of Human Rights denial of the right to a fair trial. The press did not expose the inertia of the members of Parliament who showed almost no concern for human rights — as is clear from the fact that the duration of Parliamentary discussions varied between one hour and 10 minutes in 1993 and a maximum of eight hours in 1985 and that the participation of the number of MPs varied from eight to a maximum of 34. Nor did the media emphases the gross misuse of the TADA Act which was evident from the largescale detentions in Punjab (14,451), while 14,049 persons were detained in a recognisably peaceful State Gujarat. Where it was used against tribals, trade unionists and student activitist. Here, the media regrettably failed the nation.

It however, woke up later when a famous young filmstar of Mumbai was detained under the TADA Act (a totally illegal and motivated act). Possibly because it was a story appealing to millions of film fans — here the commercial interest won: the media had forgotten the warning of philosopher Solon of Athens. Asked how people could most effectively be delivered from committing injustice, he said, "If those who are not injured feel as much indignation as those who are".

Governments conveniently invoke the sensitive ground of national security to silence the media from reporting human rights violations in affected areas. Unfortunately, the media, by and large has a tendency to accept this gratuitous advice without much demur. But this kind of yielding is totally counter to the spirit and confidence with which our Constitution gave the free press the protection it needed to fulfil its essential democratic role. The media needs to bear in kind the caution given by U.S. Supreme Court in the well-known case of *The New York Times* in "Pentagon papers" where it said about the First Amendment, which guarantees free press. "The word 'security' is a broad, vague generally whose contours should not be invoked to abrogate the fundamental law embodied in the First Amendment. The guarding of military and diplomatic secrets at the expense of informed representative government provides no real security for our Republic... For this reason, it is perhaps here that a press that is alert, aware and free most vitally serves the basic purpose of the First Amendment. For without an informed and free press there cannot be an enlightened people."

A good percentage of the press has also gone along with the vicious executive propaganda that human rights organisations are concerned with the rights of terrorist rather than that of the victims of terrorism. This is untrue, considering that established human rights bodies have unequivocally condemned the killing and taking of hostages by terrorist. Whether in Jammu and Kashmir or the northeast. The painful part is that even while the statements by the NGOs condemning the killing by terrorists of Sanjoy Ghosh, a human rights activist in Assam, were published, the prejudice against the human rights organisations continues to persist in the media.

India has ratified the Convention on the Rights of Child though after a delay of years. The abolition of child labour mandated by it did not get the backing of a majority of the media which made the untenable suggestion that the abolition could pose a problem for the poor. The media needs to remedy its remissness and launch a crusade against this evil which spans 20 million to 30 million child labourers.

Admittedly, women face discrimination and marginalisation in subtle as well as flagrant ways. They constitute 70 per cent of the world's poor. The media needs to take seriously the lament of the platform for action adopted by the Fourth World Conference of Women held in Beijing (1995), wherein it pulled up the media, pointing out that "the lack of gender sensitivity in the media is evidenced by the failure to eliminate the gender-based stereotyping that can be found in public and private local national and international media organisations".

Taking into account the ground reality that in a developing country like ours where the impact of public opinion is weak and the manoeuvring by the politician-criminal-bureaucracy nexus continues to be strong, both the media and the NGOs have a common stake in the preservation of human rights.

The media, I have no doubt, will pay extra attention to the betterment of the conditions of the people and the safeguarding of the human rights of the 40 per cent of people who are below the poverty line.

It is a truism that just as human rights cannot be safeguarded unless there is a free press, there cannot be a free press, if the human rights of the majority of the people continue to be violated, because then there will be no democracy which alone is a condition precedent to preserving both.

6.3 A Sad Day—POTO becomes POTA

When joint session of Parliament passed Prevention of Terrorism Ordinance (POTO) the government did not win; nor was the opposition defeated — it was the nation which lost temporarily the battle for civil liberties. But BJP seems to have been riding a high horse and sure of its numbers in joint session and presumably also keen to obtain approval from U.S. State department (as its spokes person has publically given) - the patronizing comments come ill from USA which is a strong ally of Israeli terrorism in the current Israeli-Palestine conflictingly the irony will not be lost on the public.

I feel considering that entire opposition had shown rare unanimous opposition it would have been act of grace and correct Parliamentary convention if government had withdrawn this controversial Bill. After all the supposed justification to fight terrorism is not a partisan programme, Central Government can not claim to have a monopoly of patriotism - such self patting will hardly pass muster. The whole purpose of such a law gets defeated when the Congress government in the majority of States vehemently deny the need of it (of course there is an element of false bluster because Madhya Pradesh and Maharashtra have a law similar to POTO. Such is the partisanship that Congress ruled Maharashtra Government has even taken the embarrassment of withdrawing POTO case against Afroz, whose arrest had been trotted by Government as the height of efficiency of State police and even foreign government had been warned of plot that Afroz was said to be engaged in blowing up House of Commons (UK). Now that Government says that POTO should not have been applied — the result is that in one up man game between Centre and Maharashtra Government the credibility and efficiency of Indian investigating agencies has taken a low dip.

The apparent urgency to pass POTA given out by Mr. Advani was to the compulsion of Resolution No. 1373 (2001) passed by Security Council is misplaced.

Central Government invocation of USA Patriot Act is inapposite. It applies to non-citizens. "This law is based on the faulty assumption that safety must come at the expense of civil liberties", is the criticism by ACLU's Washington National Office.

British Anti-Terrorist Act has also been vehemently criticized by Briitsh National Council for Civil Liberties thus "the anti-terrorism laws in this country have led to some of the worst human rights abuses in this country over the last 30 years, contributed to miscarriages of justice".

POTO is modelled on TADA, which remained in force from 1987 to 1995, and yet militancy remained at the highest in the country. Even government concedes that Terrorists Acts have come down in the last half a decade.

That the apprehension of misuse of POTO has strong basis considering the history of its predecessor TADA. The Supreme court which while reluctantly upholding TADA was constrained to observe "is heart-rending to note that day in and day out we come across with the news of blood-curdling incidents of police brutality and atrocities, alleged to have been committed, in utter disregard and in all breaches of humanitarian law and universal human rights as well as in total negation of the eonstitutional guarantees and human decency.."

How with this ancestry could anyone assure that POTA will not be misused — this boast has been belied even before ink has dried on this legislation — witness Gujarat government shamelessly making partisan arrest under POTA of minorities when by all credible reports, they have suffered the maximum; also the National Conference hypocritically abstaining in Rajya Sabha but soon thereafter arresting Yasin Malik JKLF leader with sole purpose to muddy the chances of Kashmir settlement and sabotaging chances of holding peaceful free forthcoming Kashmir elections.

The confession made before the police is made admissible, under Section 32 of POTA even when two out of 5 Judges of the Supreme Court had described a similar provisions of Section 15 of the TADA as "unfair, unjust and unconstitutional offending Articles 14 and 21 of the Constitution."

One of the most objectionable features is Section 30 of the Act which empowers the Court to issue directions that the identity of witnesses be not disclosed to the accused. This would mean that the right of the accused to show his innocence through cross-examination of the witness will be denied. Dr. Ambedkar the father of Indian Constitution could not even contemplate such a situation and said that it is not necessary to have a provision specifically providing for cross-examination because such a right cannot be taken away "Unless the provincial Government goes absolutely stark mad...defending includes cross-examination." This provision is also a denial of fair trial reorganized by all regional and international human right instruments which recognize the right of fair trial to the accused.

The question whether evidence of anonymous witnesses denies accused a right to a fair trial has been answered in the affirmative by the European Court of Human Right, which said "Being unaware of (the witnesses) identity, the defence was confronted with an almost insurmountable handicap: it was deprived of the necessary information permitting it to test the witnesses credibility or cast doubt on their credibility". The court held that that a domestic Court may not rely on the evidence obtained from anonymous sources whom the defendant has not the opportunity to challenge.

Section 48 of Act dealing with bail is a serious inroad on liberty of the citizen. Thus the reversal of burden of proof for a period of one year and before filing of charge-sheet is contrary to a basic principle of criminal jurisprudence, apart from the unfair requirement from the accused to perform the impossible task of proving at that stage that he is not guilty.

Section 18 of POTO empowers the Government to declare an organization as a terrorist organization. Significantly its provision has been included against the recommendation of Law Commission which had categorically stated that "we have not suggested herein any amendments providing for banning of unlawful organizations and for confiscation of their assets in as much has there is already an enactment in force viz, the Unlawful Activities (Prevention) Act which deals with the said aspects". Thus section 18 is not innocent but with mischievous intent.

Governments efforts to mollify Press by purporting to delete Section 3 (8), is an eyewash, because as Section 14 is continued, journalists would still continue to be covered by the Act.

Meeting the challenge of Terrorism requires determination, proper utilization of intelligence information and support of public and not these draconian laws violating the human rights of citizens.

Loud Noise that POTO even if it denies civil rights is necessary for protecting freedom can be dismissed in the words of Mr. Muggeridge, former Editor of *Punch* (UK) when he warned — "the choice for us is between security and freedom. And if we ever ceased to prefer the later, we should soon find that we had nothing of any worth left to secure anyway".

Any government shaky about its credibility has to conjure up a sense of panic in order to survive-that alone can explain B.J.P. Government rushing through with POTA, in spite of universal condemnation.

6.4 POTO will not Curb Terrorism

December 13 seemed to have changed the mindset of even the most rational. It was expected that considering the total opposition to the Prevention of Terrorist Ordinance which was promulgated on October 24, 2001, the government will allow it to lapse. Surprisingly, the Central government has re-promulgated it and built up such a panic patriotic forever that the opposition to what is now termed as Poto-2 seems to have taken a back seat.

Political cynicism alone could explain the unboundedness of the BJP-dominated government in promulgating *Poto*, which is modelled on the Terrorists and Disruptive Activities (Preventive) Act enacted in 1987 by the Congress. In fact, the BJP had protested in 1994 stating that "the Act granted powers to the Executive that were bound to be misued; political parties have been targeted by the States which have tended to misuse the law. *Tada* should be reviewed drastically, if not completely withdrawn."

The inefficacy of *Tada* was exposed when of the 76,000 arrests, the conviction rate never exceeded 0.41 per cent. The largest arrests were from Gujarat and not Punjab or the North-east which apparently were the reasons for existence of *Tada*.

Tada was challenged by the People's Union of Civil Liberties in the Supreme Court. Though its validity was upheld (1994), the Court lamented: "It is heartrending to note that day in and day out we come across news of blood curdling incidents of police brutality and atrocities alleged to have been committed in utter disregard and in all breaches of humanitarian law and universal human rights as well as in total negation of the constitutional guarantees and human decency..." The hollowness of *Tada* effectuation is shown by the fact that even assassins of Rajiv Gandhi were not convicted under the Act but under section 302 of the Indian Penal Code. The Supreme Court held that the assassination was not an act of terrorism. But it used the confession to a police officer recorded under, *Tada* as evidence under Section 302, which is inadmissible under the Evidence Act, by a reasoning which is considered to be faulty by legal pundits.

Under *Poto*, confessions made before the police is made admissible under Section 32 even when two of the five Judges of the Supreme Court had described a similar provision of Section 15 of *Tada* as "unfair, unjust and unconscionable, offending Article 14 and 21 of the Constitution". Now Poto-2 still retains the provisions of identity of the witness being withheld even from the accused, notwithstanding the judgment of the Supreme Court to the contrary in *Tada* case that the identity will be disclosed to the accused a little before the examination of the witness so as not to deny his right of cross-examination — a basic requirement for fair trial. Why, even the European Court of Human Rights has ruled that the courts may not rely on the evidence obtained from an anonymous witness.

Poto is also redundant when it is applied to banning of organisations. Section 18 of *Poto* empowers the government to declare an organisation as a terrorist organisation. Significantly, this provisions has been included against the recommendation of the Law Commission which had categorically stated: "We have not suggested herein any amendments providing for banning of unlawful organisations and for confiscation of their assets inasmuch as there is already an enactment in force viz. the Unlawful Activities (Prevention) Act which deals with the said aspects." Thus Section 18 of *Poto* appears to be with a mischievous intent.

Ironically, the People's War Group is an unlawful organisation in Andhra Pradesh but the State government has offered to hold talks with it. Does it not show that the sole aim of the government is to assume draconian power, irrespective of its utility?

There were several instances of terrorist activities in the country since the introduction of Poto, the most audacious one being the December 13 attack on Parliament. This despite being forewarned by the Mumbai police. Ironically, again, the perpertrators of the crime initially booked under various sections of crime Acts before being brought under *Poto*. So, why does one need *Poto* ?

The Central Government invocation of the USA Patriot Act is inapposite. It applies to non-citizens. "This law is based on the faulty assumption that safety must come at the expense of civil liberties", is the criticism.

The British Anti-Terrorist Act has also been vehemently criticised by the British National Council for Civil Liberties which said, "The anti-terrorism laws in this country have led to some of the worst human rights abuses in this country over the last 30 years and contributed to miscarriages of justice."

The National Human Rights Commission has given its firm opinion against *Poto*. It is the considered view for the Commission that all the actions which the government wishes to take are substantially taken care of under the existing laws.

The Opposition, though vociferously objecting to it, unfortunately did not take the simple course of passing the resolution in the Rajya Sabha disapproving it immediately after the Rajya Sabha met in November. Maybe the main opposition, the Congress, was finding itself in an embarrassing situation with the Maharashtra Control of Organised Crime Act, 1999, and the MP Special Areas Security Act, 2000, are as much attacks on the constitutional rights of the citizens just as *Poto.*

As far as journalists are concerned, under Section 14 of the revised Ordinance, they will still be under compulsion to disclose information if asked for by Investigating Officer notwithstanding the omission of Section 3 (8) in the earlier Ordinance.

There seems to be a misplaced impression amongst some well-intentioned persons that to deal with terrorism legality and constitutional compulsions have no place. Such thinking is against the very basics of a democratic republic. That terrorism cannot be wiped out by State terrorism is a truism not open to debate.

The whole exercise of issuing *Poto* is to create a psychological terror so that arbitrary action of the government is slurred over by creating a climate wherein opposition to such action may be considered as anti-national — a cheap stratagem but unlikely to succeed. If the intention of passing the Ordinance is to catch the most wanted terrorists, it certainly will not serve any purpose.

Meeting the challenge of terrorism requires determination, proper utilisation of intelligence information and the support of the public — not these draconian laws. Violating the human rights of citizens.

7

Law and Custodial Torture

7.1 Abolish Death Penalty

For decades notable people, from saints to sociologists, have wrestled with the question of whether the death penalty is consistent with human dignity. The question was raised again in India following last month's sweeping decision of the designated court to sentence 26 of the conspirators in the Rajiv Gandhi assassination case to capital punishment. This judgment now awaits confirmation by the Supreme Court. But it serves as a reminder of the inconsistencies that continue to plague India's stance on capital punishment.

The death penalty was codified as part of the Indian penal code in 1861. It was not until 1931 that this was seriously challenged when a member of the Bihar assembly unsuccessfully sought to introduce a bill seeking abolition.

Support for the death penalty remained strong. In 1946, on the eve of independence, the then Union Home Minister stated that the government did not think it wise to abolish capital punishment. Ten years later, when the government asked the states for their opinion, most expressed support for the death penalty. In its 35th report, produced in 1967, the law commission took the view that capital punishment acts as a deterrent to crime. Curiously, it conceded that statistics did not prove these so called deterrent effects. But it comforted itself by saying that neither could it be said the figures disproved this either.

There was some unease with the death penalty. One consequence was a change in the law in 1955 saying courts no longer had to explain why they had not chosen to pass or award a sentence of death. A further reform came in 1973 which provided that in case of a death sentence, special reasons for such a sentence had to be given.

The Supreme Court traditionally has not questioned death sentences. In *Jagmohan Singh* in 1973 it agree with the law commission that capital punishment should be retained.

But subsequent cases like *Ediga Anamma* in 1974 and *Rajendra Prasad* in 1979 saw dissenting voices being raised in the apex court . These led to a hearing by the constitutional bench in the case of *Bachan Singh* in 1980. The bench concluded by a four to one vote that the death penalty did not violate articles 14 or 21 of the Constitution. It was apparently influenced by the statistics provided by the government showing a rising graph of violent crime, particularly murder, armed robbery and dacoity. It was also influenced by the fact that there had been four attempts to abolish capital punishment since independence—in 1949, 1958, 1961 and 1978—but none had won over either public opinion or the legistatures.

However, the constitutional bench emphasized that the scope and concept of mitigating factors in cases involving capital punishment must receive a liberal and expansive construction by the courts. It warned judges not to be bloodthirsty. It ruled that the death penalty should not be imposed, save in the "rarest of rare cases", when the alternative remedy is unquestionably foreclosed.

However, liberal judges continued to find new grounds for not imposing the death penalty. One justification was developed in the 1983 case *Valtheeswaran* where two judges of the Supreme Court held that if a convict sentenced to death had to wait for more than two years for the execution of the penalty he or she could invoke Article 21 and demand the death sentence be quashed. This view was not taken in later case the same year where a three judge bench argued that delay alone was not good enough reason to commute a death sentence. But in 1985 a court took the view that if a person had been in jail for a period of two years and nine months with the sentence of death weighing on his mind this entitled him to having his sentence commuted to life imprisonment.

These differing judicial interpretations led to another, five judge constitutional bench being convened. In 1989 in *Trivenben*, this bench unanimously upheld the *Bachan Singh* judgment and held the death penalty to be constitutional. It struck down the contention that the suffering a condemned person experienced because of delay should be taken into count from the date of the trial court's judgment. It held that the delay could only be counted from the day the Supreme Court's judgment is pronounced. In other words when the judicial process came to an end. The court added that the time consumed by repeated mercy petitions at the instance of the convicted person should not be considered delay.

But again the judiciary found it hard to stick to a line on executions. The Supreme Court in April 1991 reduced the death sentence that it had confirmed in the 1988 *Daya Singh* case — the murderer of the Punjab chief minister, Pratap Singh Kairon — to life imprisonment because of delay. Strangely, this was done without any examination of the causes of the delay in Daya Singh's execution, apparently in defiance of the 1989 decision.

A different reaction was visible in *Dhananjoy* in 1994 when an 18 year old girl was raped and murdered by a security guard. This seemed to have so shocked the Supreme Court that the case fulfilled the rarest of rare condition and confirmed the death penalty. It argued courts must reflect public abhorrence of crime, that when courts impose sentences they must not only keep in mind the rights of criminals but also the right of victims of crime and society at large.

This cacophony of differing judicial views is bound to continue so long as the death penalty remains on the statute book. Each judge, it seems, reaches for his won interpretation of the retributive or reformative aspect of criminal punishment.

Ironically, after the rarest of rare doctrine was propounded in 1980 there was an increase in the percentage of cases in which the death penalty was confirmed by the apex court. In the decade 1970-80, the Supreme Court confirmed 37.7 per cent of death penalties. In the following decade, this figure increased to 40 per cent. Similar figures exist for High Court confirmations. In the decade ending in 1980, death sentences were confirmed in 59 per cent of cases. The following decade this rose to 65 per cent This has strengthened the case of those who complain about the vagaries and uncertainties of judicial thinking.

Amnesty International, a strong opponent of the death penalty worldwide, cites the Baldus report prepared in the United States to argue capital punishment is socially oppressive. It found that if a homicide victim was white, his or her killer was four times more likely to get the death sentence than if the victim were black.

The death penalty was abolished in the United Kingdom in 1965. At present 35 countries have abolished the death penalty for all crimes. About 18 countries have abolished capital punishment for all but exceptional circumstances such as wartime crimes. Twenty-seven countries no longer carry out executions.

In effect, 40 per cent of the countries of the world have abolished the death penalty in law or practice.

A survey conducted by the United Nations in 1988 concluded that research has failed to provide any evidence that executions have a greater deterrent effect than life imprisonment. It cannot be disputed that the outcome of any trial demands to a fairly large extent on the quality of legal advice that the accused receives. This loads the scales in favour of the rich who find it easier to avoid the death penalty than the poor. The arbitrariness, sometimes approaching freakishness, of the sentencing mechanism in India persuades one to agree that retaining the death penalty is less justice than a violation of human rights.

7.2 Human Rights and the Police

It is a common perception that human right violations will continue to persist as long as there are no significant police reforms. But tho Deputy Prime Minister and Home Minister, L.K. Advani, proclaimed without embarrassment at the seminar organised by a human rights organisation in New Delhi on October 4 that his "Government had the political will to bring police reforms but in a different perspective from that of human rights activists". Mr. Advani rebuked the activists: "For you it is important from the point of view of human rights. For me it is important from the point of governance."

Now this assumption of Mr. Advani that human rights are antithetical to governance is a dangerous mind set in a society governed by rule of law, apart from being legally and sociologically flawed. Failure to protect human rights is the surest index of poor governance. One of the most urgent measures to protect human rights is to effectuate police reforms. But Mr. Advani's concept of police reforms would bode ill for human rights because he went out of his way to warn that if the police were reformed from a human rights perspective "then there is resistance from within". "The tendency to put the police in the dock is not fair." This approach of Mr. Advani is undemocratic. It is no that the people are prejudiced against the police. It is their lawless behaviour that angers the people of India.It is unfortunate that Mr. Advani should think that good governance demands a lukewarm response to human rights. If that view prevails it would be a tragedy because good governance anywhere is judged by one universal rule - how much is it able to promote human rights. But then Mr. Advani's approach fits in with his divisive agenda, which requires total police connivance like we are witnessing in Gujarat under Narendra Modi.

Terrorism has never been curbed by state terrorism, (the latter is never permissible both under our Constitution and international human rights law) but only by public opinion turning against the senseless killings, rapes, and extortion by terrorists.

It is legally unacceptable for any state or official to assert that the victims must suffer in silence human rights violations by state agencies on the specious ground that it will demoralise the latter. On the contrary, it must be emphasised that if we are to have real peace, there must be double guarantee of no violations, either by the state agencies or by terrorists.

In this connection the observations of Britain's Secretary for Northern Ireland (in 1990) are worth recalling: "Our adherence to the rule of law, in the face of the most atrocious provocation, sustains our civilisation... It is one of the terrorists' main objectives.... to provoke the authorities to measures that will be judged oppressive and cause us to lose the confidence and support of the community at large...."

The inter-American Court of Human Rights has affirmed the obligation of the state concerned to investigate, prosecute and punish crimes against humanity. A consequence of that state obligation is the concomitant legitimate expectation (if not a right) on the part of the victim to see justice done.

In India, the public has lost faith in Governments of different political hues as reforms have not been undertaken because that would mean placing the police outside the cloths of the politicians who will then not be able to use them against opponents.

A history of various attempts at police reforms and the fate of the respective commissions will show an inbred resistance among all Governments to embark on real reforms. The Government of India appointed a National Police Commission in 1977 to undertake a review of the entire system. The Commission remained in existence till 1982 and submitted eight comprehensive reports to the Government, containing recommendations covering almost all aspects of police organisation and work. But such was the cloak of secrecy over them that the Peoples Union for Civil Liberties and others had to move the Supreme Court for making the reports public, in the face of the stout resistance from the then Government.

No real action was taken for the next decade and a half till Inderjit Gupta as Union Home Minister in the United Front Government wrote to the State Governments in 1997 expressing his sadness that they had so far not even made any attempt to implement many of the basic and salutary recommendations of the National Police Commission to bring about the required changes in police performance and behaviour pattern. In the note accompanying the letter, Gupta suggested that keeping in view the major aberrations which have crept into the police system and its malfunctioning all over the country, some important recommendations of the National Police Commission need to be implemented urgently at the State level to check any further deterioration in the policing system affecting the lives and liberties of the citizens: (i) constitution of a statutory commission in each State called the State Security Commission; (ii) laying down broad policy guidelines and directions for the performance of preventive tasks and service-oriented functions by the police.

The State Security Commission should have the Minister in charge of Police as Chairman and six more members. Two of these should be from the State Legislature (one from the ruling side and the other from the opposition) and four should be appointed by the Chief Minister, subject to the approval of the State Legislature, from amongst retired High Court Judges, retired senior Government officers and eminent social scientists or academicians.

The National Human Rights Commission (NHRC) had also called for reforms as it felt that "an efficient, honest police force is the principal bulwark of the nation against violations of human rights". And one of measures for this purpose was to provide a statutory tenure of office for the Chief of Police in the State.

Thereafter the Rebeiro Committee was constituted in May 1998. But its recommendations remained in cold storage. Again we have the Padmanabaiah Panel constituted by Government in January 2000. But the same inertia continues.

We have regular seminars in this regard. But somehow the basic point is swept under the carpet—namely, that police reforms are an urgent necessity. If the police are to act as a friend of the public and not an instrument of oppression, they must be rescued from the clutches of politicians by constituting security commissions in the State. But no Government wishes to deny itself the power to use the police for political manipulations. Tolstoy wrote of the hypocritical sympathy expressed by Russian landed gentry for the serfs: "I sit on a moving back, chocking him and making him carry me, and yet assure myself and others that I am very sorry for him and wish to ease his lot by all possible means except by getting off his back". The present rulers are worthy descendants of the Russian aristocracy — let them at least now learn from what happened to the Tsar.

7.3 Death Penalty in USA

For decades sociologists have wrestled with the question whether death penalty is consistent with human dignity. The most formidable challenge to the retention or death penalty is the arbitrariness and freakishness in the sentencing mechanism.

A study has revealed that the awarding of death sentence depends to a considerable extent on the native system and social philosophy of the Judges constituting the bench. It has also been found that death penalty in practice operates in discriminatory manner as it strikes mostly against the poor and deprived sections of the society. Notwithstanding our Supreme Court has upheld it though cautioning that it should be imposed in the rarest or rare cases. But this is too vague and leaves a great margin for judicial adhocism and arbitrariness.

The evil of discrimination in death sentencing is enhanced in societies which have a mixed racial population like U.S.A. where belatant and open racial discrimination dominates the sentencing procedure. This has been admirably brought out in the recent compilation of international commission of Jurists. This report of Mission (June 1996) under the Chairmanship of eminent jurist Mr. F.S. Nariman, is chillingly revealing and hardly complimentary to the working of Criminal jurisprudence in U.S.A.

Thirty-eight of the fifty states of U.S.A. have enacted or re-shaped laws allowing for application of the death penalty to a series of specified crime. Despite the existence of legislative safeguards and prescribed procedures, the Mission has found that, in practice, overwhelming evidence exists in the large majority of cases indicating class and/or racial disparity in the charging, sentencing and imposition of the death penalty. As one knowledgeable elder statement pithily remarked "If you're poor and black. You die". Others, including Judges stated that capital sentencing was unequal and that in their experience, where the social status of the defendant corresponded to that of the members of the jury invariably the death sentence was not imposed.

The Mission encountered no serious refutation of the fact that demand for the death penalty by District Attorneys — and imposition of the death sentence by juries or Judges — on African Americans and other minorities was disproportionate to their percentage among the general population.

As a result, the Racial Justice Act was first introduced in the US Congress in 1988. It sought to give condemned prisoners a federal right to challenge any death sentence that "furthers a racially discriminatory pattern" based on the race of either the defendant or the victim. Though the racial Justice Act has undergone several changes it is not yet enacted into law. A failure to do so constitutes a breach of the US Government's express ratification of the ICCPR and the ICERD — particularly of Articles 6 (1), 6 (2) and Article 26 read with Article 2 of the Political Covenant (ICCPR), and of Articles 2 (1) and 5 (a) of the Race Convention, (ICERD).

The Mission is of the considered opinion that in the absence of a nation-wide law framed on the pattern of the Racial Justice Act, the administration of capital punishment in the United States continues to be discriminatory and unjust — and hence "arbitrary" — and thus not in consonance with Articles 6 and 40 of the Political Covenant and Articles 2 (c) of the Race Convention.

Nariman Report points out that despite legislative elimination of racial segregation and antidiscrimination laws, racism remains a major factor within the United States today. It is most pronounced, with serious consequences, in the criminal justice system. It quotes U.N. Special Rapporteur on Contemporary Forms of Racism, Racial Discrimination, Xenophobia and Related Intolerance who has stated "racial factors affect the judicial process, from the moment of arrest right through to the trial. Here again, the figures speak for themselves. For example, although men of African — American origin make up 6 per cent of the United States population, they represent 44 per cent of prison inmates. It is common knowledge that one out of four black males aged 20 to 29 is either imprison, on parole or on probation ... the various studies and reports which confirmed that racism plays a significant role in death penalty sentencing".

The Mission was also informed that in some cases prosecutors. Wishing to secure a jury that identifies with the victim (primarily white). Will sometimes use peremptory strikes to exclude from the jury those African — Americans who have been selected for the venirement.

Amnesty International (AI) in its publication "When the State Kills" also has come to the same conclusion of arbitrariness and racial discrimination in death sentencing, when it found that black defendants especially in Southern States, have often been convicted by all-white juries after prosecutors have used their powers of peremptory challenge to exclude black prospective jurors.

Decisions leading to an eventual death sentence may be based on factors beyond the circumstance of the crime itself, including financial and community pressures, the race and social status of the offender and victim, and where the crime was committed."

Other horrifying facts mentioned by AI quoting "Baldus Study" shows that white — victim homicides were over four times more likely to result in death sentences than black-victim homicides. Further blacks comprise 12 per cent of the national population but 41 per cent of prisoners under sentence of death. The evidence suggests that race — especially that of the victim — has an important bearing on the likelihood of a death sentence being imposed, particularly in the southern states. Although blacks and whites are the victims of homicide in almost equal numbers, most offenders who are sentenced to death are convicted of murdering whites (86 per cent in 1987). Forty five of the 98 prisoners executed between January 1977 and May 1988 were black or Hispanic, and 84 of the 98 had been convicted of killing white victims.

That racial discrimination continues to play significance role in death sentence has also been commented upon by one of the four dissenting Judges in McCleskey case where the judge lamented that statistics would show that the cases involving black defendants and white victims are more likely to result in a death sentence than cases featuring any other racial combination of defendant and victim..... There was a significant chance that race would play a prominent role in determining if he lived or died.

Mr. Anthony Lewis one of legal commentators in USA has condemned the decision of the USA Supreme Court and as termed it has "effectively condoning the decision of racism in a profound aspect of our law".

With the above unedifying facts of discrimination and denial of impartial justice and racial equality the professions of U.S.A. Government to its commitments to Human Rights and universal brotherhood can hardly carry any conviction.

7.4 Amnesty to Police not Constitutional

The Union Home Minister, Mr. L.K. Advani's announcement to grant amnesty to the security force personnel accused of human rights violations has been received with shock in troubled Kashmir. Described as a "slap on democracy", the move has evoked strong resentment with condemnation from all quarters.

Human rights activist and former Delhi High Court Chief Justice, Mr. Rajindar Sachar, today described Mr. Advani's move as "unconstitutional and having shades of Hitler".

"Mr. Advani's statement will have the unfortunate effect of making the security forces act like the Gestapo (the espionage service of Hitler)," he said in a statement here.

Existing special legislation, such as the Armed Forces Special Power Act, provided "unwarranted" power to security forces to even shoot down a person.

But the law certainly did not provide protection for "excessive use of force." Such a statement from the Home Minister bode ill for a democratic and civilised Government, he said.

7.5 Change Evidence Law

It is universally accepted that the ability of the State to protect human rights is an important indicator of the quality of life enjoyed by citizens in any country. This was the principle on which the UN General Assembly adopted and proclaimed the Universal Declaration of Human Rights on Dec. 10, 1948. Article 5 of the declaration mandates that no one shall be subjected to torture or cruel, inhuman or degrading treatment of punishment.

Article 7 of International Covenant of Civil and Political Rights proclaims that no one shall be subjected to torture.

The preamble expressed the desire of member States to make more effective the struggle against torture or other forms of cruel, inhuman or degrading treatment even when it is meted as some form of punishment.

Torture is defined to mean any act by which severe pain or suffering, whether physical or mental, is intentionally inflicted on a person for such purposes as obtaining from him or a third person information or a confession, at the instigation or with consent or acquiescence of a public official.

That in spite of these mandates of international law, we continue to have growing incidents of custodial deaths and cases of torture. Amnesty International has reported that 415 deaths took place in India in police custody from 1985 to March 1992. The government has denied some of the instances. The denial of the Union Government, however, carries little conviction in face of the reports in the Press that 46 persons died in custody between January and March of last year alone.

It is a matter of anguish that notwithstanding continuation of this evil, public response is muted and indifferent, mainly because these victims of police infainy belong to the poorer strata of society— hardly a tribute to our public conscious.

I know the police in their defenclead plead that they resort to torture because they arc under pressure from their superiors including politicians to show visible results and obtaining forced confessions is the easy way out. But this is indefensible. Article 2 of the Convention Against Torture clearly says that no exceptional circumstances whatsoever, even if these be of a state of war or a threat of war, internal political instability or any other public emergency, may be invoked as justification of cases of torture. Article 2 (3) of the Convention further warns that an order from a superior officer or a public authority may not be invoked as a justification of torture.

Article 14 of the Convention further obligates that each State party shall ensure in its legal system that a victim of torture obtains redress and has a enforceable right to fair and adequate compensation. Sections 330 and 331 of the Penal Code make punishable those persons who cause hurt for the purpose of extorting a confession. But as the Law of Evidence stands at present the burden on the victim to prove his case is almost impossible to discharge. The reason is that police officers alone can give evidence as regards the circumstances in which a person comes to receive injuries while in their custody. Bound by ties of a kind of brotherhood they often prefer to remain silent in such situations and when they choose to speak, they put their own gloss upon facts and pervert the truth. The result is that persons, on whom atrocities are perpetrated by the police inside the 'sanctum sanctorum' of the police station, are left without any evidence to prove who the offenders are. Disturbed at this situation the Supreme Court as far back as 1985 recommended that the law as to the burden of proof in such cases may be re-examined by the legislature so that handmades of law and order do not use their authority and opportunities for oppressing the innocent citizens who look to them for protection.

The Law Commission in its 113th report also recommended the amendment of the Evidence Act so as to provide that a prosecution of a police officer for an alleged offence of having caused bodily injury to a person, if there was evidence that the injury was caused during the period when the person was in police custody, the court may presume that the injury was caused by the police officer having the custody of that person during that period.

The Government as usual ignored that wholesome advice because possibly this may hamper the police to go on induling in illegalities at the bidding of their political masters.

The anguish of the Supreme Court at the inaction of the Government was expressed in a recent case of custodial death. The court held that if the deceased was taken into police custody and thereafter injury or death took place the burden is on the police to explain what happened.

The court also fashioned a new tool to mould a relief to award compensation because according to its view for the unalwful acts of the instrumentality of the State the liability to pay must be placed on the State, as it must repair the damage done by its officers. The Court has firmly held that a custodial death is perhaps one of the worst crimes in a civilised society governed by the rule of law.

All of us must remind ourselves that the police torture if not checked immediately will mean the destruction of rule of law — the very foundation of our social fabric with inevitable undesirable consequences.

7.6 Is Police Unnecessarily Brutal?

The recent killing by UP police of a second year post-graduate medical student near Agra while returning in a car along with a friend has again highlighted the lack of concern for the safety of citizens and the brutal attitude of the police towards the citizen. And the only provocation stated by the police is that car did not stop when warned to do so. The explanation by the complainant not to stop namely that since it was late at night they, suspected that it might be a hold up by gangster is perfectly sound. But even if the signal was disobeyed, there is no law under which firing could be resorted to. With two mobile vans at the spot, the car could have easily been followed and stopped. But such has been the arrogance of the police, possibly due to its nexus with the politicians and criminals, that it considers itself master of all it surveys.

The belated admission by chief minister Farooq Abdullah that the alleged militants who were killed by the local police and the security forces following Chhatishsinghpora killing were in fact innocent civilians has exposed the police brutality. It has also exposed the political protection enjoyed by them .The tragedy is that whenever such police brutality takes place a large number of civilians are willing to swallow the police line that the deceased were all militants, gangster or infiltrators.

Similar police criminality was evident in the killing of businessmen in Connaught Circus by the Delhi Police. The explanation then was that they thought they were chasing some gangsters. Years have passed; yet the guilty have not been suitably punished. Hashimpura (Meerut) killing of Muslim youths over a decade ago has still not resulted in the punishment of personnel from UP Home Guard and police even though they were found guilty by the CBI.

The right to life, guaranteed under Article 21 of the Constitution, though loudly proclaimed by every government, is violated by the minute. Unless the media and the public opinion create an atmosphere where police killing is *perse* accepted as a crime, with consequential punishment immediately, police brutality will continue to shame our country.

Each day, the police undertakes millions of actions in detecting crime and maintaining law and order. Relatively rarely in terms of this volume of work, there is an aberration, a loss of control, or an error of judgement. These aberrations are highlighted, the entire police force is pre-judged, and this is done completely out of context of the objective circumstances under which the police operate. The issue of 'police brutality' is now being raised in the context of the killing of a medical student by the Mathura police. This incident clearly reflects, at once, high levels of public insecurity — which is why the couple in the car refused to stop when flagged down — and a botched police reaction. Unfortunately, in a situation where daily incidents of terrorism and the most heinous crimes are reported, there is a very thin line between over-reaction and failure of response. An under-equipped force always tends to overreact and the use more force than necessary. With sophisticated communications and a network of pursuit vehicles, no policeman would consider using his weapon just because a car refuses to stop.

The fact is, the people get the police force they pay for. Considering the circumstances under which it operates, the dedication of the Indian police is exemplary. Nearly a thousand policemen lose their lives fighting crime and terror each year. Their families are paid a pittance in compensation. Working conditions are abysmal. Yet, the majority of these underpaid, under-trained, under-equipped and over-worked men display exemplary commitment. Moreover, police response must be assessed within the context of the collapse of the criminal justice system, a complete absence of fear of law, judicial hostility and an entire presumption loaded against the police. At the same time, amendments in laws in the post-Independence era have divested the police of a role in prosecution there are virtually no convictions, and the few that actually materialise take decades. The whole system has become a mockery of justice. It is necessary to look at the whole context, instead of taking an isolated incident to condemn the police.

8
Environment in Developing Countries

8.1 Environmental Laws in Developing Countries

That there is direct link between Human Rights and Environment is no longer arguable. Environmental awareness has become universal. With the opening of International Trade and globalization of economy, contentious matters of environmental laws call for deeper examination, more especially in the context of World Trade Organization (W.T.O). It is now broadly accepted that environmental sustainability and human rights are mutually dependent-making use of this awareness the developed countries are applying great pressure on developing countries to agree to apply the same environmental standards. It is here that a vital question of principle and equity arises.

The developed countries are trying their best to include environmental standards (ostensibly as a part of social clause) and to interlink it with Trade. In this, the Governments of the countries of the North have been joined by their Trans-national Corporation, their trade unions and their NGOs active in the field of environment.

No one disputes that pollution free environment is as necessary for survival in developing part as the developed part of the world. But in the guise of environmental cleanliness, developed world is insisting on environmental laws which are disproportionate for the economic growth of developing countries. They are being asked to apply high cost environmental regulations so that their exports are not able to compete against the developed countries. The environmental damages which are caused by the MNCs in developing countries are denials of Human Rights. During Mr. Narasimha Rao, Prime Ministership an Australian Government delegation visited India to negotiate export to India its Industrial waste, considered hazardous to environment and human health. This trade negotiation was in spite of the fact that the parties to the Basal Convention had agreed that waste disposal to developing countries be banned immediately. It is a welcome sign that Mr. Soz, Minister for Environment, Government of India has now publicly announced that no hazardous waste will be allowed to be imported in the country notwithstanding the pressure from the rich nations.

The insidious attempt to deliberately link environment with international trade is one of single most important weapon in the hands of developed countries against the developing countries. It is this aspect which requires deep consideration, namely, how alibi of environmental jurisprudence should not be used as a trade barrier against the developing countries.

The reality is that it is the developed countries that have benefited from environmentally offensive international trade in the last hundred years, and even today are the principal offenders. This context is being paid little attention – on the other hand there is insistence that the underdeveloped world should accept the same environmental standards on their own.

That it is inequitable and impractical to ask the developing countries to enforce the same rigid environment standards as the developed nations was recognized in a study by GATT on the subject of trade and environment which had concluded that interference with trade is seldom if ever the best way of achieving a particular domestic environmental objective. That this approach is grossly inequitable is recognized in Principal 11 of the 1992 Rio Declaration on Environment and Development which says "Standards applied by some countries may be inappropriate and of unwarranted economic and social cost to other countries, in particular developing countries". To the same effect is the exhortation by internationally knownly economist Professor Jagdish Bhagwati who says that "the view that "International Standards" should be set for all, ignores the fact that there are legitimate reasons for diversity in environmental regulation across countries".

The cynical disregard for environmental cleanness (though loudly shouting its commitment by rich countries) is hollow if one notes that since 1989 more than 500 attempts have been made to export toxic waste from OECD countries to non-OECD countries. OECD members generate 98 per cent of all hazardous waste.

Third World governments are against social and environmental clauses in WTO because they function as protectionist measures in trade and therefore can be used to deny market access to developing country's exports.

This is precisely why Agenda 21 adopted at the Rio Conference stressed that a supportive external economic environments is crucial to the promotion of sustainable development. It aptly noted that the development process will not gather momentum if the developing countries are weighed down by external indebtedness, if development finance is inadequate, if barriers restrict access to markets and if commodity prices and the terms of trade of developing countries remain depressed. The record of the 1980s was essentially negative on each of these counts and needs to be reversed.

The concern of the West for improving the conditions in developing world is shallow. The reality is that unequal trade costs the developing nations US $ 500 billion annually, ten times what these countries receive in aid. Ironically, 64 per cent of the aid allegedly given to the poor is tied, which supports the economy of the richer countries more than that of the poor.

The brazenness of this unconcern by the developed nations is again highlighted by the latest guidelines finalized by Japanese government for its policy to be made effective from 1998, namely; Nations seeking Japanese Official Development Assistance (ODA) for environmental and anti-pollution projects will now have to make obligatory purchases of goods and services from Tokyo.

That environmental insistence is a neat way of trade advancement, is clear from the fact that Japanese government plans to limit "tied ODA loans" to projects related to anti-pollution and other environmental protection projects and measures.

The new policy of Japan has however, attracted much flak with analysts. Since Japanese prices are on an average 30 to 50 per cent higher than international market prices, linking aid with purchases automatically mean less proceeds from aid money. Aid recipients will also have to deal with the menace of overcharging or padding of bills.

In fact environment related manufacturing industry is the fastest growing in the developed world.

The simple conclusion which then suggests itself is that environment cannot be privileged over trade within a world economy which produces development and underdevelopment as an integral part of its movement.

8.2 Environment and Global Warming

Environmental awareness is on increase. To that extent it is a welcome sign. But there is other angle which calls for caution, namely to be alert to see that environmental lobby of the West does not stifle the industrialization and growth of economy of developing countries.

It is in that context that the danger of the depletion of Ozone Layer leading to Global warming necessitating control on the emission of Green House Gases (G.H.G.), (the worst being carbon dioxide (CO_2)).

As of February 1998, 165, countries have ratified the Montreal Protocol (1987) which sets out the time schedule for freeze and reduction of some of the Ozone Depleting Substances (ODS).

The threat of Global Warming resulted in the United Nations Framework Convention of Climate Change (FCCC), which has entered into force on 21.03.1994. Convention has been ratified by 119 countries.

Notwithstanding the industrialized countries loud proclamation of concern at reducing CO_2 emission the whole exercise by them is a make believe. Thus the European Union which had insisted prior to Kyoto meet of 15 per cent cut for industrialized countries lamely agreed under U.S.A. Government pressure at reduction target of only 5.2 per cent over 1990. Now as industrialized countries by 1996 had already reached emission of CO_2 below 4.5 per cent of 1990 level the emission reducing commitment by North is idle formality.

According to the World Resources (1994-95), CO_2 emission per capita of Six major countries that of United States is more than 5 MT of carbon followed by Japan of about 2.3 M.T. while that of India is the lowest at about 0.02 MT.

USA alone is responsible for about 25 per cent of the world's Green House Gas emissions. It has ironically increased the emissions by 6 per cent during the period 1990-95 that is even after Montreal Protocol had been signed. The developed countries make two-thirds to three-fourths of current emissions.

Though the production of GHG had declined by 75 per cent from the base year 1996, a new problem has arisen in the matter of growth of illegal trade and ironically the problem is most acute in the United States where large illegal imports of GHG is being done.

As far back as in the 1992 at the Earth Summit the principle of Polluter pays was broadly accepted, though, of course, the steps taken in pursuance of this do not show that the acceptance was a genuine one. 80 per cent of the current emissions comes from the industrial nations which have only 20 per cent of world population. The Global Warming is a world wide phenomenon not restricted to any part of the world. From that it must follow that human beings in all parts of the world have an equal interest and right to see and demand that global warming does not go further but is reduced so as to reach a tolerable limit. But the responsibility for that has necessarily to be taken by the developed countries because they are the biggest polluters. Some calculations to show that taking the average cost of reducing emission even at a minimum of US Dollars 20 per ton, the south is actually making subsidy of about 60 billion US Dollars to the North. It is this amount which the rich North must make available to the South if it wants that the south should reduce considerably its emission of G.H.G. - in the absence of such help, the burden cannot be borne by the developing countries.

Apparently to assist developing countries, a multilateral fund commonly known as Global Environment facility has been established by the parties to the Montreal Protocol purportedly to assist the developing countries to meet the control measures as specified in the Protocol. Developed countries are to subscribe to this fund and which is operated through UNDP which has approved only 189 Million US Dollars for global work programme for the period from June 1991–1997. India has so far received only 11.6 million US Dollars under this portfolio, while net incremental cost for the total phase out of the ODS in India has been estimated at 1964 million US Dollars. Here is thus a serious gap of resource crunch. If developing countries were to utilize their scarce resources on reducing emissions of D.S. as required by North, development and provision of even subsistence standard for millions will suffer irretrievably.

Thus even by any test of sustainable development, equity and consistency with the convention it has to be recognized that the energy needs of the developing countries are very great; that increased energy consumption and economic growth will be essential if living standards of the poor are to be raised; that without accelerated development in many countries domestic environmental degradation will worsen, and that the current threat from anthropogenic climate change is caused much more by the affluent than the poorer nations. For all of these reasons, the Convention is clear that continued growth of energy and use of fossil fuels in developing countries is quite consistent with the Convention.

The development needs of developing countries must take priority and would mandate that the developed countries should reduce their GHG emissions considerably. This demand is reasonable considering that the developing countries per capita consumption levels is 1/10th and in the case of electricity less than 1/20th of those of the rich countries. Over 2 billion people are without electricity in developing countries. Therefore, any programme or the strategy worked out at the International Convention must recognise the growing need for commercial energy in developing countries. Even the World Bank has recognized that where the objectives of developing countries conflicts with global environmental goals, such as the mitigation of greenhouse gases, the development must take priority.

That it is inequitable to ask the developing nations to accept the same environmental standards as the North was recognized in Principle 11 of the 1992 Rio Declaration on Environment and Development which has said "Standards applied by some countries may be inappropriate and of unwarranted economic and social cost to other countries, in particular developing countries".

The reality must be accepted, namely, that this insistence from the Governments of North for observing such strict similar environmental standards by developing countries is unfair and is at the insistence and lobbying by environmental related manufacturing industry of North which wants a ensured sale for its products. This is highlighted by the latest guidelines finalized by Japanese government for its policy to be made effective from 1998, namely; Nations seeking Japanese Official Development Assistance (ODA) for environmental and anti-pollution projects will now have to make obligatory purchases of goods and services from Tokyo.

That environmental standard insistence is a neat way of trade advancement, is clear from the fact that Japanese government plans to limit "tied ODA loans" to projects related to anti-pollution and other environmental protection projects and measures.

It is thus a truism that so long as there is such horrendous gap between the standard of living of the developed world and that of developing world, insistence on the observance of same environmental standards is a sure way of perpetuating misery and deprivation to the millions in developing countries.

9
Globalisation-Negation of Human Rights

9.1 Poverty Globalisation

The rouge of poverty was highlighted in a message given on 17th October in observance of International day for the Eradication of poverty by the UN Secretary-General, who reminded us as to "how many times have we said that it (poverty) was incompatible with human dignity. But billions of people are still trying to survive on less than three dollars a day, with no drinking water, health care, or access to education, still denied the jobs that would help them escape their impoverished state, and thus, still deprived of some of their must basic rights".

Freedom of an individual which is postulate of Human Rights obviously can have no meaning so long as the poor in the country do not have their economic conditions improved and the discrimination based on privilege do not become memories of the past rather than becoming more and more aggressive as the time passes on.

Unfortunately, the solutions being suggested are illusion. Thus the must touted claim by the propagandists of globalization that it will accelerate progress in developing countries is belied by UNDP's Tenth Human Development Report of 1999, which says that "market dominated globalization has led to growing marginalisation of poor nations and people, growing human insecurity and growing unequal with benefits accruing almost solely to the richest people and countries and that the global gap between the haves and have-nots is widening.

HDR 1999 has commented tersely "the benefits of globalization in the past decade have been so unevenly shared that the very word has come to acquire in certain quarters a pejorative tinge". The present situation must cause concern to all Human Rights activists.

The richest fifth have an income 74 times that of the poorest fifth.

One per cent of the wealth of the 200 richest people, or $ 8 billion, could provide universal access to primary education for a year — but no political party is seeking to correct this perverted balance — the result a denial of human right of universal education.

The assets of three richest people are more than the combined GNP of the 48 least developed countries.

About 220 million urban dwellers, 13 per cent of the developing world's urban population, lack accees to safe drinking water and about twice that number lack access to even the simplest of latrines.

Attacking Poverty, World Development Report (2000) argues that each country must devise its own poverty reduction strategy. These strategies need to address three issues:

"Empowerment: strengthening the participation of poor people in local decision-making that affects their lives, and removing social barriers that result from distinctions of gender, race, ethnicity, and social status. Promoting global financial stability and opening the markets of rich countries to the agricultural goods, manufactures, and services of poor countries".

Throughout the world, poor people are often unable to participate in the decisions that affect their lives.

Even the chief economist at the World Bank admit "No reasonable person doubts that economic growth is crucial. The argument that market-oriented reforms lead to growth and that growth leads to poverty reduction is correct, but too simplistic. Experience has also shown that growth leads to larger and quicker reductions in poverty if measures are taken to empower the poor and to enhance their security.

Calling globalization "the central challenge we face today", world leaders attending the United Nations Millennium Summit in the evening of 8 September 2000 had to recognize that "For while globalization offers great opportunities, at present its benefits are very unevenly shared, while its costs are unevenly distributed".

H.R.D. 2000 has commented acidly that Global inequalities in income increased in the 20th century by orders of magnitude out of proportion to anything experienced before. The distance between the incomes of the richest and poorest countries was about 3 to 1 in 1820, 35 to 1 in 1950, 44 to 1 in 1973 and 72 to 1 in 1992.

The "global marketplace" is not necessarily a place of equality, with benefits and rewards equitably shared by all those who participate in it. In the case of the Asian "tigers" the consequences of financial liberalization have been mixed at best and absolutely catastrophic at worst. The North American Free Trade Agreement (NAFTA) has led to serious social and political problems in certain regions of the America. Unemployment, homelessness and reduction in social services are not confined to any one geographical area.

To speak of globalisation with regard to increased integration of the world economy is misleading; there is a process of concentration of capital which only benefits three principal regions (North America, Europe and East Asia), whilst the rest of the globe (particularly Africa) becomes more and more marginalized. (We can include India along with Africa).

The situation deteriorates for the disadvantaged when the deregulation is followed by a reduction of social services and collective equipment. In order terms, globalisation entails not only a growing inequality between regional groups and countries, but also within the nation itself.

Other things being the same, growth leads to less poverty reduction in unequal societies than in egalitarian ones. If poor people get a small share of existing income and if inequality is unchanged, they will also get a small share of the new income generated by growth, muting the effects of growth on poverty. Evidence confirms this; when initial inequality is low, growth reduces poverty nearly twice as much as when inequality is high.

This view implied a trade off — more growth could be bought for the price of more inequality, with ambiguous effects on poor people. More recent thinking — and empirical evidence — weaken the case for such a trade off.

Incomplete financial sector reforms contributed to the East Asian crisis. During the 1990s several emerging economies in East Asia liberalized their domestic financial markets and lifted capital account restrictions. In the Republic of Korea and Thailand especially, a surge of capital inflows, often through newly formed nonblank financial institution, placed heavy financial stresses on banks.

But incautious and excessively rapid reforms can culminate in crises.

Even in the west there are protests at the fear of unemployment because of globalisation. There is greater danger of such a situation in our country. Unfortunately the policy makers and the political parties in our country continued to be oblivious to such a dangerous situation. This is where peoples power has to be mobilized and for this academics professionals should play active role.

A century ago Swami Vivekananda warned the Indian elite, that unless they carry the masses with them in all efforts at national regeneration, no great progress can be made. The neglect of the masses... Chronic poverty under which they were held down, have been the main cause of India's degradation and cried in anguish "I call him a traitor who having been educated, nursed in luxury by the heart's blood of the downtrodden millions of toiling poor, never even takes a thought for them.... Who thinks of raising these sunken downtrodden millions? A few thousand graduates do not make a nation, a few rich men do not make a nation".

How sad that even after a century that reproach by saintly soul should continue to shame us.

9.2 Can Globalisation Reduce Poverty?

The scourge of poverty was highlighted in a message given last October, in observance of the International Day for the Eradication of Poverty by the UN Secretary-General, who reminded us of "how many times have we said that it (poverty) was incompatible with human dignity. But billions of people are still trying to survive on less than three dollars a day, with no drinking water, health care, or access to education, still denied the jobs that would help them escape their impoverished state, and thus, still deprived of some of their most basic rights".

Freedom of an individual which is endorsed by human rights precepts obviously can have no meaning so long as the economic conditions of the poor are not improved and discriminations based on privilege end. Unfortunately, the solutions being suggested seem illusions. Thus, the assertion by the propagandists of globalisation that it will accelerate progress in developing countries is also belied by UNDP's Tenth Human Development Report (HDR), which states that "market dominated globalisation has led to growing marginalisation of poor nations and its peoples, with growing inequality and the benefits accruing to the richest people and countries.

HDR 1999 too has commented tersely that "the benefits of globalisation in the past decade have been so unevenly shared that the very word has come to acquire in certain quarters a pejorative tinge". The present scenario must cause concern to all human rights activists. The gap between the haves and the have-nots is staggering: the richest fifth have a income 74 times that of the poorest fifth.

Attacking poverty outright, the World Development Report (2000) argues that each country must devise its own poverty reduction strategy. These strategies need to address primarily three major issues, namely empowerment, strengthening the participation of poor people in local decision-making that affects their lives, and thirdly removing social barriers that result from distinctions of gender, race, ethnicity, and social status.

Experience has also shown that growth leads to larger and quicker reduction in poverty if measures are taken to empower the poor and to enhance their security. Calling globalisation "the central challenge we face today", world leaders attending the United Nations Millennium Summit on 8 September 2000 had to recognise that "while globalisation offers great opportunities, at present its benefits are very unevenly shared, while its costs are unevenly distributed".

The HRD 2000 has commented acidly that global inequalities in income increased in the 20th century by orders of magnitude out of proportion to anything experienced before. The discrepancy of incomes of the richest and poorest countries was about 3 to 1 in 1820, 35 to 1 in 1950, 44 to 1 in 1973 and 72 to 1 in 1992.

The "global marketplace" is not necessarily a place of equality, with benefits and rewards equaliably shared by all those who participate in it. In the case of the Asian "tigers" the consequences of financial liberalisation have been mixed at best and absolutely catastrophic at worst. The North American Free Trade agreement (NAFTA) has led to serious social and political problems in certain regions of America. Unemployment, homelessness and reduction in social services are not confined to any one geographical area.

To speak of globalisation with regard to increased integration of the world economy is misleading; there is a process of concentration of capital which only benefits three principal regions (North America, Europe and East Asia) whilst the rest of the globe—particularly Africa—becomes more and more marginalised. And we can include India along with Africa. The situation deteriorates for the disadvantaged when deregulation is followed by a reduction of social services. In other words, globalisation entails not only a growing inequality between regional groups and countries but also within the nation itself.

Other things being equal, growth leads to less poverty reduction in unequal societies than in egalitarian ones. If poor people get a small share of the existing income and if inequality is unchanged, they will also get a small share of the new income generated by growth, muting the effects of growth on poverty. When initial inequality is low, growth reduces poverty nearly twice as much as when inequality is high. This view implied a trade-off: more growth could be bought at the cost of more inequality, with ambiguous effects on poor people. Mor recent thinking and evidence, however, weaken the case for such a trade off.

Incomplete reforms in the financial sector contributed to the East Asian crisis. During the 1990s several emerging economies in East Asia liberalised their domestic financial markets and lifted capital account restrictions. In the Republic of Korea and Thailand especially, a surge of capital inflows, often through newly formed nonbank financial institution, placed heavy financial stresses on banks. But reckless and excessively rapid reforms can culminate in crises.

Even in the West, there are protests at the fear of unemployment because of globalisation. There is greater danger of such a situation in our country. Unfortunately, policy makers and political parties in our country are unaware of such an implication.

9.3 Protect the Family Treasure

How ideological considerations have ceased to play any part in politics is apparent from the innate, personalised, low-level of election debates. Possibly that is because both the Congress and the BJP are the faithful hangers-on of economic liberalization and thus indifferent to the dangers of globalization.

I am not suggesting a closed economy or an-era of licenses and permits controlled by the bureaucratic-political nexus. But I am pained that the public sector-bul-wark against the onslaught of multinational corporations (MNC's) – is being deliberately demolished. All this is being justified on the slogan of benefits of globalization and free market, notwithstanding the warning given by the UNDP Human Development Report 1999 that "market-dominated globalization has led to growing marginalisation of poor nations and people, growing human insecurity and growing with benefits accruing almost solely to the richest people and countries.

The new rules of globalization – and the players writing them—focus on integrating global markets, neglecting the needs of people which markets cannot meet. The process is one of concentrating power and marginalizing the poor. The rapid expansion of global markets—the conditions for people, corporations and nations to compete globally, the urge to privatize and downsize public action in search of economic efficiency— creates an environment in which the needs of human development can easily be neglected. Reduced public spending weakens institutions of redistribution, leading to inequalities.

Care is also squeezed by reductions in public spending. And free market prices do not capture the full environmental costs of production and consumption, putting a squeeze on the natural environment.

A typical case of perverted priorities and lack of care for the underprivileged is manifest in the systematic government policies of demolition of the public sector, on the national exchequer. Consider the reality—in the pre-New Economic Policies period (1985-86 and 1989-90), the Government gave about Rs. 25,537 crores as budgetary support to the public sector Undertaking (PSU's) whose contribution to the Central exchequer was Rs. 70,893 crores, besides generating internal resources of Rs. 20,755 crores. In 1991-92, the budgetary support was Rs. 3,617 crores whereas the contribution to the public exchequer was Rs. 20,366 crores.

These false assumptions by the Government are made for facilitating the loot of the family treasure of the PSU's – take the case of Modern Food Industries Ltd. (MFIL) – by the MNC's. MFIL was only getting a budgetary support of Rs. 1 crores annually (of which half is equity and half loan, and on the latter an interest of 16 per cent was paid to the Government) and the support has also been totally discontinued since 1997.

MFIL, set up in 1965, is now manufacturing bread and related items at 14 bakery units located all over India. Mid-day meal is provided by MFIL to school children under various government schemes. It is also supplying bread to hospitals and the military. Privatization will affect the employment of 2,500 directly and more than one lakh people indirectly.

That the anti-working class sentiment is shared by all political parties becomes apparent when it is recognized that it was the United Front Government which in August 1996 set up a Public Sector Disinvestments Commission to draw a comprehensive long-term disinvestments programme for the PSU's. In February 1997, the Commission recommended that the Government disinvest 100 per cent of shareholding. However, none of the alleged weaknesses justifying this recommendation can withstand a moment's scrutiny. The weakness of underutilization of production facility is falsified, the report itself noticing the capacity utilization of bread, energy food and extruded food as 90,115 and 130 per cent respectively.

The charges of MFIL having a poor public image compared to organized competitors is hollow, considering that the report itself mentions that of the 25-30 per cent share of the organization sector, MFIL has 10-12 per cent against Britannia's (MNC) 7-8 per cent. The recommendation of the Commission being so self-contradictory, the then Minister for Food (1997) opposed it and the matter was referred for a further examination by the then Prime Minister, Mr. I.K. Gujral.

Noting happened for a year and suddenly in August 1998 the Vajpayee Government disinvested 50 per cent equity in MFIL to a strategic alliance partner – a euphemism for an MNC, notwithstanding protests by trade unions. The protest was so contemptuously ignored that the Government decided to increase the disinvestments of 74 per cent in January 1999 and invited bids up to September 21, 1999.

The Commission has deliberately ignored one of the terms of reference which specifically provides that appropriate measure be taken to protect the interests of the employees, including encouraging employee participation in the sale process. Yet the Government is going ahead with disinvestments.

There is also a Constitutional objection to inviting bids without the Government first coming to an agreement with the employees. MFIL is a Government company and its employees are public servants enjoying Constitutional protection- MFIL is a state under Article 12. Their pay scales and wages are governed by the pattern for Central Government employees. There is reservation for the SC's/ ST's/ ST's. All this will disappear after disinvestments. This will amount to transfer of the service of the employee to a new employer – a non-government company. This is not permissible because the employees cannot be transferred to a new employer without their consent. Such a consent having not been obtained, the Government cannot go ahead with disinvestment.

Bringing in the MNC's by disinvestment is fraught with serious consequences. MFIL has been supplying bread to the defence force for more than three decades. These forces will now have to depend on the MNC's for getting bread not only in normal situations but also during war and in strategic areas. This will not be in the interest of the nation. The MNC's will obliterate the tiny and small bakeries. They are trying to control agriculture and seeds production, and if they take control of a large PSUs such as MFIL, they will achieve monopoly and dictate terms on food and food products to the people.

No wonder, the MNC's are evincing a keen interest in snatching MFIL, because according to a survey, the projected market in bakery products by 2005 will reach $3 billion. Those advocating privatization in the name of globalization need to be reminded of the warning given by the HDR 1999 that "when the market goes too far in dominating social and political outcomes, the opportunities and rewards of globalization spread unequally and inequitably – concentrating power and wealth in select group of people, nations and corporations, marginalizing the others."

The new Government will have to take a decision and it is hoped that the MPs will force a reversal of this bonanza being made to the MNCs and prevent an immeasurable harm being done to the public sector.

May I remind the apologists of undiluted globalization of the restraining words Mahatma Gandhi, in the contest of an analogues situation? "I do not want my house to be walled in all sides and my windows to be stuffed. I want the cultures of all the lands to be blown about my house as freely as possible. But I refuse to be blown off my feet by any."

9.4 The BALCO Deal Investment and Privatisation Disinvestment and Parliament

The Sale of BALCO by the Central Government continues to make headlines. There are too many dark (not even grey) areas which have not been illuminated. It is not disputed that BALCO is a profit-making PSU. There is no logic for the sale except that which apologists for globalisation put out — that the public sector has to be dismantled, even when it is doing fine. For persons like me, the sale of a PSU in a core sector such as aluminium is unthinkable irrespective of the question of profitability or otherwise, because I would consider this against the mandate of our Constitution which promises economic and social justice and is against concentration of economic power in a few individuals. Unfortunately, the Congress (I) the main Opposition, is also sold on privatisation. This reduces the whole controversy to a bargaining game of sorts — a far cry from the kind of Indian state we dream of.

The Government has not come out with all the facts. Responsible trade unions have alleged that BALCO made a profit of Rs. 55.89 crores and paid the Government Rs. 18 crores and dividend and Rs. 291.57 crores as taxes and duty last year. BALCO is said to have two captive power plants of about 250 MW and would be worth Rs. 500 crores even in the present condition. The Government justification that prices were on the decline is unconvincing considering that the country experienced a shortage of around 1,48,390 tonnes in 2000 itself. Even the Government has admitted that BALCO has a market share of 15 per cent.

Sterlite's Director is naturally in raptures at the deal and admits: "that BALCO acquisition is expected to complete the value chain from bauxite to high value added foils and provides Sterlite group with critical mass". He gloated "that Sterlite turnover from the aluminium business will now go up to over Rs. 1,600 crores from Rs. 800 crores in the Indian aluminium industry."

A serious consequence is that after acquiring BALCO, Sterlite will control 20 per cent of the market share in the aluminium industry. There is not even a remote explanation from the Government how it has entered into such a deal, which even under the truncated Monopolies and Restrictive Trade Practices Act, 1969, will amount to a monopoly. In such a situation, the Central Government is obliged under the Act to prohibit such a situation as being against the public interest and to even order the division of such undertaking. If the Government goes ahead with the sale of BALCO, it may run foul of challenge before the MRTP Commission. I am not sure that any prospective buyer would, normally like to take that risk, but of course, considering the dirt-cheap price at which BALCO is being sold, he may nevertheless consider taking a gamble. Also a sale like this which creates such a large market share runs counter to the principle of free competition which is said to be the basis of globalisation.

How ironic a gap between profession and practice.

Now, monopoly is checked by such unabashedly capitalist countries such as the U.S., Canada and Australia. The Europe an community has even more stringent standards against such mergers which lead to a substantial market share for a company product, which would have the effect of lessening competition and operate to the detriment of the public. Such a monopoly of market share runs foul of Anti-Trust Legislation passed as far back as 1914 in the U.S. That mergers nevertheless continued to the detriment of the public by lessing competition led the U.S. to pass the Anti-Trust Improvement Act, 1996, which requires those planning acquisitions to file notifications with the Federal Trade Commission and to delay consummation for a prescribed period to give an opportunity to the Department of Justice to review the proposed transaction and prevent consummation of transactions that violate anti-trust laws. It is well settled that immunity from the anti-trust law is not lightly implied. This reflects the role of an anti-trust policy in the maintenance of free competition.

In the Philadelphia Book case, the U.S. Supreme Court stated the position thus: "Specifically, we think that a merger which produces a firm controlling an undue percentage share of the relevant market, and results in a significant increase in the concentration of firms in that market, is so inherently likely to lessen competition substantially that it must be enjoined in the absence of evidence clearly showing that the merger is not likely to have such anti-competitive efforts. Furthermore, the test is fully consonant with economic theory". That "competition is likely to be greatest when there are many sellers, none of which has any significant market share" is common ground among most economists, and was undoubtedly a premise of congressional reasoning about the anti-merger statute. Though in that case the controlling interest was 30 per cent, the court was cautious enough to say that it was not attempting to specify the smallest market share which would still be considered to threaten undue concentration. The Court thus noticed a dominant view much favoured a finding that a much smaller market share in one corporation would tend to lessen competition and thus be against public interest. Thus it was mentioned that Kaysen and Turner suggest that 20 per cent should be the line of *prima facie* unlawfulness. Stigler suggests that any acquisition by a firm controlling 20 per cent of the market after the merger is presumptively unlawful, Markham mentions 25 per cent. Bok's principal test is increase in market concentration, and he suggests a figure of 7 per cent or 8 per cent. Needless to say, the fact that a merger results in a less than 30 per cent market share, or in a less substantial increase in concentration than in the instant case, does not raise an inference that the merger is not violative of the Anti-Trust Legislation.

In a close parallel case of the Aluminium company of America, the U.S. Supreme Court held that the acquisition by a producer of 27.8 per cent of the market of a producer of 1.3 per cent of the market violates the Anti-Trust Act as amended, which prohibits corporate stock or assets acquisitions, the effect of which may be substantially to lessen competition or to tend to create a monopoly in any line of commerce in any section of the country.

The Government cannot avoid this issue by saying that there is no definite proof that such a sale of BALCO will lessen competition — it only needs to be reminded that in law to prevent monopolisation, the test is of probabilities and not certainties.

A further serious matter that needs to be examined is the effect of Article 244 of the Constitution read with the Fifth Schedule which prohibits non-tribals holding land in scheduled areas from transferring their lands in favour of persons other than the tribals and any act contrary to this regulation will make the transfer null and void. Whatever immunity may have been enjoyed by BALCO being Government Company, will cease when 51 per cent of it is sold to non tribals — the result may be that land which at present belongs to BALCO will have to be restored to the tribals because it is situated in a scheduled tribal areas.

Another important constitutional aspect is the federal principle of our governance, BALCO is in the State of Chhatisgarh. The Chief Minister has publically raised an objection to it. The Governor has described it as mindless disinvestment of a financially-sound PSU. Surely, a harmonious working of the Constitution requires the Centre to hold full and total consolations with the State? The Centre just cannot treat the State as a vassal. The State may as we feel that privatising an industry in a tribal area is to the detriment of that neglected section of the community. It may well feel that private management will not give a fair deal to these illiterate disadvantaged populace. Surely the Centre cannot act like a Viceroy of the British Empire. If it does it may run foul of the Constitution with its attendant complications. Sobriety is a worthwhile habit — the Central Government is not exempt from it.

The Indefensible action of the Tata-controlled VSNL Board in taking Rs. 1,200 crores of VSNL money and investing it in Tata Teleservices (TTSL) has raised crucial questions regarding the principle, the methodology and the philosophy behind the privatisation drama the Centre is engaged in. All Governments since 1991 have spread the canard that the break-up of the USSR showed that socialism as a political philosophy is unworkable notwithstanding the mandate in the preamble of our Constitution that India is a socialist Republic. This is a distortion. The USSR failed not because socialism cannot prevail unless imbued with a democratic perspective. Stalinism and not socialism was the cause of the break-up of the USSR.

The public sector is being deliberately maligned by some votaries of liberalisation, though the reality is otherwise. During the pre-New Economic Policy period (1985-86 and 1989-90), the Government gave about Rs. 25,537 crores as budgetary support to the PSUs contribution to the Central exchequer was Rs. 70,893 crores. In 1991-92, the budgetary support was Rs. 3,617 crores and the PSUs' contribution to the public exchequer Rs. 20,366 crores.

Prior to its disinvestment, Modern Food Industries Ltd. was getting an annual budgetary support of Rs. one crore, of which half was equity and half loan, and on the latter an interest of 16 per cent was being paid to the Government. After its take over by Hindustan Lever, MFIL is now a supplicant before the Board of Industrial and Financial Reconstruction.

In the name of competition, insurance has been opened to the private/MNC sector. But this competition is an eyewash. In the U.S., where there are 3,500 general insurance companies, 15 firms (0.4 per cent) control 50 per cent of the market. Six per cent together control 95 per cent.

The BALCO disinvestment was in favour of Sterlite

Industries, which had been blacklisted by the SEBI and could not operate in the equity market. A perverted explanation was that Sterlite was blacklisted and not BALCO; this conveniently overlooked the fact that as BALCO was controlled by Sterlite no prudent investor would risk his money in it.

Recently, the IPCL disinvested in favour of Reliance. Even in a country like the U.S. this is considered a prohibited monopolistic practice. Action is taken for breaking up such monopolies — witness the proceedings against Microsoft. But yet the explanation is that a monopoly by itself is not objectionable and that it can be safely left to be dealt with under the monopoly legislation even when Parliament has been unable to enact a mild and not so satisfactory competition law. The fact of Reliance being prosecuted under the Official Secrets Act was ignored with the unworthy explanation that it did not impinge on the security of the state.

The Government's faith that globalisation policies are the answer to the development of poor countries is not shared by the UNDP's Tenth Human Development Report of 1999, which says, "the benefit of globalisation of the past has been so unevenly shared that the very word has come to acquire in certain quarters a pejorative tinge." Recently, Joseph Stiglitz, former World Bank economist, fairly conceded that "globalisation is an unfair game, with the rules written by rich advanced industrial countries for rich industrial countries", Noam Chomsky said it was time "history appreciated the harmful effects of the fundamentals of corporate globalisation which undermine democracy". The public sector is accused of corruption, and in a few instances rightly. But listen to what Transparency International (TI) says: "Our new survey leaves no doubt that a large number of multinational corporations from the richest nations are pursuing a criminal course to win contracts in the leading emerging market economics of the world". And in this connection let us not forget our local patriotic corporations who have notched up Rs. 80,000 crores as bad loans euphemistically called "non-performing assets". That privatisation will expose the employees hard earned money to the rapacious greed of private employers is amply proved by the disclosure that as of March 2001, in the Employees Provident Fund not more than 40 per cent (Rs. 796.97 crores) of the total demand for the year and arrears (Rs. 1,981.07 crores) was remitted by the employers to the employees, account. The rest is still with the employers.

Seventy per cent of the Indian population is primarily engaged in agriculture in the rural areas. To improve their lot, subsidies and concessions to the agriculture sector are essential, but under the cover of the World Trade Organisation and globalisation serious constraints have been placed on Third World Governments, forcing them to open their markets for unrestricted imports from the developed world. The assault on the indigenous market through the removal of quantitative restrictions, causing a surge of imports, has threatened the very fabric of the Indian economy. The net effect will be the pauperisation of the peasantry and the working class both in the unorganised and organised sectors. Mr. Stiglitz has condemned it strongly, pointing out that "while preaching free market doctrines abroad, the U.S. bails out its airlines and increases agricultural subsidies at home. Even before these increases, subsidies to agriculture by the advanced industrial countries were enormous — exceeding the total income of Sub-Saharan Africa. The rich effectively close their markets to many goods that represent the comparative advantage of the poor."

The Human Development Report 2001, has pointed out that over half a billion people in South Asia, or 40 per cent of the total population of India, Pakistan, Bangladesh, Nepal, Bhutan, Sri Lanka and the Maldives have only become poorer under globalisation. It further said that "the poor were not considered by powerful nations when embarking on globalisation and there is now substantial evidence that India's success at reducing the incidence of poverty during the 1970s and 1980s was halted, if not reversed, during the 1990s. The rich-poor and urban-rural divides have only widened".

The recent change in our patent law spells doom for cheap medicines. The Government is already moving to private health policies which will make it impossible for the average Indian to support his healthcare needs.

The purported excuse of the Central Government that WTO rules compel it to change the patent law even when there is a paucity of affordable medicines causing health hazards is unconvincing. In this context, it should be noted that the U.S. when subscribing to the WTO treaty, put in a caveat that if any of the rules of WTO were repugnant to any U.S. legislation, the latter would prevail. Why is the Central Government reluctant to take the same stand? All these factors mandate that there should be a re-examination of the controversial policy of disinvestment in the public sector.

There is a serious controversy over whether the Government can disinvest shares in the Bharat Petroleum Corporation Ltd. (BPCL) without Parliament's approval. Though the Attorney-General has agreed with the Government view that it is not needed, the matter is too grave, affecting Parliament's sovereignty, to permit it to rest there. The proper course would be to refer it to the Supreme Court under Article 143 of the Constitution.

Prior to 1976, Burmah Shell operated two companies in India—one refining crude oil and the other selling petroleum products. It was acquired by the Central Government under the Burmah Shell acquisition of Undertakings Act, 1976. The Preamble to this 1976 Act recited the objective for such a legislations: "And whereas it is expedient in the public interest that the undertakings in India of Burmah Shell Oil should be acquired in order to ensure that the ownership and control of the petroleum products distributed and marketed in India by the said company are vested in the state and thereby so distributed as best to subserve the common good." This Acquisition Act had used words almost similar to those of Article 39-A of the Constitution from the Directive Principles of the State Policy which provides that the "state shall in particular direct the policy towards securing that the ownership and control of the material resources of the community are so distributed as best to subserve the common good". By virtue of Section 7 of the 1976 Act the Central vested its title and ownership in a Government Company — BPCL.

The Government's apparent justification for avoiding going before Parliament is based on the specious argument that under the Companies Act any shareholder (even the Government) has the freedom to dispose of its shareholding in the manner it likes. But this assumes wrongly that the BPCL is a private preserve of the Executive and can be placed on a par with a private company.

The Supreme Court has observed that : "The Government carries on various trades and business activity through the instrumentality of the state such as Government Company or Public Corporations which being state instrumentalities are state within the meaning of Article 12 and, as such, they are subject to the observance of fundamental rights embodied in Part III as well as to conform to the Directive Principles in Part IV of the Constitution ... and society has a stake in their proper and efficient working."

The argument that the BPCL being registered under the Companies Act is governed solely by it is fallacious. The BPCL came into existence by virtue of the 1976 Act. Parliament's mandate was that the management and control be exercised directly by the Government or through a Government company it may be the that the Government overdid the control and did not allow full autonomy and interfered with the day-to-day working of these public sector undertakings. But that is an aberration which has to be corrected by the proper implementation of Government policy. It cannot justify a breach of the policy underlying the 1976 Act.

Even the separate entity plea under the Companies Act wears thin because of the principle of lifting of the veil, recognised under the Companies Act both in England and in India. The courts have shown themselves willing to "lift the veil" where the device of incorporation is used for some illegal or improper purpose, because "the life of the law has not been logic it has been experience". The Supreme Court has held that the Government may act through its instrumentality or agency of natural persons or it may employ the instrumentality or agency of juridical persons to carry out its functions. It has been held that the Government, in many of its commercial ventures and public enterprises, is resorting more and more frequently to this resourceful legal contrivance of a corporation because it has many practical advantages and at the same time does not involve the slightest diminution in its ownership and control of the undertaking. In such cases, the true owner is the state, the real operator is the state and the effective controller is the state and accountability for its actions to the community and Parliament is of the state. The doctrine of lifting of the veil thus marks a change in the attitude the law had originally adopted towards the concept of the separate entity or personality of the Corporation, so as to meet the requirements of different economic problems. It may be said that as the Executive has formed a Government company in the first instance by resorting to the Companies Act, it is free to change the policy and decide to disinvest and even change the management because originally it was the Executive's policy.

But the cases of the BPCL and other Government companies which owe their existence by virtue of an Act of Parliament are totally different.

The reason is that it was Parliament which initially determined the policy of how the use of petroleum products, their distribution and marketing in India is to be carried out and it laid down under Section 7 of the 1976 Act that the Central Government or a Government company would be the owner. It was by virtue of this provision that the BPCL was made the owner of these assets which had come from Burmah Shell. If now the Government of India wishes to transfer those assets, management and control to a private investor it is not a case of merely exercising its power as a shareholder to transfer the shares under the Companies Act. By doing so it would be perverting the very rationale of the 1976 Act and making a mockery of the objective of the legislation retaining the Government as the owner of the petroleum products.

It may also be mentioned that the Centre is under pressure from the multinational corporations to change the labour laws to facilitate a "hire and fire" policy. In the case of Government companies, the Supreme Court has held that a rule for terminating employment by giving notice is arbitrary and hit by Article 14 of the Constitution. The Government, therefore cannot bring in this change in the BPCL, and other Government companies. The Centre's present action in seeking to convert the BPCL into a non-Government company would be *ultra vires,* the reason being that it is seeking to violate Parliament's mandate indirectly and is also seeking to change the law regarding employees and Government control. Thus, it is seeking to exercise power for a purpose opposed to the mandate given by the 1976 Act.

Even if the Centre is convinced that the BPCL should be managed by a private company, it can facilitate this only after Parliament's approval. It cannot resort to an indirect manner of getting around Parliament's mandate by seeking to disinvest its majority shareholding.

Of course, it is needless to emphasis the serious consequences of disinvestment in the BPCL and other Government undertakings. The Government has reportedly asked oil PSUs to contribute interim dividends of Rs. 2,600 crores to the national exchequer (the BPCL's share is Rs. 60 crores) to meet its fiscal deficit and for using subsidies for the weaker sections.

Is it not a cruel joke that the surplus generated by the PSUs is sought to be gifted through disinvestment to the very foreign oil giants which were driven out by the 1976 Act? Why cannot the Opposition in the Rajya Sabha pass a resolution disapproving of these disinvestments if it is serious about opposing it? The public has a right to know.

9.5 Insurance Bill : Ominous Portents

The announcement by the Prime Minister, A.B. Vajpayee, that he will give immediate attention to the economy is welcome. But the Finance Minister, Yashwant Sinha's priority for passing Insurance Bill this very session of Parliament is a matter of concern. Any such attempt will mean flouting the will of the electorate who has demanded that there be a caring state which will provide him with immediate basic necessities rather than the grandiloquent chimera of prosperity to be ushered in by illusory investment through foreign-owned insurance and banking.

The claim that globalisation helps in the flow of foreign investment in developing countries has been belied by the fact that since 1991 the net transfer of flows out of developing countries has amounted to $60 billion.

When life insurance was nationalized in 1956, C.D. Deshmukh, the then Finance Minister, said insurance in the developing country must be seen as an essential service which a welfare state should provide to its people and not as a business proposition or additional source of investment to those who put their money in the stock market.

The capital contribution of the government to the Life Insurance Corporation was a mere Rs. 5 crores.

When general insurance was nationalized in 1973, Y.B. Chavan, the then Finance Minister, declared:

This step has been taken to serve better the needs of the economy by securing development of general insurance business in the best interests of the community and to ensure that concentration of wealth does not result in common detriment.

Against this background, I fail to see what urgency or special considerations have motivated the new government to go in for immediate privatization of insurance. I can understand multinationals waiting greedily for a harvest of the vast investible funds of the LIC, which now stand at over Rs.105 lakh crores.

The argument that the public sector is a drag on the economy is calumny. The LIC made an investment of Rs.7000 crores in the Sixth Plan and about Rs. 13,000 crores during the Seventh Plan; it rose to Rs. 56,097 crores during the Eighth Plan. The LIC has also invested in a social sector like housing to the tune of Rs.10,000 crores and in electricity to the extent of Rs. 8000 crores. A sum of Rs. 30,000 crores in insurance funds has been earmarked for infrastructure development as part of the Ninth Plan. Since 1981-82 the government's share of the additional surplus has been over Rs. 100 crores. During the year ended March 1997, the LIC paid Rs. 199 crores to the government as its share of valuation surplus. It distributed to policy-holders a bonus of over Rs. 3700 crores in 1996-97. The figure rose steadily from Rs. 2250 crores in 1992-93.

The complaint of poor customer service is partly correct and it certainly needs to be improved. But it is simplistic to imagine that mere privatization will automatically improve the situation. If full autonomy is given to the LIC and government interference removed, the management and employees could work out a solution, both safeguarding the legitimate interests of the workers and improving customer service. The LIC settles daily, on an average, over 16,000 claims and pays about Rs. 19 crores. The percentage of the LIC's outstanding claims payable during 1993-94 was only 4.86, in terms of the number of claims. While the growth rate in general insurance in India in the mid-eighties was 18 per cent, in the US it ranged between 3.2 and 6.2 per cent.

In a developing country like India, public sector is the only instrument through which the social sector can be strengthened. The gross direct premium even in general insurance projected for 2030 AD is Rs. 13,000 crores. No amount of this fund will be available for public use if privatization takes place, but the money will go to the private investors.

It is futile to suggest that foreign companies will meet the social obligations which the LIC and the General Insurance Corporation are honouring. K.C. Mittal, one of the members of the Insurance Regulatory Authority, has gone so far as to suggest that such a stipulation is unlikely but said the foreign companies will be expected to give some consideration to the untouched regions like rural areas. It is amazing that the government should throw away money-earning institutions at the whims of the foreign investors, and reduce itself to the role of begging for money which belongs to its own citizens.

Suggestions that competition would give better service and wastage would be minimised because of the private interest have been proved wrong by the experience of the developed countries. Thanks to fierce competition, caution and the principle of commercial feasibility have been wantonly ignored. In the US because of the risky investments, one life insurance company goes into liquidation every month. Over 370 general companies have become insolvent since 1982. Even Lloyds of London, supposed to be the last word on stability and solvency, suffered a loss of over $38 billion in 1991.

Free competition exists only in theory. There are 3500 general insurance companies in the US but only 15 (0.4 per cent) of them control 50 per cent of the market. Six per cent together control 95 per cent.

It is not as if the developed countries are characterised by open markets. They themselves prohibit foreign imports of insurance for domestic risks. The share (in percentage) of foreign-licensed insurers' business in the domestic markets are: the US and Japan three each; the UK, France and Switzerland five each.

According to a report by the UNCTAD Secretary, general insurance in America has almost suffered a serious collapse. In the nineties a Senate Sub-Committee report on rising insolvencies of insurers, submitted to the House of Representatives, detailed the

> Scandalous mismanagement and rascality of pirates operating insurance companies and ill-effects of frauds and incompetence leading to bankruptcies among 50 large-sized companies in the course of the last five years.

The report by John D. Dingell, Chairman of the Sub-Committee on Oversight and Investigations, reads like a fiction of white-collar crime capable of bankrupting huge companies and possibly the entire industry.

The stark experience should dispel any wrong notion about controls through a regulatory authority. Moreover, the shabby treatment given by the Department of Telecommunications to the Telecom Regulatory Authority of India does not encourage a level-playing field in the functioning of the government machinery.

Insurance is not a sophisticated industry which may require the involvement of multinationals in order to obtain the latest technology. If we are keen on following the latest trends in the insurance business, we could directly employ some of the foreign experts at a pittance of cost rather than letting Indian money and capital be secreted abroad and thereby depriving the country of vast investible funds—on false slogans of the benefits of globalisation. The UN Under Secretary-General for Economic and Social Affairs has warned:

> the world's economic system was alert enough to protect the rich but too tardy to protect the poor and that the goal was not to have a global economy that ended up as welfare state for the rich. Rethinking was needed on how to make the system more equitable and mindful of long-term concern.

Will the BJP and the Congress-I, political rivals but partners in the scheme of global economy, heed the warning? And what are the other parties, trade unions and social activists doing to meet this challenge to the sovereignty and economy of our country. The poor await an answer.

9.6 Protection of Consumer Rights

Authors address at 29th World Marketing Congress for Strategies in Banking. Insurance and Financial Institution, (2002).

The recognition of consumer is late entrant in the jurisprudence of Indian Law makers. For too long the doctrine of caveat emptor (let the buyer beware) what the dominant philosophy underlying legal circles. It was always of doubtful validity. But it is totally in appropriate in the present circumstances.

History tell us that the interests of the sellers and the buyers have invariably pulled apart, the former trying to obtain the highest price and the latter hesitating to be exploited. Consumer's resistance is an age-long pull although it may have been lighted and limited only to ineffective resentment.

Now the marketing of goods and services is conducted on an organized basis and by trained business executives. The untrained consumer is no match for the businessman who attempts to persuade the consumer to buy goods or services on terms and conditions suitable to vendor. The consumer therefore, needs protection by law.

But gradually with representative democracy taking over awareness protecting the small consumer started growing.

In the environment of modern economic development, corporate sector no longer functions in isolation. This implies that the claims of various interest will have to be balanced not on the narrow ground of what is best for the shareholders alone but from the point of view of what is best for the community at large.

It was only in 1969 that Parliament enacted (The Monopolies and Restrictive Trade Practices, (M.R.T.P.) Act, 1969). With a view to ensure that the operation of the economic system does not result in the concentration of economic power to the common detriment and to prohibit such monopolistic and restrictive trade practices as are prejudicial to public interest.

Its ineffectiveness to protect consumer interest was

highlighted in a Report of "High Powered Expert Committee" appointed by the Government of India in 1978 – (commonly known as Sachar Committee Report), which commented as follows :

"Our Act at present contains no provision for protection of the consumers against false or misleading advertisement or other similar unfair trade practices. There is now greater recognition that consumers needs to be protected not only from the effects of restrictive practices but also from practices which are resorted to by the trade and industry to mislead or dupe the customers."

The Committee therefore proposed that a separate chapter should be added to the Act defining the various unfair trade practices. But it was only in 1984 that these provisions were added to MRTP Act.

However soon after realizing the urgency the Parliament enacted the Consumer Protection Act, 1986. The rationale was emphasized by the Supreme Court (1994) in Lucknow Development case, as "The law of consumer protection has come to meet the long felt necessity of protecting the common man from wrongs for which the remedy under the ordinary law for various reasons has become illusory." The importance of the Act lies" in promoting welfare of the society in as much as it attempts to remove the helplessness of a consumer which he faces against powerful business, described as a network of rackets, or a society in which 'producers have secured power' to 'rob the rest' and the might of public bodies which are degenerating into storehouses of inaction. The enactment in these unbelievable yet harsh realities, appears to be a sliver lining, which may in course of time succeed in checking the rot."

The functioning of the Act has brought out some welcome features bringing relief to the consumers. The Supreme Court by holding that building construction is a service within the meaning of the Act has provided reprieve to the small apartment buyer against big shark of builders who were in many cases taking small investors for a ride. The Supreme Court refreshingly held that though—The proceedings before them are legal proceedings. However, it held that in view of the object of the

Act, it would be appropriate that these Forums created under the Act are at liberty to proceeding with the matters in accordance with the provisions of the Act rather than relegating the parties to an arbitration proceedings pursuant to a contract entered into between the parties.

Another issue which was creating a problem was the exclusion from consumer definition a case of a purchase for commercial purpose. That has now been clarified by Supreme Court holding that if a person purchases goods even to sell but provided he was self employed he would be a consumer which really means that a petty shopkeeper or even a craftsman would be considered a Consumer within the Act, and could seek his remedy against his supplier.

Under the Act a person is a consumer if he pays for the services. The result is that in a hospital run by the Government the persons who are not charged for consultation by the Doctors are without a remedy even if the treatment is given deficient. However, if a person has taken paying rooms he would be entitled to proceed against negligent medical service. This seems to discriminate between the poor and the wealthy which feature should be removed because in a country like India vast number of services can only be available to the poor if it is made free to them but to make the service free without giving them a remedy against a bad service would be an unfair discrimination. This is more so since the Supreme Court has held that medical service and Doctors are covered in the definition of a service to a consumer and the patient is entitled to proceed against a Doctor if his complaint is that there is a negligence in the service given to him by a Doctor. There is also a lacuna that there is no provisions for an execution of an order by the Consumer Court. This naturally is a great hindrance in the execution of the order. It has been suggested that the Commission under the Act should have the power to punish for contempt on similar laws as provided in Section 13 of the MRTP Act.

There are however some omissions which need to be rectified in the Act so as to make it a more effective instrument. Thus unlike the MRTP Commission, the consumer courts still lack the power to issue interim injunction. This is a big lacuna because in order to tackle unfair trade practices, particularly false or misleading advertisements and protect the interests of consumers, the consumer commission should have the power to issue interim injunctions preventing the trader from pursuing such a practice, pending disposal of the case.

Section 14 of the Act empowers the Consumer Courts to award compensation if there is a negligence on the part of the opposite party. This requirement of fault or negligence acts against the interest of an average consumer because he has under neither the resources nor the wherewithal to be able to prove the actual negligence in any product that he may have purchased. The defect in any product may be hidden and the test of the negligence is to be pursued the manufacturer can avoid of the proceedings by pleading that he is not aware of it. This is a serious lacuna in most of the countries in Europe and America the defects in the products is automatically treated as a negligence on the part of the manufacturer entitling the consumer to receive compensation. The concept of the product liability which mean that if the product is proved to be not complying with the quality or the performance claimed for it, the same will be deemed to be a proof of negligence and the manufacture would be automatically held liable and it will not be open to him to plead otherwise. Such a concept needs to be provided under our Act.

The adoption of a theory of strict liability in defective-product cases is justified on the following grounds: as handicrafts have been replaced by mass production with its great markets and transportation facilities, the close relationship between the producer and the consumer of a product has been altered. Manufacturing processes, frequently, valuable secrets, are ordinarily either inaccessible to or beyond the ken of the general public. The consumer no longer has means or skill enough to investigate for himself the soundness of a product, even when it is not contained in a sealed package, and his erstwhile vigilance has been lulled by the steady efforts of manufacturers to build up confidence by advertising and marketing devices such as trademarks. Consumers no longer approach products warily, but accept them on faith, relying on the reputation of the manufacturer or the trademark. Manufacturers have sought to reward that faith by increasingly high standards of inspection and a readiness to make good on defective products by way of replacements and refunds. The manufacturers' obligation to the consumer must keep pace with the changing relationship between them; it cannot be escaped because the marketing of a product has become so complicated as to require one or more intermediaries.

The classes of persons who have been held subject to strict liability in tort have included manufacturers, wholesalers, distributors, retailers, home developers, and vehicle leasing services.

The result will be that if the product was placed on the market in a defective condition originally, and this can be proved, the mere fact that the injury occurred a long time later would not excuse the manufacturer or seller from liability if the injury was caused by the defect, rather than by the mere passage of time.

A contract exempting a person from liability for future negligent acts is subject to the objection that it tends to induce a want of care, and such agreements are often declared invalid on the ground of public policy. It would seem that the Uniform Commercial Code in U.S.A. has the effect of prohibiting a disclaimer of liability for negligence in connection with a sale of goods.

In a sense, liability based on breach of an express or implied warranty in a products liability case is also liability without fault; the injured party need not prove negligence on the part of the manufacturer or the seller of the defective product.

Some Corporate friendly may maintain that in these heady day of globalization and neo economic liberation such like legislations are an unnecessary intervention in the functioning of the market, and that consumers need no special protection; all can he safely left to the market. But the perfect market is an economist's dream and consumer's sovereignty a myth. In real life, products are complex and of great variety and consumers and retailers have imperfect knowledge. Suppliers may often have a dominant buying position. As a consequence, bargaining power in the market is generally weighed against the consumer.

As a matter of fact even in the land of free Economy USA, the working of Federal Trade Commission has labeled practices not known before. It has found that a situation has developed in which the public must be prevented from being made victims of false claim of products blatantly advertised, even though it may not have an adverse effect on the competition. The effort is to shift the emphasis on detection and eradication of frauds against the consumers, particularly belonging to weaker sections of society. If a consumer is thus falsely induced to enter into buying goods which do not possess quality and do not have the cure for ailment advertised it is apparent that the consumer is being made to pay for quality of things on false representation. Obviously such a situation cannot be accepted.

We need only recall how tobacco industry kept concealed internal reports which showed a direct connection between tobacco consumption and lung cancer.

Also the recent most example of MacDonald agreeing to pay at least 10 million US Dollars to American vegetarians for having concealed the use of Beef flavour in its preparations.

As a matter of fact the philosophy of consumer protection is no longer confined to the usual concept of retail purchases and their quality. The concept is now widened to include whether the society is able to make available consumer goods at affordable price for low earning large segment of population.

Also included is the concept whether consumerism is not being equated with only meeting the requirement and looking after the needs and peculiarities of the affluent section of the society, with consequential neglect of majority which is poor.

The Consumer protection has taken such a qualitative a jurisprudence aspect that the UN Guidelines for consumer protections were laid down in 1985 with subsequent amendments. The guidelines recognize that proper distribution facilities for the enlargement of consumer goods were important part of the success of the consumer movement. It, specifically provides that the Government should have a policy to ensure distribution of essential goods and service especially in rural sector and that necessary storage and retail facilities along with education and awareness were prerequisite for success of such a movement.

The UN Guidelines for consumer protection have given guidelines especially for developing countries in various areas of health and well-being of the consumer, i.e., food, water, etc. It has advised the Government to adopt that while formulating a policy in regard to food, government should take into account the needs of all consumers for food security. In this context, we in India, have a serious problem where notwithstanding the minimum of 25 per cent to 30 per cent of population being below the poverty line to whom food purchase is grave problem, but food is not being made available to them notwithstanding the bursting storage of foodgrain running over to millions of tonnes involving the cost of storage alone running into hundreds of crores. Suggestions have been given by a large number of NGOs to start a project for food for work in which public works are started by the Government so as to give the good as part of the pay. Surprisingly, the matter still remains at the discussion stage of Inter-Governmental Agencies. This is a grave violation of Consumer Protection guidelines framed by the UN.

Similarly, in regard to water UN Guidelines mandate that the Government should ensure supply distribution and quality of drinking water and strengthen the National Policy in this regard. Unfortunately here also the present situation in India is woeful. According to one Government estimate about 57 per cent of the total population is not covered by supply of safe drinking water. The per capita norm for water consumption should be 300 litres per day whereas on an average, the urban population is supplied only 145 litres per capita per day in Class-I cities. As many as 31 per cent of the households have to walk up to 100 feet to collect water and many among the poor – women and children – had to cover the distance not once but several times a day to collect the daily requirements. That for the overwhelming majority of the slum dwellers, the availability of water may be lesser than 20 litres per capita per day.

ECOSOC resolution of 28th July, 1995 resolved that housing should also be included and strong policy for higher resources consuming sector be laid down. It recommended that the Government should develop appropriate policy to provide for shelter to the consumer in rural areas and urban and semi-urban towns.

The housing shortage in our country is estimated about 30 million units of which 16.7 millions units are in urban areas.

Out of this 15.02 million houses are needed for Low Income Group (LIG) and Economically Weaker Section (EWS). The distressing reality however is that in India over 45 per cent of households have only one room per capita. Area available to the bottom 40 per cent is 58 sq. metre. Even the Delhi Municipal Corporation prescribes the requirement regarding the minimum size of a habitable room as 60 sq. metre.

A study conducted by the Delhi Development Authority shows that a hut of 2.5 × 3 metres accommodates about four persons. In Delhi nearly one-third of the total population live jhuggi jhopri bustees. (Tin/plastic shacks).

The inequity in the provisions of infrastructure and basic services across the States and size and categories of settlements has been accentuated as a consequence of the programme of structural adjustment and consequent withdrawal of the State. To meet these requirements of consumers for such essential services Government reliance on market and free enterprise is misplaced.

This is corroborated by UNDP 10th Human Development Report which says "market dominated globalization has led to growing marginalisation of poor nations and people, growing human insecurity and growing inequality with benefits accruing almost solely to the richest people and countries and that the global gap between the haves and have-nots is widening."

Another guideline deals with for, the provisions of medicine for the poor. The present bad situation is going to become worse with the introduction of product patent instead of process patent having to be enforced because of the membership of WTO by the Government. The estimate of switch over to the Product Patent will mean increase of the medical expenses to the extent of thousands of crores for providing medicine even in the Government hospitals and dispensaries apart from increase in cost to individuals for their private purchases. This will be the severest attack on the protection to consumer in his need for medical facilities.

National Commission has had rather strong words (in my opinion only party justified) at the banking workers on going on illegal strike and presenting ingress to the bank customers. The

Commission was dealing with a strike called by All Indian Bank Employees. It observed "the Commission feels unhappy to observe that the striking workers have been totally indifferent to the interests of the consumers the depositors, account holders and the borrowers, whom the bank including its workmen are expected to serve. Not only was the strike against the Bank management illegal, the strikers also unlawfully denied ingress into and egress out of the Bank premises to willing workers, officers and customers....... The cheques issued by the opposite on the Reserve Bank of India were found to be defaced and were in consequence dishonoured........ The Commission feels that all these were clearly anti-consumer acts. Unless there is a better appreciation of the obligation of the workmen/employees to the bank's clients and a realization that "innocent clients" should not be made to suffer, and that in public sector banks, such strikes hardly affect the bank management, the Consumer Protection Act will remain largely ineffective for the consumers in this sector." No doubt, these observations need to be seriously heeded to by workmen.

I wish however, also to point out another misworking in Banking Sector which has anti-consumer implication so far as the small depositor or loanee is concerned. According to Union Governments statement Banks have over Rs. 1,25,000 crores that is euphemistically called non-performing assets but are in common parlance bad and irrecoverable loans advanced to the big corporate sector. In spite of public pronouncement no effective steps have been taken or spelled out by the Union Government for their recoveries. Such a situation is not a mere question of Revenue. It has close connection to consumers Protection, because such large outstandings prevent the Bank for meeting the genuine business, personal, housing finance needs of small customers consumers of the Banks. I do not know whether National Commission could consider advising the Government how to look after the interest or give protection to this small consumer of Banking service.

Another average consumer who needs protection is one who seeks cover under Insurance policies. No doubt the premium and service to the insured are the first priorities along with safety of the dues to the assured. In the days of nationalized insurance of Government control and guarantee acted as a cover for protection of the interest of the insured. Now that this line has been opened, the powers under the Consumer Protect Act may have to be invoked often. We are, however, assured that because of competition among various companies consumers will be safe and get better service and in this context example is given of U.S.A. and the benefit of open market competition. But unfortunately even a cursory examination of situation in U.S.A. occasions misgiving regarding greater consumer protection. The situation is rather to the contrary – free competition exists only in theory. There are 3,500 general insurance companies in the U.S. but only 15 (0.4 per cent) of them control 50 per cent of the market. Six per cent together control 95 per cent.

According to a report by the UNCTAD Secretary, General Insurance in America has almost suffered a serious collapse. In the Nineties a Senate sub-committee report on rising insolvencies of insurers, submitted to the House of Representatives, detailed the "scandalous mismanagement and rascality of pirates operating insurance companies and ill-effects of frauds and incompetence leading to bankruptcies among 50 large-sized companies in the course of the last five years". The report by Mr. John D. Dingell, chairman of the sub-committee on oversight and investigations, reads like a fiction of white-collar crime capable of bankrupting huge companies and possible the entire industry.

In any study of consumer protection inevitably sociological question regarding the nature of consumer society, the contradictions within the country and intra countries are frequently raised. No absolute may be possible, but the various important currents arise and which need to be closely examined when planning for a consumer society – the questions posed being does such a society lead to real happiness. Also connected with it would be the question of development stage of various countries in the world and the acceptance of the reality that in developing countries consumerism must provide for the necessities of life, like food, shelter – as against the concept in developed world, where basic necessities having been provided already, consumerism is concerned with enjoying facilities of gadgets and other items of luxury living, with consequential tools of advertisement, etc. being put more to use in trying to establish a particular type of consumer society.

According to Prof. Galbraith, "production, inequality and insecurity were the economic problem of the 19th century in the developed world but these problems are no longer in that society but according to him, new problems have arisen because of the expansion of production because the society is in a rat-race in which people have to be persuaded by high-powered advertising and hidden persuasion to buy the goods which the businessmen think up to produce. Real scarcity has been succeeded by contrived scarcity. Economy depends on reiterating the contrivance. Luxurious living which drives the whole machine, becomes the necessary cost of production so that the margin of resources available for social uses such as defence as unduly small in relation to the national income."

The bottom line of the environmental position is that it does not seem possible, based on any known technology, for the people of China, India, or other large populations in the developing world to imitate the consumption patterns of the North.

That foreign investment and the mantra of globalization will raise the level of developing countries is a myth flying in face of reality. Clive Pointing in his book "creating the affluent society has pointed out:

"Development aid, despite official rhetoric to the contrary, has been modest and is frequently tied to the commercial interests of the donor country. Multilateral development agencies such as the World Bank have often supported projects that have caused major social and economic damage; massive hydroelectric, dams that have flooded agricultural land and displaced huge numbers of people are just one example. Economic necessity leads many. Third World countries to concentrate on the production of crops and minerals for export, even when these export industries interfere with local food production and damage the environment.

Economic growth since the Second World War has increased the gap between the industrialized world and poorer countries. During most of the 1980s, the Third World transferred more money to the industrialized world in debt interest than it received in new loans and aid. Austerity programmes imposed on debtor nations by the International Monetary Fund have placed the heaviest burdens on the poorest people. The World Bank officially estimates that 800 million people worldwide (excluding China) exist in conditions of absolute poverty, including 20 per cent of the world's children.

The emergence of an affluent society has thus been accompanied by a huge shift in the pattern of wealth distribution worldwide. The industrialized countries utilize the vast majority of the world's resources to support *unprecedented high levels of consumption.* Internal inequity has persisted, but international inequality has greatly increased, together with a large increase in the worldwide impact of pollutants." (Emphasis supplied).

It is commonly known that with the production of goods goes the persuasion that assures their purchase. Advertising, as in several essays here told, is an essential feature of the economic process. But this economic reality has long been denied. In the orthodox view consumer sovereignty reigns supreme. Questioning this assumption has persisted for all these years and recently even more vehemently.

To make this image more concrete the amount spent annually on advertising in the United States is about $150 billion. This is approximately equal to the total spent in the nation on higher education. But the time they are eighteen, most children will have spent more time watching television than they will have spent in school.

Public services, especially those for the poorer citizens, enjoy no such promotion. As a result, the modern, economy has an inherently un-equal and unsocial distribution of resources between its private and public sectors – wonderfully expensive television programmes, poor schools; spacious, handsomely furnished houses, filthy streets; abundant automobiles, dense traffic jams and poor public transportation.

A variety of specific connections have been suggested by thinkers who see the ethos of the consumer society as exacerbating the effects, or the feelings of poverty. For example, poverty is created by a desire for more (Marshall Sahlines, Part I); poor people and poor countries, make inappropriate decisions on what to consume, and reduce their savings and investment, because they are misled by seeing the consumption of richer people and nations (Rangnar Nurkse, Part V); and the driving force of profit-seeking capitalism creates pressures for poor countries and poor individuals to make and purchase comodities that respond to wants manufactured by consumer-society-dominated media, rather than putting their efforts and resources into serving true needs (Russell Belk and Nathaan Keyfitz, Part IX).

(*Consumer Society*, Edited by Neva R. Goodwin).

Let me end with the somber picture pointed by Prof. J. K. Gallbraith when he says "with the development, perhaps one should say exploitation, of the modern consumer economy has come a marked change in social concern as regards consumer products. There was once the consumer movement – a determined investigation of, and report on, the value and utility of various consumer products and supporting public regulation and, education. This continues but with a diminished sense of social urgency. The poor still need guidance on what they buy, including protection against consumer scams. For the more affluently supplied there is no similar urgency. There is no social need for according guidance on the purchase of a Cadillac or a Marcedes Benz or for that matter, designer jeans or a vast range of other affluent products. As consumer necessity yields to fashion and persuasion, concern for consumer protection and choice inevitably recedes. This is recognized in part, but far fully, in either public discourse or practice.

9.7 Poverty : The Worst of Human Rights Violations

Of the many violations of human rights that can be listed, none is worse but less spoken of in fashionable seminars on human rights—I am referring to "poverty" the mother of all human rights violations.

No doubt human rights violations manifest themselves in various forms—brutality of police, or gender injustice, pollution and environmental degradation, social ostracism of the Dalits—but ultimately the answer to all these must be found in our commitment to the elimination of poverty.

The horror of poverty was highlighted in a message given on October 17, 1999 in observance of the International Day for the Eradication of Poverty, by the United Nations Secretary-General, Mr. Kofi Annan: "How many times have we said that it (poverty) was incompatible with human dignity."

"But billions of people are still trying to survive on less than Rs. 130 a day, with no drinking water, health care, or access to education, still denied the jobs that would help them escape their impoverished state, and thus, still deprived of some of their most basic rights."

During the Cold War human rights were said to be restricted to what we call the political right of freedom of speech. Association and economic rights were said to be something necessary, but not a part of human rights. This is a myth.

Fortunately, this myth of conflict between political or economic rights or artificial prioritisation of such rights in developed or developing countries was exploded when the Vienna Declaration and Programme of Action at the World Conference on Human Rights (1993) affirmed that human rights were the birth right of all human beings and their protection and promotion were the first responsibility of the Government and that all the human rights were universal, indivisible and interrelated.

Bread and liberty are two sides of the same coin, and deprivation of either must inevitably damage the fabric of the other. The freedom to agitate for bread, and sustenance to fight for one's liberties are concomitant.

Freedom of an individual, which is the postulate of human rights, obviously can have no meaning so long as the poor in the country do not have their economic conditions improved and the discrimination based on privilege do not become mere memories instead of becoming more and more aggressive as time passes on. The present situation must cause concern to all human right activists.

The richest fifth have an income 74 times that of the poorest fifth.

One per cent of the wealth of the 20 richest people, or $8 billion, could provide universal access to primary education for a year—but no political party is seeking to correct this balance—the result is a denial of the human right to universal education.

The assets of three of the richest people are more than the combined GNP of the 48 least developed countries.

In Delhi, nearly one third of the total population lives in juhggi jhompri bustees. This is a shortage of 40 million houses. Those preferring artificial sympathy to the homeless express helplessness because of the huge outlay of Rs. 123,000 crores required for this purpose. But curiously these very worthies maintain a deafening silence about Rs. 55,000 crores in bad debts (euphemistically called non-performing assets) owed by big business to banks and which if realised could considerably help the homeless meet their needs.

Many a time one feels distressed by some human rights organisation getting preoccupied with human rights problems which are more relevant in the European and American context—the rights of homosexuals, the rights of unmarried mothers, the right to abortion or the status of surrogate mothers—no doubt important aspects of human rights dimension in their social set up. But I do fell that the protagonists of human rights in developing countries should concern themselves on a priority basis with the actual realities of oppression of the weak and of discrimination in the social set up.

The blessing of the Government would degenerate into tyranny unless it is accompanied by a recognition that there are certain basic rights which are possessed by all the citizens. Though believers in human rights must be ever vigilant to resist any onslaught on the civil and political liberties of the individual, and there can be no compromise on their essentiality, it is necessary that these rights, so far as developing countries are concerned, must correlate with the equally important major issue which is also an aspect of human rights, namely, the development of the economy and the responsibility of the society to feed, clothe, house, keep its people free from starvation, and to be able to bring up one's children and oneself in a decent, healthy environment.

The former South African President, Mr. Nelson Mandela, speaking at the Heads of Non-Aligned Nations Conference held on 2-9-1998 in Durban highlighted the immediate need to fight poverty when he said: "We have to remake our common world anew. The violence we see all around us, against people who are as human as we are, who sit in privileged positions, must surely be addressed in a decisive and sustained manner. I speak here of the violence of hunger which kills, of the violence of homelessness which kills, of the violence of malaria and HIV/AIDS which kill and of the trade in narcotics which kills."

Unfortunately the solutions being suggested are all an illusion. Thus the much touted claim by the propagandists of globalisation that it will accelerate progress in developing countries is belied by the UNDP's Tenth Human Development Report of 1999, which says that "market dominated globalisatiron has led to growing marginalisation of poor nations and people, growing human insecurity and growing inequality with benefits accruing almost solely to the richest people and countries" and that "the global gap between the haves and have-nots, is widening." HDR 1999 has commented tersely that "the benefits of globalisation in the past decade have been so unevenly shared that the very word has come to acquire in certain quarters a pejorative tinge."

Similarly, the World Development Report for 1999-2000 says that at the start of the new millennium an estimated 1.5 billion people will subsist on the equivalent of a dollar a day.

About 220 million urban dwellers (13 per cent of the developing world's urban population) lack access to safe drinking water and about twice that number lack access to even the simplest of latrines.

Another denial of human rights is to the half of the population, that is the women. The burden of deprivation, poverty and violence is the heaviest on them.

In most countries women have neither the right to the home in which they were born nor to the home they live in after marriage. This essential homelessness of women is a major factor in limiting the valuable contribution women can make towards gaining and retaining a home and, in turn, in building society. This critical factor has the effect of perpetuation of gender inequality and poverty.

A century ago Swami Vivekananda warned the Indian elite that unless they carried the masses with them in all efforts at national regeneration, no great progress could be made. The neglect of the masses.... chronic poverty under which they were held down have been the main cause of India's degradation. "I call him a traitor who having been educated, nursed in luxury by the heart's blood of the downtrodden millions of toiling poor, never even takes a thought for them....who thinks of raising these sunken downtrodden millions? A few thousand graduates do not make a nation, a few rich men do not make a nation."

How sad that even after a century, that reproach by the saintly soul should continue to shame us.

9.8 The Danger of Privatising Insurance

The announcement by the Prime Minister, Mr. A.B. Vajpayee, that he will give immediate attention to economy is welcome. But the Finance Minister, Mr. Yashwant Sinha's priority for passing the Insurance Bill this very session of Parliament is a matter of concern. Any such attempt will mean flouting the will of the electorate who had demanded that there be a caring state which will provide him with immediate basic necessities rather than the grandiloquent chimera of prosperity to be ushered in by illusory investment through foreign-owned insurance and banking.

The claim that globalisation helps in the flow of foreign investment in developing countries had been belied by the fact that since 1991 the net transfer of flows out of developing countries has amounted to $ 60 billion.

When life insurance was nationalised in 1956, C.D. Deshmukh, then Finance Minister, said insurance in the developing country must be seen as an essential service which a welfare state should provide to its people and not as a business proposition or additional source of investment to those who put their money in the stock market.

The capital contribution of the Government to the Life Insurance Corporation was a mere Rs. 5.00 crores.

When general insurance was nationalised in 1973, Y.B. Chavan, then Finance Minister, declared "this step has been taken to serve better the needs of the economy by securing development of general insurance business in the best interests of the community and to ensure that concentration of wealth does not result in common detriment".

Against this background, I fail to see what urgency or special considerations have motivated the new Government to go in for immediate privatisation of insurance. I can understand multinationals waiting greedily for a harvest of the vast investible funds of the LIC, which now stand at over Rs. 105 lakh crores.

The argument that the public sector is a drag on economy is calumny. The LIC made an investment of Rs. 7,000 crores in the Sixth Plan and about Rs. 13,000 crores during the Seventh Plan; it rose to Rs. 56,097 crores during the Eighth Plan. The LIC has also invested in a social sector like housing to the tune of Rs. 10,000 crores and in electricity to the extent of Rs. 8,000 crores. A sum of Rs. 30,000 crores in insurance funds has been earmarked for infrastructure development as part of the Ninth Plan. Since 1981-82 the Government's share of the additional surplus had been over Rs. 100 crores. During the year ended March 1997, the LIC paid Rs. 199 crores to the Government as its share of valuation surplus. It distributed to policy-holders a bonus of over Rs. 3,700 crores in 1996-97. It rose steadily from Rs. 2,250 crores in 1992-93.

The complaint of poor customer service is partly correct and it certainly needs to be improved. But it is simplistic to imagine that mere privatisation will automatically improve the situation. If full autonomy is given to the LIC and government interference removed, the management and employees could work out a solution, both safeguarding the legitimate interests of the workers and improving customer service. The LIC settles daily, on an average, over 16,000 claims and pays about Rs. 19 crores. The percentage of the LIC's outstanding claims payable during 1993-94 was only 4.86, in terms of the number of claims. While the growth rate in general insurance in India in mid-80s was 18 per cent, in the U.S., it ranged between 3.2 and 6.2 per cent.

In a developing country like India, public sector is the only instrument through which the social sector can be strengthened. The gross direct premium even in general insurance projected for 2030 A.D. is Rs. 13,000 crores. No amount of this fund will be available for public use if privatisation takes place, but the money will go to the private investors.

It is futile to suggest that foreign companies will meet the social obligations which the LIC and the General Insurance Corporation are honouring. Mr. K.C. Mittal, one of the members of the Insurance Regulatory Authority, has gone so far as to suggest that such a stipulation is unlikely but said the foreign companies will be expected to give some consideration to the untouched areas like rural areas. It is amazing that the Government should throw away money-earning institutions at the whims of the foreign investors, and reduce itself to the role of begging for money which belongs to its own citizens.

Suggestions that competition would give better service and wastage would be minimised because of the private interest have been proved wrong by the experience of the developed countries. Thanks to fierce competition, caution and the principle of commercial feasibility have been wantonly ignored. In the U.S., because of the risky investments, one life insurance company goes into liquidation every month. Over 370 general insurance companies have become insolvent since 1982. Even Lloyds of London, supposed to be the last word on stability and solvency, suffered a loss of over $38 billion in 1991.

Free competition exists only in theory. There are 3,500 general insurance companies in the U.S. but only 15 (0.4 per cent) of them control 50 per cent of the market. Six per cent together control 95 per cent.

It is not as if the developed countries are characterised by open markets. They themselves prohibit foreign imports of insurance for domestic risks. The shares (in percentage) of foreign-licensed insurers, business in the domestic markets are: the U.S. and Japan three each, the U.K., France and Switzerland five each.

According to a report by the UNCTAD Secretary, general insurance in America has almost suffered a serious collapse. In the Nineties a Senate sub-committee report on rising insolvencies of insurers, submitted to the House of Representatives, detailed the "scandalous mismanagement and rascality of pirates operating insurance companies and ill-effects of frauds and incompetence leading to bankruptcies among 50 large-sized companies in the course of the last five years". The report by Mr. John D. Dingell, chairman of the sub-committee on oversight and investigations, reads like a fiction of white-collar crime capable of bankrupting huge companies and possibly the entire industry.

The stark experience should dispel any wrong notion about controls through a regulatory authority. Moreover, the shabby treatment given by the Department of Telecommunications to the Telecom Regulatory Authority of India does not encourage a level-playing field in the functions of Government machinery.

Insurance is not a sophisticated industry which may require the involvement of multinationals in order to obtain the latest technology. If we are keen on following the latest trends in the insurance business, we could directly employ some of the foreign experts at a pittance of cost rather than letting Indian money and capital be secreted abroad and thereby depriving the country of vast investible funds — on false slogans of the benefits of globalisation. The U.N. Under Secretary General for Economic and Social Affairs, has warned, "the world's economic system was alert enough to protect the rich but too tardy to protect the poor and that the goal was not to have a global economy that ended up as welfare state of the rich. Rethinking was needed on how to make the system more equitable and mindful of long-term concern".

Will the BJP and the Congress (I), political rivals but partners in this scheme of global economy, heed the warning? And what are the other parties, trade unions and social activists doing to meet this challenge to the sovereignty and economy of our country. The poor await an answer.

9.9 Disinvestment and Parliament

There is a serious controversy over whether the Government can disinvest shares in the Bharat Petroleum Corporation Ltd. (BPCL) without Parliament's approval. Though the Attorney-General has agreed with the Government view that it is not needed, the matter is too grave, affecting Parliament's sovereignty, to permit it to rest there. The proper course would be to refer it to the Supreme Court under Article 143 of the Constitution.

Prior to 1976, Burmah Shell operated two companies in India—one refining crude oil and the other selling petroleum products. It was acquired by the Central Government under the Burmah Shell acquisition of Undertakings Act, 1976. The Preamble to this 1976 Act recited the objective for such a legislations: "And whereas it is expedient in the public interest that the undertakings in India of Burmah Shell Oil should be acquired in order to ensure that the ownership and control of the petroleum products distributed and marketed in India by the said company are vested in the state and thereby so distributed as best to subserve the common good." This Acquisition Act had used words almost similar to those of Article 39-A of the Constitution from the Directive Principles of the State Policy which provides that the "state shall in particular direct the policy towards securing that the ownership and control of the material resources of the community are so distributed as best to subserve the common good". By virtue of Section 7 of the 1976 Act the Central vested its title and ownership in a Government Company — BPCL.

The Government's apparent justification for avoiding going before Parliament is based on the specious argument that under the Companies Act any shareholder (even the Government) has the freedom to dispose of its shareholding in the manner it likes. But this assumes wrongly that the BPCL is a private preserve of the Executive and can be placed on a par with a private company.

The Supreme Court has observed that : "The Government carries on various trades and business activity through the instrumentality of the state such as Government Company or Public Corporations which being state instrumentalities are state within the meaning of Article 12 and, as such, they are subject to the observance of fundamental rights embodied in Part III as well as to conform to the Directive Principles in Part IV of the Constitution ... and society has a stake in their proper and efficient working."

The argument that the BPCL being registered under the Companies Act is governed solely by it is fallacious. The BPCL came into existence by virtue of the 1976 Act. Parliament's mandate was that the management and control be exercised directly by the Government or through a Government company it may be the that the Government overdid the control and did not allow full autonomy and interfered with the day-to-day working of these public sector undertakings. But that is an aberration which has to be corrected by the proper implementation of Government policy. It cannot justify a breach of the policy underlying the 1976 Act.

Even the separate entity plea under the Companies Act wears thin because of the principle of lifting of the veil, recognised under the Companies Act both in England and in India. The courts have shown themselves willing to "lift the veil" where the device of incorporation is used for some illegal or improper purpose, because "the life of the law has not been logic it has been experience". The Supreme Court has held that the Government may act through its instrumentality or agency of natural persons or it may employ the instrumentality or agency of juridical persons to carry out its functions. It has been held that the Government, in many of its commercial ventures and public enterprises, is resorting more and more frequently to this resourceful legal contrivance of a corporation because it has many practical advantages and at the same time does not involve the slightest diminution in its ownership and control of the undertaking. In such cases, the true owner is the state, the real operator is the state and the effective controller is the state and accountability for its actions to the community and Parliament is of the state. The doctrine of lifting of the veil thus marks a change in the attitude the law had originally adopted towards the concept of the separate entity or personality of the Corporation, so as to meet the requirements of different economic problems. It may be said that as the Executive has formed a Government company in the first instance by resorting to the Companies Act, it is free to change the policy and decide to disinvest and even change the management because originally it was the Executive's policy.

But the cases of the BPCL and other Government companies which owe their existence by virtue of an Act of Parliament are totally different.

The reason is that it was Parliament which initially determined the policy of how the use of petroleum products, their distribution and marketing in India is to be carried out and it laid down under Section 7 of the 1976 Act that the Central Government or a Government company would be the owner. It was by virtue of this provision that the BPCL was made the owner of these assets which had come from Burmah Shell. If now the Government of India wishes to transfer those assets, management and control to a private investor it is not a case of merely exercising its power as a shareholder to transfer the shares under the Companies Act. By doing so it would be perverting the very rationale of the 1976 Act and making a mockery of the objective of the legislation retaining the Government as the owner of the petroleum products.

It may also be mentioned that the Centre is under pressure from the multinational corporations to change the labour laws to facilitate a "hire and fire" policy. In the case of Government companies, the Supreme Court has held that a rule for terminating employment by giving notice is arbitrary and hit by Article 14 of the Constitution. The Government, therefore cannot bring in this change in the BPCL, and other Government companies. The Centre's present action in seeking to convert the BPCL into a non-Government company would be *ultra vires,* the reason being that it is seeking to violate Parliament's mandate indirectly and is also seeking to change the law regarding employees and Government control. Thus, it is seeking to exercise power for a purpose opposed to the mandate given by the 1976 Act.

Even if the Centre is convinced that the BPCL should be managed by a private company, it can facilitate this only after Parliament's approval. It cannot resort to an indirect manner of getting around Parliament's mandate by seeking to disinvest its majority shareholding.

Of course, it is needless to emphasis the serious consequences of disinvestment in the BPCL and other Government undertakings. The Government has reportedly asked oil PSUs to contribute interim dividends of Rs. 2,600 crores to the national exchequer (the BPCL's share is Rs. 60 crores) to meet its fiscal deficit and for using subsidies for the weaker sections.

Is it not a cruel joke that the surplus generated by the PSUs is sought to be gifted through disinvestment to the very foreign oil giants which were driven out by the 1976 Act? Why cannot the Opposition in the Rajya Sabha pass a resolution disapproving of these disinvestments if it is serious about opposing it? The public has a right to know.

9.10 Sanctions Against South Africa—Reality or Myth

The news that President Bush of United States has removed the embargo and the sanctions imposed on South Africa is most distressing and will gravely affect the struggle against Apartheid. Reactions of some of Indian leaders and Organisations have bordered on extreme optimism and suggestions for opening up the association with South Africa are being mentioned. I believe this approach to be faulty. As a matter of fact Mr. Nelson Mandela and African National Congress have disapproved of American Government's decision to end sanctions.

It is necessary to appreciate various facets of sanctioning mechanism before rushing in to welcome South Africa in the comity of civilised Nations. The sanctions were imposed as a result of worldwide resentment at the open hostile racial regime of South Africa. On paper many countries imposed sanction and even though USA was compelled by virtue of public opinion to impose sanction, it has always been recognized by knowledgeable circles that it had limited effectiveness. Reference in this connection will be relevant to the decision of Sub-Commission on Prevention of Discrimination and Protection of Minorities (to be called the Sub-Commission) as far back as Sept. 1973, to appoint a Rapporteur to evaluate the adverse consequence for the enjoyment of Human Rights of assistances in particular through investment of foreign capital and military aid given to the racist regime in South Africa. Ever since then Sub-Commission has been updating the date and problems of Blacks in South Africa.

It has been established that since 1984 a number of large transactional corporations (TNCs) have sold their South Africa subsidiaries or affiliates or announced their intention of doing so. There is evidence, however, that several of the disinvesting companies maintain non-equity ties with the host country thus defeating the very purpose of the idea of disinvestment action. Non-equity ties are established in three ways: first, through the licensing of production to another company based in South Africa or in a third country: Secondly, through the licensing of production to a company that has been newly created; Thirdly, through the licensing of production to a specially created trust. This type of arrangement enables the departing firm to continue its presence indirectly in the host country and ensure continuity in the transfer of technology.

Of the 1,226 transnational corporations identified as operating through subsidiaries or affiliates in South Africa, 563 disposed of their equity interests between 1984 and 1988, that is, 46 per cent of the total number of TNCs in South Africa. Today, TNCs with equity interests in South Africa/Namibia account for slightly over 50 per cent.

It should be pointed out here that restrictions on direct investments in South Africa through news and decrees are the most common economic measures taken by Government's In the area of direct equity investments. A typical feature of most of these laws is that they permit existing levels of investments, but prohibit further investment through the new infusion of transfer of capital, or expansion of activities. TNCs have apparently for public consumption ordered disinvestments from South Africa. But it is wrong to consider that that has resulted in total cut off from doing any business in South Africa.

Kodak also announced that its products would not be available to South African clients through any sources. However, Kodak re-established its direct presence in South Africa in 1988 with the acquisition of Sterling Drug Inc., and Kodak products are still available in South Africa, although it is not clear how they get there. Therefore, a shut-down of operations does not necessarily mean end to future commitments to South Africa. Thirteen of the 32 companies disinvested in this manner maintain on-going relations in one form or another with South Africa. In short, some of these disinvesting multinationals subsidiaries in reality remain firmly rooted on the spot through ingenious devices such as voluntary mergers and easy acquisitions.

The case of General Motors shows the stratagems employed to defeat sanctions. It is believed that the interests of

General Motor in South Africa was sold to its local management on terms which required an adjunction of Rs 100 million from the parent company, and the subsidiary was sold to legal management under the direction of an American former executive of General Motors. It is widely assumed that the contract, none of the details of which are known includes a buy-back clause which would allow the parent to return openly when circumstances permit.

Structural flaws in the South African economy have long made it dependant on foreign funds to finance economic growth, making it extremely vulnerable to economic sanctions. The South African economy has been in decline for two decades, although this has been hidden by heavy foreign borrowings and occasional gold price boosts. Sanctions have only exacerbated this decline.

An impression may go around as if sanctions imposed on South Africa had completely cut it off from all source of foreign investments and aid. In reality, it is not so. In the later period of 1985 the South African Government took two measures to counter the impact of the financial sanction. First it imposed an unilateral moratorium on the payment of the principal of short-term international debt falling due during the next four months and extended this to the end of March 1986. Second it reimposed the dual exchange rate system abandoned in 1983 which seeks to make capital placement in South Africa more attractive by increasing the cost of withdrawing it. It also worked out three successive agreements with its creditors in 1986, 1987 and 1989. In this way, South Africa sought to retain some of this funds and to buy time in which to reestablish the country creditworthiness. The second and third agreements provided for 'exit options which would allow for the conversion of short term frozen debt into long term 10 years exit options with lenient debt repayment terms circumvent financial sanctions by functioning as new loan.

In this process, South Africa was helped by shortcomings in the measures adopted by Foreign Government. Some of the loopholes and shortcomings in the measures of imposition of sanctions have been identified as failure to adopt comprehensive mandatory sanctions because of the opposition in the United Nations Security Council.With regard to trade, South Africa was able to evade sanctions by diverting imports and exports through third countries and offshore facilities. South African products have been sold under false labelling and also obtaining false certificates of origin and transformation as in the case of coal channelled to Europe through Rotterdam and Antwerp. Another devise to evade sanctions was to restrict the range of products that bans are supposed to cover. The Iron & Steel is usually interpretted as excluding iron ore and ferro-alloys, both of which are major South African Exports. Japan bans the import of South African iron and steel but imports large quantities of iron ore.

Similarly, the United States continues to import South African uranium hexafluoride which it considers as falling outside its ban on uranium ore and oxide.

Sanctions-busting is also a result of the expansion of South African investment abroad. 34.8 per cent going to EEC countries and 3.2 per cent to other European countries mainly Switzerland.

Another loophole is that ban on foreign direct investment is applied only to new direct investments and excludes non equity links. South Africa has been able to evade this by rescheduling and conversion of short and medium term debt into long term loans which are technically not considered as new loans but serve the same purpose. A report by the Centre against the Apartheid indicates that some 30 per cent of South Africa's trade is currently backed by Foreign Governments through their official export credit agencies of which the biggest insurers are the United Kingdom and Japan.

Trade figures for the period 86-88 show that there has been a marked increase in exports to South Africa from the wealthiest countries: 72 per cent increase for the Federal Republic of Germany, 50 per cent for Japan, 54 per cent for Britain, 41 per cent for the United States and 44 per cent for France. Payment for these exports would only have been possible if South Africa's major trading partners had provided guaranteed exports credits. Overall, the sanctions measures adopted, particularly by South Africa's major trading partners, are far from satisfactory. Their impact has been greatly reduced by their failure to restrict imports of strategic mineral and by keeping certain channels open for technology transfer and credit.

It is necessary to study closely the result of South Africa

experiment, especially when Government of India's latest economic package seems to put all its faith in the investments and aid expected from Multinationals. Experience has shown that such faith is totally and mispleased elsewhere. In India's case result can be no different.

10
International Humanitarian Law

10.1 International Humanitarian Law

The main instruments of international humanitarian law are the Geneva Conventions of 12th August, 1949 for the protection of war victims. These treaties which are universally accepted, protect the wounded, the sick, prisoners of war and civilians in enemy hands. They also protect medical services, namely medical personnel, medical units and establishments, and medical means of transport.

As a matter of fact this concern for humanitarian aspect we read in our ancient epics like Mahabharata that rules of conduct as to the timing and not attacking the unarmed were strictly laid down. The laws of Manu, a compilation of encyclopedic scope, and which British Professor J., Duncan M. Derret, a known authority on Hindu Law describes it as a text "which constitutes India's greatest achievement in the field of jurisprudence and who regards this work as one of the world's premier compositions in ancient law, more valuable in every sense than Hammurabi and able to hold its own in comparison to the covenant and Priestly codes of Moses.[1] Thus Manu describing the duties of King warn against unusual and cruelty even against an enemy in warfare and has this to say, "fighting in a battle, he should not kill his enemies with weapons that are concealed, barbed, or smeared with poison or whose points blaze with fire. He should not kill anyone who has climbed on a mound, or an impotent man, or a man who folds his hands in supplication, or whose hair is unbound, or anyone who is seated or who says, I am yours; nor anyone asleep, without armour, naked, without a weapon, not fighting, looking on, or engaged with someone else nor anyone whose weapons have been broken, or who is in pain badly, wounded, terrified, or flying — for he should remember the duties of goods men.[2]

Although the four Geneva Conventions of 1949 are very comprehensive, they do not cover the full range of human suffering caused by war. There are gaps in important areas, for instance in the provisions relating to the behaviour of combatants and the protection of civilians from the effects of the hostilities.

To remedy these shortcomings, two Protocols were adopted in 1977. They supplement, but do not replace, the Geneva Conventions of 1949. They are the Protocol additional to the Geneva Conventions of 12th August, 1949, and relating to the Protection of Victims of International Armed Conflicts (Protocol I);

Protocol additional to the Geneva Conventions of 12th August, 1949 and relating to the Protection of Victims of Non-international Armed Conflicts (Protocol II).

Instances are mentioned condemning the role of Kauravas in killing Abhimannyu and that of Bhim (otherwise great worrior) in killing Duryodhana by fouling the rule and method of attacking the opponent.

Protocol I imposes constraints on the way in which military operations may be conducted.

Protocol I gives a reminder that the right of the parties to a conflict to choose methods and means of warfare is not unlimited and that it is prohibited to employ weapons, projectiles and any other device that may cause superfluous injury or unnecessary suffering.

Protocol I defines legitimate targets in case of military attack. Furthermore it

(a) Prohibits

Indiscriminate attacks and attacks or reprisals against the civilian population and individual civilians.

Most conflicts since the Second World War have been non-international. Protocol 11 applies only to internal armed conflicts of a certain intensity in which dissident armed forces, under responsible command, exercise control over a part of the national territory.

Protocol II

(a) Sets forth

The fundamental guarantees to which all persons not, or no longer. Taking part in hostilities are entitled.

Additional Protocols I and II of 1977 are binding on a large number of States, but it is essential that they attain universal recognition, for only when all States have pledged compliance with their humanitarian rules, and are clearly aware of their mutual commitments, will it be possible to ensure equal protection for all the victims of all armed conflicts.

Article 48 - Basic rule provides that in order to ensure respect for and protection of the civilian population and civilian objects, the Parties to the conflict shall at all times distinguish between the civilian population and combatants and between civilian objects and military objectives and accordingly shall direct their operations only against military objectives.

Indiscriminate attacks are prohibited. Among others, the following types of attacks are to be considered as indiscriminate:

An attack which may be expected to cause incidental loss of civilian file, injury to civilians, damage to civilian objects, or a combination thereof, which would be excessive in relation to the concrete and direct military advantage anticipated.

International humanitarian law is increasingly perceived as part of human rights law applicable in armed conflict. This trend can be traced back to the United Nations Human Rights Conference held in Tehran in 1968 which not only encouraged the development of humanitarian law itself, but also marked the beginning of a growing use by the United Nations of humanitarian law during its examination of the human rights situation to certain countries or during its thematic studies.

A particularly important development which influenced later human rights law was the creation of the International Labour Organization in 1919 which made major efforts, through the development of treaties and the installation of supervisory mechanisms, to improve economic and social (including health) conditions for workers.

Third World States have in particular pointed out that in order to be able to show proper respect for economic and social rights, the appropriate economic resources are required, and that for this purpose they have a right to development.

The most important general observation to be made is that, like human rights law, humanitarian law is based on the premise that the protection accorded to victims of war must be without any discrimination.

First, it prohibits the starvation of civilians as a method of warfare and consequently the destruction of their means of survival (which is an improvement on earlier customary law). Secondly, it offers means for improving their chance of survival by, for example, providing for the declaration of special zones that contain no military objectives and consequently may not be attacked.

The next "hard-core" right is that no one shall be subjected to torture or to cruel, inhuman or degrading treatment or punishment. Humanitarian law also contains an absolute prohibition of such behaviour, and not only to states but this prohibition explicitly in all the appropriate places but goes still further, since a large part of the Geneva Conventions can be said in practice to be a detailed description of how to carry out one's duty to treat victims humanely.

The protection of children and family life is also given a great deal of importance in humanitarian law.

Respect for religious faith is also taken into account in humanitarian law, not only by stipulating that prisoners of war and detained civilians may practise their own religion, but also by providing for ministers of religion who are given special protection. In addition the Geneva Conventions stipulate that if possible the dead are to be given burial according to the rites of their own religion.

Overall, the cases that have been decided by the Committee in respect of asylum seekers have moved the law on refugee protection in a positive direction.

A restrictive application of the rules of procedure and the adoption of higher evidentiary burdens will impede the development of human rights and refugee law and must be guarded against. An Expert Workshop on Human Rights and Refugees sponsored by LNHCR and held Athens in December, 1998, took note that under funded and overburdened human rights treaty bodies will be unable to deal with claims fairly and expeditiously which will be "to the detriment of vulnerable individuals, to the state parties and to the integrity of the human rights system itself". The Workshop report went on to conclude that there is an "urgent need for states to develop and rationalize refugee and human rights procedures national ly and regionally, if they were to comply fully with their obligations under both refugee and human rights instruments". Indeed as the Export Workshop suggested, it is a narrow interpretation of the 1951 Refugee Convention which is driving rejected asylum seekers to human rights treaty bodies and there would be no need for asylum seekers to have recourse to Convention Against Torture and other such mechanisms if states honour the spirit of their obligations under the refugee instruments.

In its conclusions and recommendations, the Expert Workshop noted the need to train officials at all levels in international human rights law and to ensure their awareness of the views and comments adopted by the treaty bodies. It further stated that all officials should be familiar with the approach adopted by the CAT which considers that discrepancies in statements made by victims of torture are not uncommon, as long as the inconsistencies do not raise doubts about the general veracity of the application.

Another Article 22 decision that involved a rejected asylum seeker is that of Mr. Tahir Hussain Khan who was a member of the Baltistan Student Federation, which was a political movement claiming independence for Kashmir. In this case the Committee found that the state party, Canada, had an obligation to refrain from forcibly returning the applicant, a citizen of Pakistan of Kashmiri origin, to Pakistan.

International humanitarian law is applicable in all armed conflicts and protects persons and property actually or potentially affected.

In establishing the principle of damages for violation of its rules, it sets out to place upon the Contracting Parties an obligation they cannot avoid. They must meet it after the cessation of hostilities.

The obligation to make reparation is incumbent upon any party to the conflict, regardless of the final outcome. Based on the principle of equal treatment among other things, IHL cannot allow a distinction to be drawn between victims dependent upon the winner and those dependent on the loser. All persons who have suffered any harm or wrong in violation of the treaty provisions are entitled to the same treatment regardless of the party to which they belong.

Consequently, the right to restitution, compensation and rehabilitation for victims of gross violations of human rights and fundamental freedoms has become a subject on the international human rights agenda.

Responsibility arising from the violation of international humanitarian law is incumbent not only upon individuals but also upon States. According to the 1949 Conventions, "No High Contracting Party shall be allowed to absolve itself or any other High Court Contracting Party of any liability incurred by itself or by another High Contracting Party in respect of breaches referred to in the preceding Article."

The interlinking of human rights and humanitarian law can also be seen in the work of bodies responsible for monitoring and implementing international law.

In this connection, it is interesting to note that in recent years the Security Council has been citing humanitarian law more and more frequently in support of its resolutions. The latest example of this tendency can be found in Resolution 808 (1993) on the conflict in the former Yugoslavia, in which the Security Council decided to establish an international tribunal "for the prosecution of persons responsible for serious violations of international humanitarian law committed in the territory of the former Yugoslavia since 1991."

During its invasion of Grenada that year the United States had bombed a mental asylum, killing several patients. In its petition, the organization asked the Commission to interpret Article I of the American Declaration on the basis of the principles of humanitarian law. The Commission declared the petition to be admissible. In dealing with the fundamental aspects of the issue, therefore the Commission had to base its decision on a provision drawn up in the spirit of human rights in order to apply that provision to an armed conflict.

This objective was behind the adoption in 1990 of the Declaration of Minimum Humanitarian Standards, the so-called Turku Declaration. This text makes it clear from the outset that its drafters are determined not to take a position on any dichotomy between humanitarian law and human rights law. It proclaims principles "which are applicable in all situations, including internal violence, disturbances tensions and public emergency, and which cannot be derogated from under any circumstances".

The most politically sensitive aspect of human rights law, namely. political rights and mode of government, is totally absent from humanitarian law, what will probably not be avoided, however, are the political influences that lead States to insist on the implementation of the law in some conflicts whilst ignoring others. This, however, is not new and it is to be hoped that a greater interest in humanitarian law will tend to bring about more demands for it to be respected in all conflicts.

In this regard the history, the establishment and the manner of working out a mechanism for International Criminal Court (ICC) would show the contradictions the motivation and the manner in invoking international humanitarian law in actual practise.

In 1937, the League of Nations adopted a Convention against Terrorism, whose Protocol contained a Statute for an ICC. However, the Convent never entered into effect because of insufficient ratifications.

In 1948, UN General Assembly directed the International Law Commission (ILC) to study the possibility of establishing a permanent international criminal court. Because of the compulsions of a bipolar world no progress was made. But in a unipolar world and under US persuasion, the idea was revived when in 1992 the General Assembly requested the ILC to draft a statute for a permanent ICC. This item was also mooted at the Vienna Conference of Human Rights in 1993 and though conflicting views were expressed, the UN Security Council proceeded to establish two ad hoc war crimes tribunals, one for former Yugoslavia in 1993 and another for Rwanda in 1994.

In 1994, the ILC submitted a draft statute to the General Assembly which established a preparatory committee. There was much skepticism. among nations as to the real purpose and efficacy of ICC especially when seeing the functioning of adhoc Tribunals set up for Yugoslavia and Rwanda. That the reach of the ICC could be a false hope became manifest from what was happening in Kosovo. It was no secret that Yugoslavia was supporting the Serbs in unleashing violence against the ethnic Albanian, while at the same time a UN representative was holding closed door partly with Yugoslavia leaders to find a solution.

In 1995 when the US failed to stop the war in Bosnia in spite of behind the scene negotiations with Yugoslavia, NATO jets (in itself an act of aggression) attacked Bosnian Serb military positions. The result was that President Milosevic was nominated by the Bosnian Serbs to negotiate with the UN. It was only the internal uprising by people that threw out Milosenic and not the threat of a warrant of arrest issued by the Tribunal.

Though prospects were dim, but at last a change in the attitudes of Governments eventually led to the conclusion of the Rome Statute on 17th July, 1998. This treaty, when ratified by 60 countries, will establish the ICC. But there is still a long way to go when ICC can start working. Sixty ratifications are needed for the treaty to enter into force and for the court to be set up. But so far only 27 have ratified it.

The option of signing the International Criminal Court treaty without ratifying it expired on December 31, 2000. One hundred and thirty-nine governments signed by the deadline - whether ICC will get the requisite number for ratification remains an open question.

Some commentators feel that the International Criminal Court (ICC) represents one of the most important advancements in human rights protection since the adoption of the 1948

Universal Declaration of Human Rights and the most significant step for international justice since the Nuremberg Tribunal, and that the Court will be an effective mechanism for bringing to justice those responsible for the most serious human rights crimes: genocide, war crimes and crimes against humanity.

In my view, however, the various provisions, and reservation in the statute do not inspire confidence of ICC (even when it comes into force) of being an impartial, non political and effective instrument for protecting Human Rights across the borders of the countries. I am afraid the various in built limitations will only lead to selective justice where the whims of big powers will determine what particular cases would be investigated. How else to explain that in spite of the report of the special committee appointed by UN General Assembly (1989) to investigate Israeli human rights violations of Arab population of the occupied territories, no one has suggested an ad hoc crime tribunal as in the case of former Yugoslavia and Rwanda.

Not even the current brutal violent and unprovoked bombing by Israel against Palestinians has persuaded the Security Council dominated by U.S.A. to even suggest an International Tribunal to investigate Israeli Govt. crimes.

Recently the Baghdad Conference, Follow up and Coordination Committee, held its fourth meeting in Baghdad on 11-12 November 2000 under the presidentship of Mr. Tariq Aziz, Chairman of the Committee and Deputy Prime Minister of Iraq. It stated strongly that the ban was creation of Anglo-American plot against the people of Iraq which has been exposed among the international fraternity.

There were 110 representatives who officially attended the Baghdad Conference.

The committee appreciated efforts exerted to develop the initiatives aiming at breaking the air ban imposed illegally by the US on Iraq.

The committee appreciates the resolution of the 104th, Inter Parliamentary Conference in Jakarta calling for lifting the embargo off Iraq. The Fourth Meeting renewed its demand to the UN Secretary Council to implement its obligations towards Iraq by lifting the embargo.

It has now been conclusively documented how because of embargo, millions of children in Iraq are the victims of malnutrition, many hundred of thousands are dying because of lack of medicine and medical facilities. These acts by group of nations under the leadership of U.S.A. are plain acts of aggression.

Now Article 5 is the principal provision setting out the crimes within the Court's jurisdiction. It lists four crimes - genocide, crimes against humanity, war crimes and the crime of aggression.

There is no explanation of the crime of aggression or of its elements as a matter of individual criminal responsibility. By the Final Act of the Conference the Prep Corm is to prepare proposals for a provision on aggression, including the definition; the Elements of Crimes, including aggression; and the conditions under which the Court shall exercise its jurisdiction with regard to this crime. It will, therefore, be seen that regrettably though in theory the Rome Statute covers aggression, the word aggression has not been defined and the jurisdiction over this 'crime of crimes' must await such definition through an amendment process. Critics are, however, skeptical. They say that such an amendment might never happen. I agree, because if it was so defined how could USA have escaped being arraigned guilty.

The provisions on complementarily, mean that an individual suspected of criminal activities under his or her national law may be tried by the national jurisdictions.

Whatever an ICC acquires permanence or not, the gatekeeper and lead role played by the permanent members of the Security Council will remain secure.

Further any special privilege given to the UN Security Council would amount to granting special privileges to a select group of five states wielding veto power to decide upon a particular situation on purely political considerations favoured by those states only, while they themselves would always be outside the pale of the inherent jurisdiction of the Court.

India tabled an amendment to list nuclear weapons among those weapons whose use is banned for the purposes of the Statute. This was not accepted. India says that the message this sends is that, at the level of plenipotentiaries, the international community has decided that the use of nuclear weapons is not a crime. What is worse, the Statute does not list any weapon of mass destruction among those whose use is banned as war crime. Several Asian and European countries have also expressed serious concern over the exclusion of weapons of mass destruction, in particular the use of nuclear weapons.

Though the draft Statute contained an exhaustive list of weapons of mass destruction under the list of prohibited weapons, fierce opposition by major military powers such as the US, China and Russia resulted in the exclusion of nuclear weapons. In the end, all the weapons except poisoned weapons, asphyxiating gases and dum-dum bullets were actually dropped from the list.

This was a motivated decision because smaller nations could make poison gas and could pose danger to the hegemony of big powers.

The Court itself has no practical means to enforce its orders and decisions. The ICC has no police force of its own. It is therefore entirely dependent on states to investigate cases and transfer suspects to the Court.

The Prosecutor has very limited power to conduct investigations. For instance, he cannot compel witnesses or carry out exhumations. In the event of non-compliance, the ICC does not have the power to order state compliance itself but has to turn to the Assembly of states parties or if the referral is from the Security Council, it can turn to the Council for assistance.

Unlike the Statute of the ICTY, the Rome, Statute does not give the Prosecutor the authority to conduct investigations independently of national authorities.

By Article 1, the Court is established as a permanent

institution with power to exercise its jurisdiction over persons for the most serious crimes of international concern, as referred to in the Statute, 'and shall be complementary to national criminal jurisdictions'. This general functional jurisdiction is universal in scope. The limitation of the Court's jurisdiction to 'the most serious crimes of international concern, as referred to in the Statute' is an immediate source of ambiguity.

In this respect the ICC is much weaker than the ICTY and ICTR, both of which have concurrent jurisdiction with national courts and may choose to exercise primacy over them by requesting deferral to their competence. This is problematic because if a state wishes to cover up certain crimes, it would assert its jurisdiction or engage in a sham investigation. In such a situation, the ICC would not be made by it under Article 17 of the crimes, it would assert its jurisdiction or engage in a sham investigation. In such a situation, the ICC would not be made by it under Article 17 of the Statute that the state is unwilling or unable to act, it could proceed with the investigation. In the meantime, crucial evidence may be lost.

Article 124 of the Statute permits states at the time of ratification to make a declaration that they do not accept the Court's jurisdiction over war crimes for a seven-year period. According to the Amnesty International, such a declaration undermines the very purpose of the Court by giving states immunity from international justice over war crimes for seven years, as this provision effectively gives the soldiers a "license to kin with complete impunity"

As a result of the insistence of the US and France, the final text stipulates that the state may withhold information or prevent an individual from giving evidence if, in its view, it would prejudice its national security interests. The US proposal prevailed over the one from the UK, which would have allowed the Court to order a state to disclose information, if it was acting in bad faith. Further, a very vague provision could allow states not to co-operate on the basis of inconsistency with their own "fundamental national law", such as constitutional provisions.

Even while acknowledging it as an historic step forward for international justice. Amnesty International says that the Statute still requires radical surgery to ensure that the Court will be just, relevant and effective. I would regretfully be forced to echo with Amnesty International when it has characterized 1CC as "Crippled at Birth?"

10.2 Instead of Building Bunkers, the Government Should First Provide Basic Amenities

I was appalled at a news item last week that an insane exercise is being carried out by the Health and Transport Ministries to build bunkers and provide safe covers to ministers and senior government officials and their colleagues in case of a nuclear attack by Pakistan at Delhi. The Delhi Government is even reported to have proposed a 'war book' to inform the citizens that there will be no survivors in such an eventuality. Just who has authorised. This senseless study? And how does the Delhi Government arrogate to itself this authority? Only if it is meant to spread panic among the citizens, will such a venture succeed. Such an exercise would be termed sheer lunacy if it were not also reflection of the stupidity and vanity of these 'minions' in power.

It is a matter of shame that an administration that cannot ensure even proper water and power supply arrogates to itself the right to conduct such a highly sensitive defence study. With hindsight, however, we know that there must be the temptation to be able to spend millions, with a large chunk of it obviously remaining unaccounted. Do these worthies have the least idea that it is universally recognized that there is no defence against the madness of nuclear attack? Those who wish to indulge in such an adventure should know that there is no defence against nuclear destruction except the fear of the well-tested concept of MAD (Mutually Assured Destruction), which kept the US and the Soviet Union from the suicidal step even in the sixties when their relations were at their worst. It would be worthwhile to remember Khrushchev's retort when the US President boasted that USA could destroy the Soviet Union ten times over with its nuclear strike. Khrushchev replied that he accepted the claim but was fully satisfied with his capability to destroy USA just once. The Delhi Government would do well to instead concentrate on the basic amenities. When Sheila Dikshit took over, we were told that the new government would take steps to involve Resident Welfare Associations across the city to effect a turnaround. Yet, nothing happened in this regard. It is all very well to sanction funds for the repair and maintenance of roads, for instance. But all that happens is that though the funds enter the books and the CAG conducts an audit five years later, nothing changes. The government should instead involve the locals in every area and get them to monitor the maintenance of civic amenities. Without the active involvement of RWAs, the civic agencies are getting away with fraud of the worst kind. Let the government get these things in order before indulging in madcap schemes such as building bunkers and the like.

11
Human Rights and Election

11.1 The Quota Within : Don't Split up the Women's Bloc

The betrayal of women by all political parties, including the communists who have avoided passing the Women Reservation Bill on specious grounds, shows to what depths our politicians have sunk.

Some legal advisors to Sonia Gandhi are reported to have made the untenable suggestion that the Bill may be unconstitutional because it is discriminatory. The suggestion is laughable, and I can only hope it has been wrongly reported. As a matter of fact, though a constitutional Amendment Bill is to be preferred out of abundant caution, even ordinary legislation for reservation will be constitutionally permissible.

Article 15 (1), which includes every kind of state action including political activity, forbids the state from discriminating on the ground of sex, but makes an exception by Clause (3) to emphasise that it shall not prevent the state from making special provisions for women. This would authorise the state to act in a manner that brings about effective equality between men and women so as to improve the status of women.

Though women constitute about 50 per cent of the population, their strength in the Lok Sabha has been almost negligible right from 1952 when they numbered 14, to about 43 at present.

The Supreme Court has upheld as constitutional a government order reserving 30 per cent of jobs for women employees. It also supports reservation in the managing committees of Cooperative Societies as well as the nomination of women to Municipal Boards.

The argument that the women's quota will be monopolised by urban women is a red herring. There are about 200 OBCs in the Lok Sabha. It is a stark reality that it is not their public service, but merely the caste configuration that has preferred them. Similar results will follow even after reservation for women. The only difference will be a big chink in the male bastion. That is the real reason for opposition by male MPs.

In my view, provision of a sub-quota for OBC women runs the risk of being held as un-constitutional. Reservation of seats is guaranteed only for SC/STs in Article 330. The framers of the Constitution did not intend further fragmentation of the legislatures on caste lines.

But reservation for women as a group, who have suffered similar and sometimes even worse injustices and deprivations than the SC/STs, will be permissible under Article 15 (3).

A sub-quota for Muslim women would violate secularism, a basic feature of the Constitution, and even an amendment would be illegal. Article 325 provides for one general electoral roll for every constituency and mandates that no person shall be ineligible for inclusion on grounds of religion. In the Poudyal case the Supreme Court, while upholding the constitutionality of seat reservation for the Buddhist Sangha in the Sikkim legislature, has at the same time warned: "It is true that the reservation of seats of the kind and the extent brought about by the impugned provisions may not, if applied to the existing states of the Union, pass constitutional muster."

Two other judges however struck down the reservation, emphasising that it would amount to discrimination because a person would be denied the right to be included in the rolls because of religious affiliation and would for similar reasons be ineligible to contest from that seat. Thus if seats were reserved for Muslim women and even if they were to be elected by a common electoral roll it would still be discriminatory and violate Article 15 (1) because it would deny a non-Muslim woman the right to contest that seat. This would amount to destroying one of the basic tenets of our Constitution as provided by Article

325, and would be impermissible.

If sub-quotas are to be permitted then how can a similar demand from SC/ST women be resisted? The result would be the elimination of the identity of women as a group, reducing them to an appendage of caste and religion.

Reservation for women would check the muddy politics that their menfolk have brought about. It would bring social consciousness to political life. It will also help in breaking the criminal-politician nexus—the real danger to our democracy.

In my view, the introduction of the Bill will unleash a powerful agent of social change. But, I'm afraid, the strategy of women's organisations has been faulty from the start. Holding seminars or lobbying political leaders in their offices or on television will not help. All women's organisations, irrespective of political affiliation, should form a common platform with a single agenda. It must become a mass social movement and send out a message to all political parties, assuring them that women will withdraw their support in the next election if they do not support the Bill now.

Such a mobilisation should be easy to manage, considering that a recent opinion poll shows that 78 per cent of the population is in favour of women's reservations and the majority against sub-quotas. This is a welcome sign as it indicates that society is accepting women as a group in its own right, and not as an appendage of either the male community, caste or religion.

Women activists have a ready made army in over a million women Panches. Women's organisations should not allow themselves to be divided by sub-quotas. A split in the women's rank will only make it easier for males to retain their dominance and defeat the laudable objective of developing a women-oriented political agenda. Opponents of the Bill refuse to treat women as equals. It is this mindset that is sought to be destroyed by the Bill, which selfish politicians are resisting while pretending to fight for social justice.

Crimes against urban women are no less heinous than those against rural women. Women as a class cannot be bifurcated in the matter of injustice. The creation of artificial sub-quotas within this suppressed section is a conspiracy of male chauvinism to perpetuate its dominance.

The figures at the National Crime Records Bureau too appear discouraging. The overall average conviction rate for rape offences has been consistently lower than other less serious crimes such as burglary and theft. For example, in 1994, of every 100 rape cases that went for trail, 80 remained pending. Of the remaining 20 cases, there were about 5 conviction and 15 acquittals.

Do the courts realise this gender bias? "Yes," says Justice Sachar. "At the People Union for Civil Liberties (PUCL), we had taken the case of a woman and questioned the Hindu Minority and Guardianship Act. Seeing a prima facie "unconstitutional" aspect the court had issued a notice to the Attorney General. Citing the Mathura case where the law had to be changed when women took to streets, Justice Sachar says that only mass mobilisation can bring about a change in the legal system.

11.2 Higher Representation for Women in House to Curb Gender Injustice

Former Delhi High Court chief justice and human rights activist Rajinder Sachar has said that higher representation for women in Parliament through reservation can help eliminate gender bias in the administration of justice.

Justice Sachar, in an interview with *The Times of India Human Rights Cell* said, laws in our country are gender biased and "gender injustice" means violation of human rights of an individual which are sacrosanct."

He made this comment when his attention was drawn to the rise in crimes against women (a rape every 54 minutes, a dowry death every 92 minutes, molestation every 26 minutes and an act of cruelty every 33 minutes according to the figures compiled by the National Commission for Women) and the legal system's apparent unsympathetic attitude reflected by, for example, the following:

l Under Mitakshara law, only a male member of the family can be a coparcener and can inherit the ancestral property.

l Under Hindu Minority and Guardianship Act 1956, only

the father is considered as the natural guardian of the child. The mother is only an ordinary guardian.

l Under the Muslim law (Personal law) monogamy is a rule for the wife but polygamy is allowed for husbands.

l In the 1979 Mathura case, involving custodial rape, the Supreme Court, as in the Bhanwari Devi case, pronounced the theory of "easy character" of victim and reduced the punishment of the rape convict. (This law, however, has been amended now).

l Betraying complete lack of understanding of female psychology. Section 497 of the IPC makes adultery an offence only in case of a person who has had sexual intercourse with a married woman, despite this section being violative of Article 21, guaranteeing personal liberty.

Ms Padma Seth, legal adviser National Commission for Women, says, "there is no denying that laws are gender biased. However, even in cases where the law is gender neutral, justice is not meted out because of slack enforcement. For instance, we have equal pay for equal work which is never enforced."

The figures at the National Crime Records Bureau too appear discouraging. The overall average conviction rate for rape offences has been consistently lower than other less serious crimes such as burglary and theft. For example, in 1994, of every 100 rape cases that went for trial, 80 remained pending. Of the remaining 20 cases, there were about 5 conviction and 15 acquittals.

Do the courts realise this gender bias? "Yes," says Justice Sachar. "At the People Union for Civil Liberties (PUCL), we had taken the case of a woman and questioned the Hindu Minority and Guardianship Act. Seeing a prima facie "unconstitutional" aspect the court had issued a notice to the Attorney General. Citing the Mathura case where the law had to be changed when women took to streets, Justice Sachar says that only mass mobilisation can bring about a change in the legal system.

11.3 For Whom the Polls Toll

The timing of the general election, with its attendant economic and administrative consequences, has led to a great deal of confusion. One had assumed that since there was only a caretaker government in place, elections would be held immediately. But the Election Commission, by citing the problem of the general revision of electoral rolls—which can be completed only by the end of July — has put a question mark over this possibility. CEC M.S. Gill's off-the-cuff observation that he would prefer simultaneous elections for Parliament and state assemblies acted as a further damper.

Now elections to the state assemblies are due only from December 1999 to March 2000. The refusal by the chief minister to recommend the early dissolution of their assemblies evidently means that the Parliamentary election will have to be held by itself because it cannot be delayed beyond this October. The Election Commission cannot force the state assemblies to be dissolved earlier.

One of the reason given for delaying the general elections to September/October is stated to be the need to update electoral rolls. Section 21 of the Representation of People Act, 1950 states that unless otherwise directed by the Election Commission the electoral rolls shall be revised before each general elections with reference to the qualifying date which is January of 1999. So that general revision will still not include those who have qualified after January 1999. Of course all of them can get themselves included in the electoral roll before the last date for making nominations (Section 23) which need not be before the last week of May if it is decided to hold the election by the last week of June.

Thus the concern for 18-year-olds currently on display need not prevent an early election. Let the political parties do this exercise if they are keen for the inclusion of new names. It is understood that the Election Commission has called a meeting of various political parties. It will be good if a consensus is arrived at about the timing of the general elections. But in case of difference, it is not the Election Commission, but the Central government which has powers to fix the date under the law. This follows from Section 14 of 1950 Act, which provides that for the purpose of holding a general election for constituting a new House of the People, the President shall by notification fix dates as may be recommended by the Election Commission. Thus, though the recommendation may be made by the Election Commission, the binding decision has to be made by the

President and not the Election Commission.

The Supreme Court has held that President of India, under Section 14 of the 1950 Act, ignites, the general election across the nation by calling upon the people to choose their representatives to the Lok Sabha. It is only thereafter that the Election Commission takes over the conduct and supervision of the mammoth enterprise.

Now the President in the context of Article 74 of the Constitution has in the exercise of his function to act in accordance with such advice as is given by the council of ministers. According to the Supreme Court, even when there is dissolution of the House of the People, the President cannot exercise executive power without the aid and advice of the council of ministers.

That this interpretation may permit the cabinet to decide the date of the election which it considers most suitable for itself, is nothing strange or immoral. As a matter of fact Brazier, the British constitutional author has opined that, "The Prime Minister, by convention, now has the right to recommend a dissolution at a time which seems most propitious for him". The ground reality must be accepted that a decision to hold a general election is no less a piece of political decision-making than any other cabinet policy.

There is a tendency to read moral homilies into the desire of political parties for a particular timing to suit their convenience. This is unfair, both on constitutional principles and precedents. Moreover experience has shown that the timing of election does not automatically ensure victory. According to Brazier the modern practice is for the "Prime Minister to consult senior Ministers about a possible election date, then to inform the Cabinet of the chosen date, followed by an audience of the Queen and a public announcement. This preserves the Prime Minister's sole right to select a date".

Incidentally, opinion on the suitability of timing being openly and unabashedly expressed has been the common practice in British parliamentary elections. Norman Tebbit, in his book *Upwardly Mobile*, recounts how he had analysed the results of the local council election in May 1987 and advised Prime Minister

Margaret Thatcher to hold the general election in June 1987. And then it was held according to his advice.

Even a defeated prime minister has the right to fix the date of the general election. Former British Prime Minister, James Callaghan, wrote in his book, *Time and Chance*, about how he had lost the vote of confidence by 311 votes to 310. He went to acquaint the queen formally of the position and sought the dissolution of the Parliament to be followed by general election in May.

Of course, it would be desirable if there was an agreement on dates. But, if there is a difference, constitutionally speaking it is the duty of the government to fix a date and advise the President, who will then direct the issue of necessary notification. The work of the Election Commission comes subsequently as an implementing mechanism to hold the elections, once the government has so decided.

The uncertainty and the undesirability of a caretaker government continuing in power for six months is an unacceptable situation in our democratic set up. People have a right to demand that the period of the caretaker ministry be reduced to the minimum. As Dicey says, "No modern constitutionalist will dispute that the authority of the House of Commons is derived from its representing the will of the nation, and that the chief object of a dissolution is to ascertain that the will of Parliament coincides with the will of the nation".

Law requires about 30 days to complete the whole process. Irrespective of the desires of the various political parties, a healthy precedent must be set: the election process must be completed within six to eight weeks from the date of dissolution of the House of the People. Political parties do not own the country. People have a right to have their own elected representatives at the earliest.

11.4 A Fair Proposal for Fair Elections

The Chief Election Commissioner's suggestion that state government resign six weeks before elections has, not surprisingly, led to a spate of criticism in identical terms by all political parties including the BJP and the Congress. The reaction shows the reluctance of political parties to give up the power to misuse the state machinery for electoral gain.

The touching reference to the right of elected representatives to remain in power right till the date of the constitution of the new legislature contrasts with the present demand of various political parties to invoke Article 356, but only against rival party governments.

Unfair Advantage

The Supreme Court has ruled that services rendered by government servants, including the police, for construction of rostrums, special helipads for ministers, etc. are part of the official discharge of their duty and do not amount to a corrupt service rendering the election void. Thus, the unfair advantage over the opposition candidate is obvious.

In Bangladesh, the present prime minister, Ms Hasina Wajed, had led a mass protest against the alleged unfair elections held in 1994, in which Begum Zia had been elected prime minister. Ultimately, Begum Zia herself agreed to amend the election law. The 13th amendment provides that there shall be a non-party caretaker government during the period after parliament is dissolved or stands dissolved, till the date on which the new prime minister assumes office after the election of parliament.

The caretaker government is to consist of a chief advisor and not more than 10 advisors to be appointed by the president. The executive power of the government shall be exercised by the chief advisor, who is to be appointed from among the retired members of the higher judiciary. The advisors to be appointed are persons who are not members of any political party or any organisation associated or affiliated to any political party. They should not be over 72 years of age.

The non-party caretaker government discharges its functions as an interim government and carries on only the routine functions of such government with the aid and assistance of persons in the services of the republic; and, except in the case of necessity for the discharge of such functions, it shall not make any policy decision.

The same set of rules with necessary modification, could be

applied for elections to our state legislatures. I am not vain enough to suggest that the judiciary alone should be eligible. On the contrary, I believe that there are any number of eminent citizens who could perform this function equally well. Nevertheless, I appreciate the apprehension of the opposition because of the partisan way in which governors are selected: I would, therefore, suggest that appointment to the caretaker government be made by the chairperson of the Rajya Sabha and the Speaker of the Lok Sabha, out of a panel of names given by the outgoing chief minister and leader of opposition. The interim government should not consist of more than five ministers.

When we have had elections under governor's rule, why should there be an objection to a caretaker government with all these safeguards? The only explanation is the politician's fear to go to the polls without the power and potential for misusing the government machinery.

Faith in Masses

It is correct that the Indian electorate has on numerous occasions given a resounding slap to the ruling party. But those exceptions cannot wish away the coercion and the misuse of state machinery which make a good part of our election a mockery of democracy. It cannot, therefore, be said that this suggestion is in any way impractical or undemocratic.

The objection by political parties to the idea of caretaker governments on the grounds of their being unelected is hypocritical, considering that we had Mr Deve Gowda functioning as Prime Minister for six months without being a member of either of the Houses and without any objection being raised by any political party.

To keep faith in democracy, it is essential that like justice, elections must not only be held freely and fairly but must also be seen to have been so held. Political parties must have faith in the masses, their real masters.

11.5 Avoid Confrontation

An Unnecessary confrontational stance is being taken by the Central Government and some political parties on the March 13 Supreme Court judgment on electoral reforms, in response to the second writ petition filed by the People's Union for Civil

Liberties. It is best to get the facts right.

In 2001, the PUCL filed a writ petition in the Supreme Court on the plea that voters have a fundamental right to know the relevant particulars of candidates standing for elections. It referred to the Election Commission's observation that it is widely believed that there is a criminal nexus between the political parties and anti-social elements and that it is leading to criminalisation of politics; that the criminals themselves are now joining the election fray, and some of them have even adorned Ministerial berths and, thus, law-breakers have become law-makers. At present, there are about 700 legislators and 25 Members of the Parliament who are having a criminal record.

In this background, the Court took the view that elections would be a farce if the voters were to remain unaware of the antecedents of their candidates. Though it agreed that such tainted candidates ought to be disqualified from contesting elections, it acted with judicial self-restraint and emphasised that "at the outset, we would say that it is not possible for this court to give any directions for amending the Act or the statutory rules. It is for Parliament to amend the Act and the Rules".

The Court held that the right to information — the right to know the antecedents, including the criminal past, or assets of candidates — was a fundamental right under Article 19 (1) (a) of the Constitution and that the information was fundamental for the survival of democracy. In its judgement of May 2, 2002, it directed the Election Commission to call for information on affidavit from each candidate seeking election to Parliament or the State Legislature as a necessary part of the nomination papers on: Whether the candidate has been convicted/acquitted/ discharged of any criminal offence in the past — if any, whether he has been punished with imprisonment or fine; prior to six months of filing the nomination, whether the candidate was accused in any pending case of any offence punishable with imprisonment for two years or more, and in which charge was framed or cognisance taken by the court of law. If so, the details thereof; the assets (immovable, movable, bank balance, etc.) of a candidate and of his/her spouse and that of the dependents; liabilities, if any, particularly of any overdues of any public financial institution or Government dues; educational qualifications of the candidate.

The Court was so circumspect in not even remotely giving the impression that it was treading on legislative domain that it did not accept the arguments to provide for disqualification for non-compliance with its directions or for the consequences of filing a false affidavit.

One should have thought that these mild directions towards cleansing the political field would have been welcome, considering that even the Prime Minister, Atal Behari Vajpayee, had publicly lamented that the electoral system had been almost totally subverted by muscle power and votebank considerations of caste and community. Instead, in a hurry, the Governments brought in the Representation of the People (Amendment Ordinance), followed by the R.P. (Third Amendment Act). Section 33A required the candidate to file an affidavit along with his nomination papers, giving information on pending criminal cases, if any, against him and in which charge has been framed against him. As for information on his assets/liabilities, it could be furnished after his getting elected. The amendment also provided for penalty for filing a false affidavit. These provisions, in addition to the requirement of information to be given as per the direction of the May 2, 2001, judgment, would have been broadly accepted by the public as a welcome step towards electoral reforms.

But then, the Legislature stepped beyond its powers by incorporating in the Amendment Act Section 33B purporting to nullify the May 2 judgment by providing that directions issued to the candidates by the court as per the judgement —to provide details of information mentioned therein —need not be complied with. Frankly, no challenge might have been made if the Amendment Act had not introduced Section 33B, which may verily be called a "constitutional monstrosity". This alone was challenged by the PUCL. The Court also held only Section 33B unconstitutional and void because it is well settled that the Legislature has no power to ask the instrumentalities of the State to disobey or disregard the decisions given by the courts, or to declare that the decisions rendered by the court is not binding or is of no effect.

The result of the latest judgment is that the candidate, in addition to the disclosure to be made in pursuance of the earlier

Court judgment of May 2002, will also have to give information in pursuance of the Third Amendment Act, 2002. The directions by the Supreme Court and under the Act are supplementary. The court accepted the Government plea that though the Election Commission could insist on information as per the May 2 judgment, it was not justified in saying that wrong information furnished by a candidate would permit the Returning Officer to reject the nominations. It accordingly asked the Election Commission to revise its instruction.

Unfortunately, some political parties, without even observing the courtesy of reading the judgment, assumed a shrill posture, warning of "serious consequences" of alleged usurpation by the Court of the functions of the Legislature. The Court has done nothing of the sort.

Recently, the Election Commission issued revised instructions saying that it is only if information is not furnished as required under both the Supreme Court judgment and the Third Amendment Act will the nomination papers be rejected. But, if wrong information is given though there will not be a rejection, it will entail criminal prosecution under the Third Amendment Act. Surely, if legislators object to this, their ire should be directed at Parliament, not the Supreme Court.

Over-touchiness on the part of legislators and their treating the Court as an opponent is unedifying. The courts have never doubted that the function of making laws is that of the Legislature. But then, the Legislature also needs to appreciate the role of courts as expounded by the then Chief Justice of India, Patanjali Sastri (1952), who reminded the Executive that "what is sometimes overlooked is that our Constitution contains express provision for judicial review of legislation as to its conformity with the Constitution. If, then the courts in this country face up to such important and none too easy task, it is not out of any desire to tilt at legislative authority in a crusader's spirit, but in discharge of a duty plainly laid upon them by the Constitution... We have ventured on these obvious remarks because it appears to have been suggested in some quarters that the courts in the new set-up are out to seek clashes with the legislatures in the country".

Those words of wisdom need reiteration to serve as a beacon

light to all constitutional instrumentaliti.

11.6 A 'Foreigner' cannot be Prime Minister

The expulsion of Sharad Pawar, P.A. Sangma and Tariq Anwar was inevitable, considering the culture of sycophancy in the Congress which holds that any dissidence against a member of the 'dynasty' (even if indirectly by marriage) is a treasonable act. It is intellectually dishonest to label this issue as an outcome of communalism or xenophobia. Surely a combination of Pawar, a Hindu, Sangma, a Christian and Tariq Anwar, a Muslim, who were only a month back praised as top secularists and the first two recognized even by their opponents as of prime ministerial mettle cannot suddenly have become communal, unless of cause the premise is that anyone who does not accept the undisputed leadership of Sonia Gandhi and the Congress party's junior partners, the Communists, is automatically to be branded as communal. It is also wrong as some well meaning academics seem to suggest that the question of foreign origin is an attack on our multi- religious society.

In the United State, Article 11(4) of the Constitution provides that "no person except a natural born citizen............ shall be eligible for the office of President." Thus, Henry Kissinger, US citizen and erstwhile Secretary of State, whose brilliance and statecraft are beyond doubt, is ineligible to stand for President. Similarly Khorana, Nobel laureate, who I take it is now a citizen of the US and is settled there for decades is ineligible, having been born in India. Madeleine Albright, US citizen and the present Secretary of State whose ferocious loyalty to the US is shown by her hawkish stance in Kosovo has to remain content and accept that she can never become President of the US, having been born in Czechoslovakia. In the United Kingdom, the law provides that "no person born out of the Kingdom of England, Scotland or Ireland or the dominions thereof..... shall be capable to be of Privy Council or a member of either House of Parliament". Would the apologists of Sonia Gandhi call these legislations racial or communal?

I believe there is good reason for restricting the highest offices to natural-born citizens. A person who has spent a good part of her life in the country of its birth acquires a culture, memories and loyalties which subconsciously continue to have a permanent influence on him or her. Thus even if he or she adopts the citizenship of another country, the subconscious link with the country of birth remains powerful. A recent news item of young Indians and Pakistanis born in England and whose families have acquired British citizenship years ago, still cheering Indian and Pakistani cricket teams against the English team of their co-citizens much to the annoyance of Englishmen is of relevance in this context.

Some apologists of Sonia give the example of Annie Besant who becomes Congress president, even though not born in India. Nothing can be a more unfair to the memory of that great leader. Annie Besant, who had already made a name for herself in British political life before she came to India, spent a lifetime here to fight against British imperialism.

Annie Besant's instance is of those souls who were willing to don the mantle of sacrifice deprivation and imprisonment who did not join a race for the coveted plums of the highest executive office. Incidentally it may be emphasized that there was no separate Indian citizenship prior to 1947. Both Jawaharlal Nehru and Annie Besant had the same citizenship, namely, British.

Sonia Gandhi must be regretting having allowed herself to be persuaded to join politics at the instance of small-time political operators who had no bases of their own but wanted to use their perceived proximity to her for self aggandisement. She was enjoying the privileges of a Queen of Mother, but the moment she decided to become a reigning queen, such like situation was bound to arise.

Politics is a cruel game. One feels distressed that many well-meaning persons, though rightly against the Sangh parivar's communalism and obscurantism, are yet ignoring the equal danger of dynastic feudal zamindari politics being revived by the Congress party. The Communist wooing of Sonia seems inexplicable unless one recollects what de Tocqueville said, "In politics shared hatreds are almost always the basis of friendship."

But that is not how the evil of communalism can be fought; only a people–oriented programme to expose the hollowness of both the Congress and the Bharatiya Janata Party would be effective. One would have thought that the action of Sharad

Pawar and others would stir the Congressmen to free themselves from the shackles of dynastic leadership. But the rot has gone too deep.

11.7 Against Democracy

The Government has announced two anti-democratic amendments to the elections law; one; to provide for open voting for election to the Rajya Sabha instead of by secret ballot, and the other to remove the residency requirement of a candidate to be chosen as a representative of any state to the Council of States. These amendments, if passed, will spell the end to the law of secret voting in all democracies in the world. The amendments will also be against the basic structure of the Constitution and beyond the power of Parliament.

Article 80 (4) states that "the representatives of each State in the Council of States shall be elected by the elected members of the legislative assembly of the State in accordance with the system of proportional representation by means of the single transferable vote." Section 3 of the Representation of the People Act, 1951, provides that a person shall not be qualified to be chosen as a representative of any state or Union Territory in the Council of States unless he is an elector for a parliamentary constituency in that state or territory.

This is in accordance with the scheme and spirit of Article (1) of the Constitution which mandates that India will be a Union of States — that is, a federation of States. The State legislature under our Constitution is not a delegate of the Union Parliament. Both legislatures derive powers from the same source — the Constitution. Within its appointed sphere, the state legislature has plenary powers.

The reason given for the proposed amendment is that as each Indian is a citizen of the country and has a right to stand for the Lok Sabha from any constituency, the position should be for the same for being elected to the Rajyva Sabha. But this argument ignores that when the Constitution envisaged the Rajya Sabha, it wanted the interests of the states to be safeguarded at the Centre. The Rajya Sabha is meant to provide an opportunity to a resident member of the state to concentrate on special needs peculiar to this state which require urgent attention—apart from national concerns. Along with the principle of federalism, this demands that the states in their own right must have an effective voice in all functions at the Centre—a function performed by a person in the Rajya Sabha who must be able to understand the state's language or be familiar with its culture.

The argument that many able people are not able to enter the Rajya Sabha because of this limitation of residency in the state is an insult to the large number of capable people in each state. The proposed change will further strengthen the hold of party bosses sitting in Delhi to pick their favourites. At present, even the most autocratic party leader has to pay consideration to local sentiment. But with the proposed change, centralisation will increase and cronyism become the rule.

In the US, for both the House of Representatives (its equivalent of the Lok Sabha) and the Senate (Rajya Sabha), the Constitution provides that no person is qualified to be representative or senator if he is not an inhabitant of the state for which he has been chosen.

The other change suggested is that voting for election should not be secret. This flies in the face of Section 94 of the Representation of People Act, 1951, that no witness or other person shall be required to state whom he has voted for in an election. The reason given against preserving secrecy is that the party bosses have found that many of their candidates to the Rajya Sabha have been defeated because many state legislators do not carry out the whip of the party and even sell their votes for money. It is truly unfortunate that all the parties seem to accept without embarrassment that their legislators are unreliable, amoral and open to corruption. One would have thought that this evil which certainly exists would have forced political parties to find new ways of combating it. Instead, a way is being found to destroy the fundamental basis of democracy — secrecy of voting.

Hopefully, these amendments, even if carried out, will be still born. This is because secrecy of voting is the fundamental principle of elections in all democratic forms of government. Both Article 21 of the Universal Declaration of Human Rights and Article 25 of the International Covenant on Civil and Political Rights, 1996 (which India has ratified and is thus bound to honour) mandate that the will of the people shall be expressed in periodic and genuine elections which shall be held by secret vote.

The American Supreme Court has pointed out the danger of open voting in the following words: "Absolutely secrecy in voting reaches effectively a great number of evils, including violence, intimidation, bribery and corrupt practices, dictation by employers or organisations, the fear of ridicule and dislike or of social or commercial injury — in fact all coercive and improper influence of every sort depending on a knowledge of the voter's political action."

Secrecy of ballot can be appropriately described as a postulate of constitutional democracy. It serves a vital public interest in that an elector or a voter should be absolutely free in the exercise of his franchise.

11.8 Unfair Verdict on Undertrials

Those who have read Charles Dickens' Oliver Twist have felt intrigued as to why Dickens made Mr. Bumble say "if the law supposes that ... the law is a ass, a idiot". Similarly many may have wondered as to what provoked George Chapman (1559-1634) to say "I am ashamed the law is such an ass". But they might find it easier to do so now in the context of the recent Supreme Court decision upholding the validity of law which debars a slum dweller accused of even a minor offence from voting because he is languishing in jail, being too poor to offer bail bonds, while permitting a rich accused facing charges of murder, rape or corruption to be elected to as a member of Parliament.

A public interest litigation had challenged Section 62 (5) of Representation of People Act, 1951 which denies to undertrials who are in prison or police custody the right to vote while permitting this to persons accused of heinous offences but who are out on bail. The plea that this provision favours the rich smugglers and black marketeers who can afford bail bonds against poor undertrials failed to persuade the court to hold this provision as unconstitutional.

The court has upheld this restriction on undertrials by seeking support from the well accepted proposition that criminalisation of politics is the negation of democracy and thus subversive of free and fair election which is a basic feature of the Constitution. A lay man, however, would find absurdity in a law which at the same time permits a convicted person and sentenced to less than two years to contest elections (even from jail) and vote at an electon (if out on bail) even though sentenced for 10 years, and wonder as to how this discrimination advances the cause of fair and free elections.

The court has also justified permitting a person in preventive detention to vote by postal ballot while denying the same right to undertrials in detention by holding that preventive detention is to prevent breach of law while imprisonment on conviction or during investigation is subsequent to the commission of crime and, therefore, this classification is reasonable. Persons under preventive detention are those against whom allegations are of smuggling and of narcotic offences. But even then such a person can only be kept in preventive detention if it is justified on a review by three judges of the High Court. If in spite of this prima facie strong proof a detenue is permitted to vote at the election, what is the logic for denying the right to vote to a poor undertrial in jail, against whom there is only an allegation of guilt?

This differential attitude against an undertrial would be in conflict with normal criminal jurisprudence and specifically with Article 84 of the Standard Minimum Rules for Treatment of Prisoner, adopted by the First United Nations Congress on the Prevention of Crime and the Treatment of Offenders, held at Geneva in 1955, and approved by the Economic and Social Council to the effect that "unconvicted prisoners are presumed to be innocent and shall be treated as such".

The finding of the court, also runs counter to the right guaranteed by Article 25 (b) of human rights guaranteed under the International Bill of Human Rights, namely, the International Covenant on Civil and Political Rights, which specifically provides that "every citizen shall have the right and the opportunity, without any of the distinctions mentioned in Article 2 and without unreasonable restrictions to vote and to be elected at genuine periodic elections which shall be by universal and equal suffrage and shall be held by secret ballot, guaranteeing the free expression of the will of the electors; which specifically recognises a right to vote and to be elected at genuine periodically election." In the UK, the right to vote is denied only if a person is convicted and during the time he is detained in a penal institution. In Israel even a convicted person in jail is allowed to vote.

Notwithstanding the international law and conventions, the court felt the classification to be valid by holding that some elbow room must be available to the legislature with regard to classification. But, with respect, the court has ignored the caution given by the apex court more than 40 years ago that good faith and knowledge of existing conditions on the part of a legislature have to be presumed. That is so; yet to carry that presumption to the extent of always holding that there must be some undisclosed intention or reason for subjecting certain individuals to a hostile and discriminatory legislation is to invalidate the protection clause of Article 14 by not restraining State action.

Another justification mentioned for upholding the law is that it would mean deploying a larger police force for the conduct of elections. But it was never pleaded that undertrials should be taken personally to polling booths to cast their votes, all that was claimed was the right to vote by postal ballot, as given to smugglers and others detained under preventive law. This did not require even one extra policeman to be deployed.

But what is of distorting consequence is the reasoning that as the right to vote is subject to the limitations imposed by the statute, the challenge to any provision of the election law, therefore, cannot be made with reference to a fundamental right. This is contrary to Article 13(2) which mandates that a law which contravenes any of the fundamental lights shall be void. Thus the election law is no holy cow to claim immunity from the sweep and protection of Article 14. The guarantee of equal protection under Article 14, according to earlier Supreme Court decisions, embraces the entire realm of state action, even in the matter of granting privileges and contract. How then can it be said that the statute on election law is immune from scrutiny under Article 14 ?

11.9 Women's Reservation Bill : A Social Necessity, National Obligation

History does not repeat itself is a self-evident maxim which most people tend to accept without demur. But now we are witness to seeing history being repeated every year in Parliament in the matter of hypocrisy of all political parties in the context of the Women's Reservation Bill.

Every political party for the last six years has been assuring its support to the Bill which disarms women activists. And then a farce rather than a tragedy is played out by so-called radical politicians, jumping into the well of the House, tearing copies of the Bill and making impossible for proceedings to continue — the House gets adjourned, the Bill is thrown into the dustbin till it is revived in subsequent years with the same result. It is time this mockery stopped, considering that the Congress, the BJP and Left parties proclaim that they are for the Bill in the present form, and really want it to become law.

Women are not asking for grace and charity. Their contribution to the cause of nation-building exceeds that of men. An International Labour Organisation study shows that "while women represent 50 per cent of the world adult population and a third of the official labour force, they perform nearly two-thirds of all working hours, receive a tenth of world income and own less than 1 per cent of world property." Therefore, reservation for women is not a bounty but only an honest recognition of their contribution to social development.

An alternative to the Bill suggests to amend the Representation of People Act, 1951, to compel political parties to mandatorily nominate women candidates for at least one-third of the seats on the pain of losing recognition. This is politically flawed and not even constitutionally permissible.

It may be violative of the fundamental rights to form an association guaranteed under Article 19(1) (c) of the Constitution. The only permissible restrictions are those in the interest of sovereignty and integrity of India or public order or morality, and such an amendment would not fall within these.

That apart, this alternative will not achieve the objective behind the Amendment Bill, because even if a third of women candidates are put up by political parties, there is no guarantee that the same number will get elected.

It is freely admitted by all parties that because of the inbuilt prejudice against women male candidates will have an unfair advantage in elections. This aspect is freely admitted even by Left parties. Thus, parties will tend to allow women candidates to fight elections from their weak constituencies. Though I am all for the Bill in its present form, it is unwise to underestimate the opposition from the male constituency in Parliament. Given the present instability in political coalitions, and the material that is in Parliament, to expect one-third of the male members to accept political hara-kiri is unrealistic. They are no Gandhians. They will not give up their privileges so easily.

There is also some merit in the objection that the reservation of seats for women would mean rotation of seats at every general election with the result that the members will not be able to nurse their constituencies and also that candidates will be uncertain of anticipating their future constituencies. This will be thus breaking their link with the electorate. Notwithstanding these ticklish problems, I would have continued insisting on the present Bill. But there is another alternative which can give one-third seats to women without in any way asking the male members to make the way.

This alternative gets further strength now that the Delimitation Commission has been asked to adopt the 2001 census for delimiting the constituencies, and therefore the same inevitable consequences must follow.

Article 81 provides for the Lok Sabha to have not more than 530 members. Further amendments were made to freeze the number of Lok Sabha members on the basis of the 1971 census till another census after 2000 had been published.

Article 82 provides for the allocation of seats upon the completion of each census. As per the 1971 census, the population of India was about 54 crores. Now after the 2001 census it has risen to about 102 crores. So the strength of the Lok Sabha can be easily increased by one-third to 750 well within the requisite formula. This will take away the fear of any male member to vacate the present seat. These extra seats could be dovetailed into double-member constituencies, which will ensure the reservation of one seat for women and, even permitting two to be elected, if the other woman candidate gets the maximum of the votes polled.

This is what happened in former President Giri's case during the 1957 general election when both seats were won by Scheduled Caste members — one reserved and the other a general seat — because SC candidate got more votes than Mr. Giri.

The argument that the women's quota will be monopolised by urban women is a redherring. There are about 200 OBC candidates in the Lok Sabha. It is a stark reality that it is not their public service, but merely the caste configuration that has preferred them. Similar results will follow even after the reservation for women. The only difference will be a big chink in the male bastoin. That is the real reason for opposition by male MPs.

In my view, the provision of a sub-quota for the OBCs runs the risk of being held as unconstitutional. A sub-quota for Muslim women would violate secularism, a basic feature of the Constitution, and even an amendment would be illegal. Article 325 provides for one general electoral roll for every constituency and mandates that no person shall be ineligible for incursion on grounds of religion.

In the matter of the fight against injustice and discrimination, women as a class should not be weakened by seeking to bifurcate them on caste lines. Reservation for women would check the muddy politics that the menfolk have brought about. It would bring social consciousness to political life. It will also help in breaking the criminal-politician nexus—the real danger to our democracy.

But, I am afraid, the strategy of women's organisations has been faulty from the start. Holding seminars or lobbying political leaders in their offices or on television will not help. All women's organisations, irrespective of political affiliation, should form a common platform with a single agenda. It must become a mass social movement and send out a message to all political parties, warning them that women will withdraw their backing in the next election if they do not support the Bill now.

12
Statements and Interviews

12.1 Need for Adequate Housing in Nairobi

I have read with pain and anger this well documented Brief on pavement dwellers by YUVA and have found the information presented through the compilation of studies on pavement dwellers conducted in Mumbai between 1972 to 1985 most insightful.

I am pained by the miserly and the wretched conditions faced by the 1,50,000 pavement dwellers who were victims of horrifying circumstances, after being exposed to the elements of nature following the demolitions carried out by the Brihanmumbai Municipal Corporation (BMC) in the monsoons.

I feel angry because these demolitions have taken place even before the ink on the lofty Istanbul Declaration on Human Settlements could dry - a document to which India is a signatory: rendering thousands of families shelterless. Somehow all this is silently accepted by a citizen influenced by misinformation that makes out pavement dwellers to be semi-criminals and work shirkers. This is sheer slander. As a matter of fact, their contribution to the informal and unorganised sector is predominant.

My visits to communities which have been forcibly evicted in the past have been a heart rendering experience. Women with children, old people hardly able to walk but yet earning their livelihood somehow asked in bitterness as to why they were forcibly evicted in such a manner and whether they were not citizens of this country?

It would be wide to heed the caution posed by the Economic

Commission for Europe that says, "High level of squatter housing indicates that the formal land market does not provide affordable residential land for housing, forcing households to occupy land illegally. High levels of this indicator also suggest that evictions may not be a realistic option, but rather calls for policies and programmes that lead to strengthening tenure security in squatter settlements, thus facilitating higher levels of housing investment".

I am convinced that a wide range of civil and political rights will be compromised in the absence of measures ensuring the right to housing. It is undisputed that rights including the right to privacy, the right to equal protection and benefit of law, the right to gender equality have an inherent linkage with housing rights.

Evictions run counter to the commitments made by the Government of India to the Istanbul Declaration 1996 and to the National Plan of Action where an accepted critical objective is to enable people (especially the houseless and the inadequately housed) to have access to adequate and affordable shelter.

The usual explanation given for displacement of squatters is claimed to be the alleged need for development projects. While this outmoded philosophy of development followed by the government is itself seriously flawed; evictions conducted to make way for development projects without providing alternative land and rehabilitation runs squarely counter to the decisions of the Supreme Court and also to the National Plan of Action which accepts government responsibility for "adequate and affordable shelter to all".

I have no doubt that demolitions by the government as brought out by various studies are in breach of international obligations and moreover a breach of trust with the poor of this country. It needs to be emphasised that social concern shown to the less advantaged sections of the population of any country is the measure by which the claims of any government regarding its functioning in the interest of the poor and the people at large must be judged.

I urge the State Government and the BMC to take immediate measures of adopting a humane and participatory housing policy for the pavement dwellers of Mumbai.

The document offers useful information and analysis on which policy initiatives can be based. Respect for the human rights of these communities and the satisfactory resolution of their demands must form a priority agenda for the BMC. The state and its institutions must not be party to violations of human rights.

Finally housing must be seen not simply as the provisions of houses, but primarily as an instrument for the promotion of justice, equality and human dignity.

Mr. Rajindar Sachar Former President of the PuCl has issued the following statement

The wanton and heart rending demolition of over 100,000/- shanty shops in Calcutta by Communist Government only shows how the loud mouthed professions for the disadvantaged are not even skin deep. That families of lakhs should be deprived of their meagre livelihood and thrown on the road makes a mockery of Communists governments slogan of full employment.

Has the lure of foreign investment and the market economy made communists forget the basic rationale of a civilized society - that city is for the poor and the later are not dispensable commodity.

Such like use of force not only shows a lack of sensitivity but a deliberate attack on the human right of housing that these pavement dwellers enjoy under international human right covenants.

12.2 Regrets VHP Decision on Shila Puja Dead and Burried

The President of the Peoples Union of Civil Liberties, Mr. Rajinder Sachar, while welcoming the decision of the Vishwa Hindu Parishad to call off the proposed march to Ayodhya, has expressed regret that the VHP has decided to continue with the Shila puja.

In a statement issued, Mr. Sachar said, "as we are witnessing the terrible pain and humiliation of the communal flare-ups it has become incumbent on all right thinking people to so act that this race down to communal divide is immediately halted."

"There is no justification for foundation ceremony unless it is known where the proposed temple is to be built. The matter is before the High Court and no party can or should be allowed to disturb the status quo."

"What is, however, most curious and remains unanswered is as to how any by what justification the state government, in agreement with the Central Government, has agreed to allot any land for the purpose of laying foundation. The government must take its position clear because if there is no allotment by the government the action in laying the foundation stone would be an unlawful and illegal act making it incumbent on the state/ Central government to take all steps to prevent it" Mr. Sachar stated.

He added that if unfortunately the programme for foundation stone is not given up he would appeal to all political parties and other civil liberties organisations to have their representatives present on the spot to make certain that no harm or damage is done to the Babri mosque and to prevent the fouling of the communal atmosphere.

The Babri Masjid Dispute Drags on only because of the Weakness of Political Will

An Extensive debate has ensued on the significance of the Lucknow Bench of the Allhabad High Court directing the excavation of the area near the Babri masjid site. Some have raised the question about the competency and even impartiality of the Archaeological Survey of India to carry out the excavations. Some have pointed out that there could be many conflicting and uncertain interpretations of the finds and this exercise may turn out to be a futility.

I am not competent to comment on these technical formulations. But I have no doubt that the high court will duly take note of these warnings. It should, however, be noted that one of the issues before the high court is whether or not the Babri masjid was built after a temple was demolished. Large evidence of historical literature and circulars from the Mughal court have been – and are being – produced by both conflicting parties in support of their respective stand. I can, therefore, see no extraneous motive behind high court order per se.

But then there is genuine apprehension and I can appreciate

the fear of this precedent being used for divisive and mischievous purposes by the Sangh privar in its attempts to reopen the question of other mosques at Varanasi and Mathura. I concede that there is some danger in taking such a course. But it can be resisted successfully provided the non-BJP parties look inward and do not repeat their prevarication as in the past which has allowed the situation to develop to such present dangerous proportions.

It is well–known that the RSS's communal ideologues manufactured the question of Babri masjid in 1948. We had leaders like Jawaharlal Nehru and G.B. Pant (the chief minister of Uttar Pradesh). But somehow they allowed the matter to remain in limbo by virtue of a magistrate's order, assuming it was the best option – presumably under the stress of post-Partition India. But I feel the seed of future trouble was planted when it was decided to skirt the issue rather than face it squarely.

The matter remained dormant for about 40 years. But then the older leadership was gone, and we had, on the one hand, the central government which sought to reap benefits through the shilanyas ceremony and, on the other, a weak and divided opposition unable to react strongly. This led to the deterioration of the situation.

In July 1991, the Congress government at the Centre still refused to take a principled stand on the Ayodhya issue. It compromised its position by passing the Places of Worship (Special Provisions) Act, 1991, plausibly to foreclose any controversy in respect of any place of worship defined as temple, mosque or church. Section 4 declared that the religious character of a place of worship existing on August 15, 1947, shall continue to be the same as it existed on that day.

While this was a worthwhile legislation (though it would have been more reassuring if this act was incorporated as constitutional amendment), the pusillanimous conduct of political parties came to the fore when the act stated that since the case relating to the place commonly called 'Ram Janmabhoomi–Babri masjid' forms a classes by itself, it was necessary to exempt it entirely from the operation of the act. Had the secular force been strong, no such exemption would have been incorporated as it went against the grain of the Constitution that accords equal status and respect to all religions.

This passivity of the non-BJP political groups encouraged elements of the Sangh parivar to commit the dastardly act of the Babri masjid demolition on December 6, 1992. Even that tragedy did not spur these groups to take the only correct stand—that is, state that since the RSS had committed the unforgivable sin of demolishing a place of worship, it would not be allowed to reap any benefits. In common law, if a heir kills his ancestor, he forfeits his inheritance. In the Ayodhya case too, there was 'murder most foul, and the only response should have been that the exemption clause be deleted and the Babri masjid restored to its original Muslim owners.

But that did not happen. Various alternatives started being put forward by well-meaning but politically weak people. The easy way of letting the matter be deciding by the court was taken. The Sangh parivar purportedly claimbed down from its proclamation of the Babri masjid site being where Lord Ram was born – a claim that was a non-issue right from the start as there was no way such an ancient event could be proved. So it made a further dilution – namely, that a temple existed which was destroyed to build the Babri mosque. Had the strong, this plea should have been rejected outright and the cowardly goons who had demolished the masjid shown the boot.

Muslims, in a measure of accommodation, conceded that if it was found that the masjid was built on the site of temple. They would give up their claim because the Koran forbids Muslim to build a mosque by demolishing any other religious place. That is the issue that the court is to decided and it is in that context that the present order has been passed.

It is somewhat curious that the non-BJP parties are still not prepared to suggest the only honourable course: that the demolition of the masjid was an act of sacrilege and no such dispute can be raised in a civilized State. Once the digging is permitted, it is near impossible to stop anyone from demanding excavations to find out whether a particular Hindu temple was built on an old Jain or Buddhist temple.

History teaches us that people who continue to look backward learn no lessons. Rather, the correct and impartial reading of history will show us the people who can learn to look forward need not be condemned to relive the past. Consequently, they learn to live with each other harmoniously.

Legally, the Sangh parivar has no case even if a temple had been demolished to build the Babri masjid. (It is a different matter that Muslims on their own may not like to persist with their claim if that is the case, as it would be against the injunctions of the Koran.)

I say this in view of the precedent of the case of Masjid Shahid Ganj in Lahore decided by the Privy Council in 1940. Muslims failed to win back the masjid built in 1200 and converted into a gurdwara in 1796 as the 12-year period for reclamation had long passed. Whatever the nature of the title of the site under the mosque, by the very fact that the Babri masjid had existed for over 400 years, the VHP/ RSS cannot claim any title to the contentious site in Ayodhya.

The legal position is clear. It is only the weakness of political will that is responsible for the Ayodhya imbroglio to continue as one of the bitter disputes within the country. By keeping the Ayodhya issue alive, the country has been kept from addressing its most urgent task – how to meet the challenge of the growing pauperization of the masses. And that includes both Hindus and Muslims.

12.3 Poverty is Poverty

Sir — This is apropos of the article, 'Liberalisation does not aggravate poverty' (*The Pioneer,* October 28), by Sh Venkatramani. The writer's indifference to heart-rending poverty in the country would make us consider Milcon Friedman, the market economy proponent, as a liberal conservative, and Margaret Thatcher as a radical.

Mr. Venkatramani is angry that economists should choose to include in definition of poverty persons who are somehow able to keep body and soul together. According to him, the concept of equality is satisfied by a minuscule number eating caviar and owning Rolls Royces. The overwhelming population should be satisfied by eking out on gruel, oven without safe drinking water.

The open contempt for the poor is exhibited by gleefully admitting that "the thrill of owning a Mercedes Benz inheres in the fact that there is a bullock cart passing by you as you cruise along". The ghost of Marie Antoinette ("If they don't have bread, let them have cake") is evident in his asking us to accept that it is perfectly correct for a few to have butter while the majority of masses should remain content if they "manage to eat something and keep body and soul together by doing subsistence farming".

His naive belief in market forces is against all honest statistical findings. That markets cannot be trusted to solve serious social problems faced by less fortunate of society has been forcefully recognised in the Copenhagen Programme of Action Adopted by the World Summit for Social Development (Copenhagen, 6-12 March 1995), wherein it is emphatically stated: "But social progress will not be realised simply through the free interaction of market forces. Public policies are necessary to correct market failures, to complement market mechanisms, to maintain social stability. Such growth should promote equity and social justice.... (para 6); and that urban poverty should further be addressed by promoting public and private investment and infrastructure, in particular housing water...."

Mr. Venkatramani's view that "Poverty is not a problem of inadequate money, but problem of attitude, awareness and ability" is similar to the attitude of 17th century European feudal nobility which held that poverty was the result of poor being lazy and indolent, and not (as indeed was the truth) the exploitation of the masses that kept people poor. It is this social lie that brought about the French Revolution.

12.4 Right Bodies Accused of Bias

Sensitive to the human rights violations. Mr. Sachar, who also heads the UN's one-member sub-commission on prevention of discrimination and protection of minorities, was here to conduct a study on discrimination in housing all over the world.

Mr. Sachar said he was not one of those who would object to international human rights organizations if they were correct on the facts about rights abuse in India. "But what I want to emphasize is that similar violations are taking place in the U S, Europe and other countries and these very bodies are pointing those out" he said.

"My real objection arises from the fact that some impression is gathered by political bodies that Indian don't abhor rights abuse. That is absolutely wrong." He said major portion of the Amnesty or other reports are picked up from the PUCL's investigation of from the Indian newspapers. "We Indians are very touchy about the rights abuse and awe are on the vanguard of exposing them," Mr. Sachar asserted.

In an apparent dig at Washington's recent renewal of Chain's MFN status, he said "there are several countries in the world where human rights are violated, but you don't cut their aid." As the special repertoire of the UN Commission on Human Rights, Mr. Sachar said he visited a homeless shelter in New York and found that more than 70 per cent of the occupants were blacks.

"If you have 70 per cent homeless people in one shelter from a minority black population of 11 per cent, something is not right here he said.

12.5 Jurists Condemn Blasting of Jaipal Reddy's Home

The eminent jurists, Justice V.R. Krishna Iyer, Justice V.M. Tarkunde and Justice Rajinder Sachar, today condemned the recent blasting of the rural house of the Congress (I) leader, Mr. Jaipal Reddy, in Mehboobnagar district of Andhra Pradesh, by militants of an ultra-Left outfit.

"Mr. Reddy is widely known for his uncompromising and consistent stand for the cause of civil liberties and the rights of poor and weaker sections of the society. To have targeted the home of such a progressive activist is an unfortunate irony," they said in a statement here.

They said such acts "only weaken the very cause for which they claim to fight and strengthen the anti-poor and anti-democratic forces in Andhra Pradesh in particular and in the country as a whole".

Index

J

K

L

U

V

W